William Shakespeare

HAMLET

Edited with a Commentary by T. J. B. Spencer
Introduced by Alan Sinfield
The Play in Performance by Paul Prescott

PENGUIN BOOKS

Published by the Penguin Group

Penguin Books Ltd, 80 Strand, London WC2R ORL, England
Penguin Group (USA) Inc., 375 Hudson Street, New York, New York 10014, USA
Penguin Group (Canada), 10 Alcorn Avenue, Toronto, Ontario, Canada M4V 3B2
(a division of Pearson Penguin Canada Inc.)
Penguin Ireland, 25 St Stephen's Green, Dublin 2, Ireland (a division of Penguin Books Ltd)
Penguin Group (Australia), 250 Camberwell Road, Camberwell, Victoria 3124, Australia
(a division of Pearson Australia Group Pty Ltd)
Penguin Books India Pvt Ltd, 11 Community Centre, Panchsheel Park, New Delhi – 110 017, India
Penguin Group (NZ), cnr Airborne and Rosedale Roads, Albany, Auckland 1310, New Zealand
(a division of Pearson New Zealand Ltd)
Penguin Books (South Africa) (Pty) Ltd, 24 Sturdee Avenue, Rosebank 2196, South Africa

Penguin Books Ltd, Registered Offices: 80 Strand, London WC2R ORL, England

www.penguin.com

This edition first published in Penguin Books 1980
Reprinted with revised Further Reading 1996
Reissued in the Penguin Shakespeare series 2005

015

This edition copyright © Penguin Books, 1980, 1996
Account of the Text and Commentary copyright © the Estate of T. J. B. Spencer, 1980
Further Reading copyright © Michael Taylor, 1996
General Introduction and Chronology copyright © Stanley Wells, 2005
Introduction and revised Further Reading copyright © Alan Sinfield, 2005
The Play in Performance and revised Further Reading copyright © Paul Prescott, 2005

Set in 11.5/12.5 PostScript Monotype Fournier
Typeset by Palimpsest Book Production Limited, Polmont, Stirlingshire
Printed in England by Clays Ltd, St Ives plc

ISBN-13: 978-0-141-01307-7

www.greenpenguin.co.uk

Penguin Books is committed to a sustainable
future for our business, our readers and our planet.
This book is made from Forest Stewardship
Council™ certified paper.

ALWAYS LEARNING   **PEARSON**

Contents

General Introduction

Every play by Shakespeare is unique. This is part of his greatness. A restless and indefatigable experimenter, he moved with a rare amalgamation of artistic integrity and dedicated professionalism from one kind of drama to another. Never shackled by convention, he offered his actors the alternation between serious and comic modes from play to play, and often also within the plays themselves, that the repertory system within which he worked demanded, and which provided an invaluable stimulus to his imagination. Introductions to individual works in this series attempt to define their individuality. But there are common factors that underpin Shakespeare's career.

Nothing in his heredity offers clues to the origins of his genius. His upbringing in Stratford-upon-Avon, where he was born in 1564, was unexceptional. His mother, born Mary Arden, came from a prosperous farming family. Her father chose her as his executor over her eight sisters and his four stepchildren when she was only in her late teens, which suggests that she was of more than average practical ability. Her husband John, a glover, apparently unable to write, was nevertheless a capable businessman and loyal townsfellow, who seems to have fallen on relatively hard times in later life. He would have been brought up as a Catholic, and may have retained

Catholic sympathies, but his son subscribed publicly to Anglicanism throughout his life.

The most important formative influence on Shakespeare was his school. As the son of an alderman who became bailiff (or mayor) in 1568, he had the right to attend the town's grammar school. Here he would have received an education grounded in classical rhetoric and oratory, studying authors such as Ovid, Cicero and Quintilian, and would have been required to read, speak, write and even think in Latin from his early years. This classical education permeates Shakespeare's work from the beginning to the end of his career. It is apparent in the self-conscious classicism of plays of the early 1590s such as the tragedy of *Titus Andronicus*, *The Comedy of Errors*, and the narrative poems *Venus and Adonis* (1592–3) and *The Rape of Lucrece* (1593–4), and is still evident in his latest plays, informing the dream visions of *Pericles* and *Cymbeline* and the masque in *The Tempest*, written between 1607 and 1611. It inflects his literary style throughout his career. In his earliest writings the verse, based on the ten-syllabled, five-beat iambic pentameter, is highly patterned. Rhetorical devices deriving from classical literature, such as alliteration and antithesis, extended similes and elaborate wordplay, abound. Often, as in *Love's Labour's Lost* and *A Midsummer Night's Dream*, he uses rhyming patterns associated with lyric poetry, each line self-contained in sense, the prose as well as the verse employing elaborate figures of speech. Writing at a time of linguistic ferment, Shakespeare frequently imports Latinisms into English, coining words such as abstemious, addiction, incarnadine and adjunct. He was also heavily influenced by the eloquent translations of the Bible in both the Bishops' and the Geneva versions. As his experience grows, his verse and prose become more supple, the patterning less apparent, more ready to accommodate the rhythms of ordinary speech, more colloquial in diction, as in the speeches of the Nurse in *Romeo and Juliet*, the characterful prose of Falstaff and Hamlet's soliloquies. The effect is of increasing psychological realism, reaching its greatest heights in *Hamlet*, *Othello*, *King Lear*, *Macbeth* and *Antony and Cleopatra*. Gradually he discovered ways of adapting the regular beat of the pentameter to make it an infinitely flexible instrument for matching thought with feeling. Towards the end of his career, in plays such as *The Winter's Tale*, *Cymbeline* and *The Tempest*, he adopts a more highly mannered style, in keeping with the more overtly symbolical and emblematical mode in which he is writing.

So far as we know, Shakespeare lived in Stratford till after his marriage to Anne Hathaway, eight years his senior, in 1582. They had three children: a daughter, Susanna, born in 1583 within six months of their marriage, and twins, Hamnet and Judith, born in 1585. The next seven years of Shakespeare's life are virtually a blank. Theories that he may have been, for instance, a schoolmaster, or a lawyer, or a soldier, or a sailor, lack evidence to support them. The first reference to him in print, in Robert Greene's pamphlet *Greene's Groatsworth of Wit* of 1592, parodies a line from *Henry VI, Part III*, implying that Shakespeare was already an established playwright. It seems likely that at some unknown point after the birth of his twins he joined a theatre company and gained experience as both actor and writer in the provinces and London. The London theatres closed because of plague in 1593 and 1594; and during these years, perhaps recognizing the need for an alternative career, he wrote and published the narrative poems *Venus and Adonis* and *The Rape of Lucrece*. These are the only works we can be certain that Shakespeare himself was responsible for putting into print. Each bears the author's dedication to Henry Wriothesley, Earl of Southampton (1573–1624), the second in warmer terms than the first. Southampton, younger than Shakespeare by ten years, is the only person to whom he personally dedicated works. The Earl may have been a close friend, perhaps even the beautiful and adored young man whom Shakespeare celebrates in his *Sonnets*.

The resumption of playing after the plague years saw the founding of the Lord Chamberlain's Men, a company to which Shakespeare was to belong for the rest of his career, as actor, shareholder and playwright. No other dramatist of the period had so stable a relationship with a single company. Shakespeare knew the actors for whom he was writing and the conditions in which they performed. The permanent company was made up of around twelve to fourteen players, but one actor often played more than one role in a play and additional actors were hired as needed. Led by the tragedian Richard Burbage (1568–1619) and, initially, the comic actor Will Kemp (d. 1603), they rapidly achieved a high reputation, and when King James I succeeded Queen Elizabeth I in 1603 they were renamed as the King's Men. All the women's parts were played by boys; there is no evidence that any female role was ever played by a male actor over the age of about eighteen. Shakespeare had enough confidence in his boys to write for them long and demanding roles such as Rosalind (who, like other heroines of the romantic comedies, is disguised as a boy for much of the action) in *As You Like It*, Lady Macbeth and Cleopatra. But there are far more fathers than mothers, sons than daughters, in his plays, few if any of which require more than the company's normal complement of three or four boys.

The company played primarily in London's public playhouses – there were almost none that we know of in the rest of the country – initially in the Theatre, built in Shoreditch in 1576, and from 1599 in the Globe, on Bankside. These were wooden, more or less circular structures, open to the air, with a thrust stage surmounted by a canopy and jutting into the area where spectators who paid one penny stood, and surrounded by galleries where it was possible to be seated on payment of an additional penny. Though properties such as cauldrons, stocks, artificial trees or beds could indicate locality, there was no representational scenery. Sound effects such as flourishes of trumpets, music both martial and amorous, and accompaniments to songs were provided by the company's musicians. Actors entered through doors in the back wall of the stage. Above it was a balconied area that could represent the walls of a town (as in *King John*), or a castle (as in *Richard II*), and indeed a balcony (as in *Romeo and Juliet*). In 1609 the company also acquired the use of the Blackfriars, a smaller, indoor theatre to which admission was more expensive, and which permitted the use of more spectacular stage effects such as the descent of Jupiter on an eagle in *Cymbeline* and of goddesses in *The Tempest*. And they would frequently perform before the court in royal residences and, on their regular tours into the provinces, in non-theatrical spaces such as inns, guildhalls and the great halls of country houses.

Early in his career Shakespeare may have worked in collaboration, perhaps with Thomas Nashe (1567–*c.* 1601) in *Henry VI, Part I* and with George Peele (1556–96) in *Titus Andronicus*. And towards the end he collaborated with George Wilkins (*fl.* 1604–8) in *Pericles*, and with his younger colleagues Thomas Middleton (1580–1627), in *Timon of Athens*, and John Fletcher (1579–1625), in *Henry*

VIII, *The Two Noble Kinsmen* and the lost play *Cardenio*. Shakespeare's output dwindled in his last years, and he died in 1616 in Stratford, where he owned a fine house, New Place, and much land. His only son had died at the age of eleven, in 1596, and his last descendant died in 1670. New Place was destroyed in the eighteenth century but the other Stratford houses associated with his life are maintained and displayed to the public by the Shakespeare Birthplace Trust.

One of the most remarkable features of Shakespeare's plays is their intellectual and emotional scope. They span a great range from the lightest of comedies, such as *The Two Gentlemen of Verona* and *The Comedy of Errors*, to the profoundest of tragedies, such as *King Lear* and *Macbeth*. He maintained an output of around two plays a year, ringing the changes between comic and serious. All his comedies have serious elements: Shylock, in *The Merchant of Venice*, almost reaches tragic dimensions, and *Measure for Measure* is profoundly serious in its examination of moral problems. Equally, none of his tragedies is without humour: Hamlet is as witty as any of his comic heroes, *Macbeth* has its Porter, and *King Lear* its Fool. His greatest comic character, Falstaff, inhabits the history plays and *Henry V* ends with a marriage, while *Henry VI, Part III*, *Richard II* and *Richard III* culminate in the tragic deaths of their protagonists.

Although in performance Shakespeare's characters can give the impression of a superabundant reality, he is not a naturalistic dramatist. None of his plays is explicitly set in his own time. The action of few of them (except for the English histories) is set even partly in England (exceptions are *The Merry Wives of Windsor* and the Induction to *The Taming of the Shrew*). Italy is his favoured location. Most of his principal story-lines derive from printed writings; but the structuring and translation of these narratives into dramatic terms is Shakespeare's own, and he invents much additional material. Most of the plays contain elements of myth and legend, and many derive from ancient or more recent history or from romantic tales of ancient times and faraway places. All reflect his reading, often in close detail. Holinshed's *Chronicles* (1577, revised 1587), a great compendium of English, Scottish and Irish history, provided material for his English history plays. The *Lives of the Noble Grecians and Romans* by the Greek writer Plutarch, finely translated into English from the French by Sir Thomas North in 1579, provided much of the narrative material, and also a mass of verbal detail, for his plays about Roman history. Some plays are closely based on shorter individual works: *As You Like It*, for instance, on the novel *Rosalynde* (1590) by his near-contemporary Thomas Lodge (1558–1625), *The Winter's Tale* on *Pandosto* (1588) by his old rival Robert Greene (1558–92) and *Othello* on a story by the Italian Giraldi Cinthio (1504–73). And the language of his plays is permeated by the Bible, the Book of Common Prayer and the proverbial sayings of his day.

Shakespeare was popular with his contemporaries, but his commitment to the theatre and to the plays in performance is demonstrated by the fact that only about half of his plays appeared in print in his lifetime, in slim paperback volumes known as quartos, so called because they were made from printers' sheets folded twice to form four leaves (eight pages). None of them shows any sign that he was involved in their publication. For him, performance was the primary means of publication. The most frequently reprinted of his works were the non-dramatic poems – the erotic *Venus and Adonis* and the more moralistic *The Rape of Lucrece*. The *Sonnets*, which appeared in 1609, under his name but possibly without his consent, were less successful, perhaps because the vogue for sonnet sequences, which peaked in the 1590s, had passed by then. They were not reprinted until 1640, and then only in garbled form along with poems by other writers. Happily, in 1623, seven years after he died, his colleagues John Heminges (1556–1630) and Henry Condell (d. 1627) published his collected plays, including eighteen that had not previously appeared in print, in the first Folio, whose name derives from the fact that the printers' sheets were folded only once to produce two leaves (four pages). Some of the quarto editions are badly printed, and the fact that some plays exist in two, or even three, early versions creates problems for editors. These are discussed in the Account of the Text in each volume of this series.

Shakespeare's plays continued in the repertoire until the Puritans closed the theatres in 1642. When performances resumed after the Restoration of the monarchy in 1660 many of the plays were not to the taste of the times, especially because their mingling of genres and failure to meet the requirements of poetic justice offended against the dictates of neoclassicism. Some, such as *The Tempest* (changed by John Dryden and William Davenant in 1667 to suit contemporary taste), *King Lear* (to which Nahum Tate gave a happy ending in 1681) and *Richard III* (heavily adapted by Colley Cibber in 1700 as a vehicle for his own talents), were extensively rewritten; others fell into neglect. Slowly they regained their place in the repertoire, and they continued to be reprinted, but it was not until the great actor David Garrick (1717–79) organized a spectacular jubilee in Stratford in 1769 that Shakespeare began to be regarded as a transcendental genius. Garrick's idolatry prefigured the enthusiasm of critics such as Samuel Taylor Coleridge (1772–1834) and William Hazlitt (1778–1830). Gradually Shakespeare's reputation spread abroad, to Germany, America, France and to other European countries.

During the nineteenth century, though the plays were generally still performed in heavily adapted or abbreviated versions, a large body of scholarship and criticism began to amass. Partly as a result of a general swing in education away from the teaching of Greek and Roman texts and towards literature written in English, Shakespeare became the object of intensive study in schools and universities. In the theatre, important turning points were the work in England of two theatre directors, William Poel (1852–1934) and his disciple Harley Granville-Barker (1877–1946), who showed that the application of knowledge, some of it newly acquired, of early staging conditions to performance of the plays could render the original texts viable in terms of the modern theatre. During the twentieth century appreciation of Shakespeare's work, encouraged by the availability of audio, film and video versions of the plays, spread around the world to such an extent that he can now be claimed as a global author.

The influence of Shakespeare's works permeates the English language. Phrases from his plays and poems – 'a tower of strength', 'green-eyed jealousy', 'a foregone conclusion' – are on the lips of people who may never have read him. They have inspired composers of songs, orchestral music and operas; painters and sculptors; poets, novelists and film-makers. Allusions to him appear in pop songs, in advertisements and in television shows. Some of his characters – Romeo and Juliet, Falstaff, Shylock and Hamlet – have acquired mythic status. He is valued for his humanity, his psychological insight, his wit and humour, his lyricism, his mastery of language, his ability to excite, surprise, move and, in the widest sense of the word, entertain audiences. He is the greatest of poets, but he is essentially a dramatic poet. Though his plays have much to offer to readers, they exist fully only in performance. In these volumes we offer individual introductions, notes on language and on specific points of the text, suggestions for further reading and information about how each work has been edited. In addition we include accounts of the ways in which successive generations of interpreters and audiences have responded to challenges and rewards offered by the plays. The Penguin Shakespeare series aspires to remove obstacles to understanding and to make pleasurable the reading of the work of the man who has done more than most to make us understand what it is to be human.

Stanley Wells

The Chronology of
Shakespeare's Works

A few of Shakespeare's writings can be fairly precisely dated. An allusion to the Earl of Essex in the chorus to Act V of *Henry V*, for instance, could only have been written in 1599. But for many of the plays we have only vague information, such as the date of publication, which may have occurred long after composition, the date of a performance, which may not have been the first, or a list in Francis Meres's book *Palladis Tamia*, published in 1598, which tells us only that the plays listed there must have been written by that year. The chronology of the early plays is particularly difficult to establish. Not everyone would agree that the first part of *Henry VI* was written after the third, for instance, or *Romeo and Juliet* before *A Midsummer Night's Dream*. The following table is based on the 'Canon and Chronology' section in *William Shakespeare: A Textual Companion*, by Stanley Wells and Gary Taylor, with John Jowett and William Montgomery (1987), where more detailed information and discussion may be found.

The Two Gentlemen of Verona	1590–91
The Taming of the Shrew	1590–91
Henry VI, Part II	1591
Henry VI, Part III	1591

Macbeth (revised by Middleton)	1606
Antony and Cleopatra	1606
Pericles (with George Wilkins)	1607
Coriolanus	1608
The Winter's Tale	1609
Cymbeline	1610
The Tempest	1611
Henry VIII (by Shakespeare and John Fletcher; known in its own time as *All is True*)	1613
Cardenio (by Shakespeare and Fletcher; lost)	1613
The Two Noble Kinsmen (by Shakespeare and Fletcher)	1613–14

Introduction

THE PROBLEMS OF HAMLET

'Sblood, do you think I am easier to be played on than a pipe?
(III.2.377–8)

Hamlet is a problem for the Danish court. At the opening of the play he is still mourning the death of his father, King Hamlet, while everyone else is celebrating the marriage of his mother, Gertrude, to the new king, his uncle, Claudius. They try to discover what's bothering him. 'How is it that the clouds still hang on you?' Claudius asks (I.2.66). 'Why seems it so particular with thee?' his mother questions (I.2.75). 'How does my good Lord Hamlet?' inquires Polonius, the chief minister (II.2.171). 'How does your honour for this many a day?' asks Ophelia, Polonius's daughter (III.1.91).

Hamlet's behaviour is indeed somewhat eccentric. He moons around in black talking to himself, rails at Ophelia, whom previously he has courted, and contrives a play which criticizes the marriage of the King and Queen. He responds to questions about his state of mind with puns, riddles, pointed impertinence and pretended madness.

Hamlet's mental state is important because it threatens the Danish state. 'Madness in great ones must not unwatched go', the King declares (III.1.189). He demands that Hamlet remain at court, under observation. Ophelia is placed to sound out the Prince, but he uses her approach to indulge his disillusionment with love and marriage. Rosencrantz and Guildenstern are commissioned to uncover the problem, but they get no further. 'He does confess he feels himself distracted, | But from what cause 'a will by no means speak' (III.1.5–6).

Hamlet is irritated by the presumption of Guildenstern, who won't play the recorder because he has no expertise but supposes he can fathom the depths of Hamlet's mind.

> Why, look you now, how unworthy a thing you make of me! You would play upon me. You would seem to know my stops. You would pluck out the heart of my mystery. You would sound me from my lowest note to the top of my compass . . . 'Sblood, do you think I am easier to be played on than a pipe? Call me what instrument you will, though you can fret me, you cannot play upon me. (III.2.371–9)

Audiences and readers have also tried to pluck out the heart of Hamlet's mystery since the play was first performed at the Globe theatre, probably in 1600, three years before the death of Queen Elizabeth I. His state of mind is perhaps the most debated question in English literary culture. Since the Romantic movement of the late eighteenth and early nineteenth centuries Hamlet has become the prototype of the enigmatic, sensitive and thoughtful young man, damaged by a corrupt society yet stimulated by interaction with everyone around him. For some commentators he rises above his circumstances and is a tragic hero, for others he falls into triviality, brutality and ungodliness. Despite, or because of, all this urgent scholarly and imaginative work, both the character of Hamlet and the meaning of the play remain unresolved. The poet T. S. Eliot in his essay 'Hamlet and His Problems' called the play 'the "Mona Lisa" of literature' (David Bevington (ed.), *Twentieth-Century Interpretations* – see Further Reading).

DELAY AND REVENGE

> *. . . is't not perfect conscience*
> *To quit him with this arm?* (V.2.67–8)

Audiences and readers have a good deal more evidence of Hamlet's state of mind than Claudius and his court. We know from his first soliloquy that he is disgusted with his mother's hasty second marriage: 'O, most wicked speed, to post | With such dexterity to incestuous sheets!' (I.2.156–7). Then he meets his father's Ghost, who appears to confirm his worst suspicions about his uncle: Claudius seduced Gertrude and poisoned King Hamlet, in a particularly gruesome way. The command is: 'Revenge his foul and most unnatural murder' (I.5.25). King Claudius is right to fear Prince Hamlet.

For many commentators the key question is why Hamlet 'delays' his revenge. Tell me quickly, he exhorts the Ghost,

> that I, with wings as swift
> As meditation or the thoughts of love,
> May sweep to my revenge. (I.5.29–31)

Actually, those comparisons are oddly self-cancelling. Meditation, while it may involve flights of fantasy, is generally a rather private and self-absorbed practice; and thoughts of love may be more rewarding when they are less flighty. Neither seems an obvious analogue for decisive and brutal action.

One interpretation of Hamlet's delay is that it is not in fact excessive. He can't just rush in and kill the King; he'd be slain by the guard. When he finally stabs Claudius 'All' shout 'Treason! Treason!' (V.2.317). Then the truth about the murder would not be revealed. This is important to Hamlet – he insists that Horatio survive to tell his story. Besides, Hamlet can't be sure that the Ghost isn't malign and dishonest, sent by the devil to tempt him. With these factors in mind, we might feel that he is really quite purposeful. His plan to check on the King through the performance of the Players is brilliantly improvised, and effective: 'O good Horatio, I'll take the ghost's word for a thousand pound' (III.2.295–6). Then he lets Claudius live when he finds him alone and praying; although that may appear over-scrupulous it is not an unreasonable thing to do, if the idea is to punish the King rather than send him to heaven. When someone is skulking behind the arras in Gertrude's chamber Hamlet kills him without hesitation, believing it to be the King.

So we might say that the Prince is fairly punctual. On the other hand, the idea that he delays is firmly planted in the text when he accuses himself of neglecting his task. 'How all occasions do inform against me | And spur my dull revenge!' he exclaims (IV.4.32–3), contrasting his own prevarication with the resolution of Fortinbras and his army, who are ready to die for a small piece of territory. Perhaps he is guilty of the forgetfulness of a beast; or perhaps, contrariwise, he has taken on 'some craven scruple | Of thinking too precisely on th'event' (IV.4.40–41). Commentators have often seized upon this latter thought: perhaps Hamlet thinks too much or, at least, too much for a revenger. He is a man of reflection, a student, who is suddenly expected to behave like a man of action. If Hamlet rushed to judgement, as Othello does, there would have been no tragedy. Conversely, if Othello had investigated and considered as carefully as Hamlet does, he would not have murdered Desdemona.

Perhaps, we might conclude, there is something perverse in Hamlet's nature and situation, whereby he is rapid and decisive in everything but the accomplishment of revenge. We might attribute this to a bloody-mindedness in the nature of the universe, whereby man's best intentions are obscurely thwarted; or to some irrational blockage in the mind of Hamlet himself. We will return to these questions.

In evaluating Hamlet's speech and actions, a good deal depends on one's attitude to revenge. Christians have often quoted the biblical injunction: 'Vengeance is mine, I will repay, saith the Lord. Therefore if thine enemy hunger, feed him: if he thirst, give him drink. For in so doing thou shalt heap coals of fire on his head' (Romans 12:19–20 (Bishops' Bible, 1568, etc.)). The individual Christian, therefore, is not to take the law into his own hands. Observe that this is not a very generous programme, however: as with Hamlet's sparing of the praying Claudius, the idea is to forgo the immediate satisfaction of harming your enemy today in order that he will suffer more in the long run. Humanists, on the other hand, are likely to repudiate vengeance – divine and human – as primitive, and to look for a more productive way of dealing with disputes. They may think Hamlet's delay indicates an emergent humanism. Having studied at an international university in Germany, Hamlet has a different sensibility from that of his father, an old-fashioned warrior who wagered his kingdom in combat with Fortinbras, King of Norway, whom he slew.

Among the upper classes in Shakespeare's time it was still often supposed that one was honour-bound to avenge an affront. Hamlet believes 'honour's at the stake' (IV.4.56); so does Laertes (V.2.240–44). Claudius attempts to incorporate these unruly disputes into the business of the court; primitive warrior emotions, such as duelling and revenge, may be softened and tamed when they are filtered through the elaborate ritual of the court by the wealthy hanger-on, Osrick. This seems to be a good modernizing policy, but it is corrupted by Claudius's attempt to fix the outcome through the secret use of poison. In many plays of the period the source of the wrongdoing is a tyrannical or inadequate ruler, and this may seem to justify the personal intervention of the malcontent-avenger. There was a long-running political argument about whether subjects might legitimately intervene to quell a tyrant. Often this was couched in religious terms: the king has been appointed by God as his deputy. Actually, Protestants tended to argue that the nobility might overthrow the monarch when they were living in countries where Catholicism was enforced as the state religion, and vice versa.

In Shakespeare's *Richard II* the King seeks to draw the rivalry of Bolingbroke and Mowbray into a legal framework that will make revenge within the ruling elite redundant, but the process is corrupted by his own involvement in the murder which is at issue: King Richard encouraged Mowbray to kill Gloucester. The debate is made explicit when Gloucester's widow calls upon Gaunt to avenge her, but he counsels Christian patience:

> God's is the quarrel; for God's substitute,
> His deputy anointed in His sight,
> Hath caused his death; the which if wrongfully,

Let heaven revenge, for I may never lift
An angry arm against His minister. (I.2.37–41)

In *Richard II* these issues of principle are overtaken
by the course of events. But in *Hamlet* it is only as the
catalogue of King Claudius's crimes accumulates that
Hamlet claims that it would be right to kill him – and
even then he puts it as a question to Horatio:

He that hath killed my King and whored my mother,
Popped in between th'election and my hopes,
Thrown out his angle for my proper life,
And with such cozenage – is't not perfect conscience
To quit him with this arm? (V.2.64–8)

THIS FELLOW IN THE CELLARAGE

O, horrible! O, horrible! Most horrible! (I.5.80)

The controversy about revenge was yet more complex.
Hamlet's phrasing – 'is't not perfect conscience[?]' –
implies a Christian context. However, in various aspects
of Elizabethan thought, alternatives to Christian orthodoxy had crept in through classical culture. Roman and
Greek writings were hugely prestigious, yet they
promoted pagan religion and a relaxed attitude towards
fornication and homosexuality. An anti-Christian lust for
revenge, inspired by a ghost, is central to the tragedies
of the ancient Roman author Seneca (*c.* 4 BC–AD 65). His
works were taught in Elizabethan schools and colleges;
his plays were published in English as *Seneca His Tenne
Tragedies* by Thomas Newton in 1581. Seneca's plays seem
designed for recitation and are quite unlike the busy plots

of the Shakespearian popular theatre; their biggest influence was on closet dramas written in and for students at the Inns of Court, where lawyers were educated, and universities. However, the academic and popular traditions were not, initially, altogether separate.

The relevance of Seneca to *Hamlet* is manifest in the notoriously enigmatic remark made by the writer Thomas Nashe in 1589, ten or eleven years before Shakespeare's play. There are inferior authors who cannot read Latin, Nashe says. 'Yet English Seneca read by candlelight yields many good sentences, as "Blood is a beggar," and so forth; and if you entreat him fair in a frosty morning, he will afford you whole Hamlets, I should say handfuls, of tragical speeches' (*Preface to Greene's 'Menaphon'*). In other words, the reading of Seneca in translation has informed the writing of a blood-and-thunder tragedy based on the Hamlet story. This earlier play, of which no text has survived, is usually called the *Ur-Hamlet*. So Senecan images and themes were key parts of the intellectual and imaginative context in which *Hamlet* was fashioned.

Thomas Kyd's *The Spanish Tragedy* (1587–9) is illuminating at this point, because it has a lot in common with both Seneca and *Hamlet*, and makes explicit the conflict between Christian and pagan ideas. Kyd's play opens with a long speech by the Ghost of Andrea, describing how he has been received into Hades, the pagan underworld kingdom of the dead. There he is assigned to the care of Revenge, who tells him to sit and watch the action of the play: he will see his death avenged. Despite this classical framework the play is set in Christian Spain and Portugal. Hieronimo, pondering (like Hamlet) the justice of his cause, directly juxtaposes the Christian text '*Vindicta mihi!*' (Vengeance is mine) with the Senecan

injunction '*Per scelus semper tutum est sceleribus iter*: |
Strike, and strike home, where wrong is offer'd thee'
(*The Spanish Tragedy*, III.13.1, 6–7). Biblical and classical contexts clash again when Hieronimo claims that he
and heaven and the saints are collaborating in avenging
his son:

> Why, then I see that heaven applies our drift,
> And all the saints do sit soliciting
> For vengeance on those cursed murderers. (IV.1.31–3)

In John Marston's *Antonio's Revenge* (*c*. 1599), a play
which shares many linguistic and plot motifs with *Hamlet*,
Andrugio's Ghost mingles Senecan and Christian senti-
ments without apparent discomfort:

>   Now down looks providence
> T'attend the last act of my son's revenge.
>   . . . O, now triumphs my ghost,
> Exclaiming 'Heaven's just, for I shall see
> The scourge of murder and impiety'. (*Antonio's Revenge*,
>   V.1.10–11, 24–5)

The similarities and differences between what Shakespeare writes and what other authors do with similar
stories, themes and genres are always instructive. These
contemporary writings are not merely sources or background for *Hamlet*; they do not offer a chronicle of the
Elizabethan theatre. Pointing to the explicit disputes and
the covert embarrassments of the time, they mark out
the boundaries of the thinkable. Exploring the scope of
Senecan ideas will not pluck out the heart of Hamlet's
mystery, but it may bring us closer to the conditions that
enable the characters to make sense, as it were, to each

other and, in turn, to make sense to audiences and readers. It is through this framework that the dilemmas of Hamlet may speak to us today.

The neatest way of amalgamating the Senecan ghost and Christian imagery is to place him in purgatory, where souls destined ultimately for heaven are said to suffer for their sins:

> I am thy father's spirit,
> Doomed for a certain term to walk the night,
> And for the day confined to fast in fires,
> Till the foul crimes done in my days of nature
> Are burnt and purged away. (I.5.9–13)

However, the doctrine of purgatory was specifically rejected by the Elizabethan Protestant orthodoxy, so its appearance in *Hamlet* has encouraged speculation about Shakespeare's religious affiliations. What was he doing in the years about which we have little evidence, between his marriage in 1582 and his appearance in poetic and theatrical circles in London in 1591–2? Might he have been working as secretary or tutor in a Catholic household in the north of England? Can the universal bard have been committed, secretly, to an outlawed faith?

We need to bear in mind that almost everyone had been a Roman Catholic before the Reformation, so many people might have retained knowledge of and feeling for the old rites. Shakespeare's father, John, was a grown man by 1563, when the Thirty-nine Articles of the Church of England confirmed Protestantism as the official state religion and declared that purgatory was a pernicious Romish invention. John may have maintained his Catholic allegiance. William may have experienced a nostalgic attachment to the imagery and perspective of the old faith, or perhaps a rational respect for its intellectual ambitions.

HAMLET'S PHILOSOPHIES

There are more things in heaven and earth, Horatio,
Than are dreamt of in your philosophy. (I.5.166–7)

The development of Senecan motifs in *Hamlet*, alongside Christian attitudes, provokes two further thoughts. First, while the general tone of the play appears to align it with Senecan attitudes, the language and themes of the Players are even more Senecan – violent and bloody in theme, and ponderous and ranting in expression. For them, 'Seneca cannot be too heavy, nor Plautus too light' (II.2.399–400). Revenge, and the bombastic language that accompanies it, is for the audience the style of an older kind of play. It is a dramatic convention, in the service of the Ghost, who has a grudge; of the Players, who want to make a living; and of Hamlet, who seeks to trap his uncle. It is an attitude that has flourished in particular conditions; it is not the inevitable way to behave.

Second, we have been noticing only one aspect of Seneca, who is a radically incoherent figure. He is not just a writer of bloodthirsty tragedies; his *Moral Essays* argue for a calm, rationalist attitude towards human affairs. His outlook there is *stoic*: one must accept with tranquillity those forces one cannot control. This also is an active theme in *Hamlet*. The Prince presents himself in stoic terms when he exchanges philosophical banter with his fellow students. Rosencrantz denies that Denmark is a prison; Hamlet replies, 'Why, then 'tis none to you. For there is nothing either good or bad but thinking makes it so' (II.2.248–9). He values Horatio because he has achieved a stoic calm:

>   For thou hast been
> As one, in suffering all, that suffers nothing,
> A man that Fortune's buffets and rewards
> Hast ta'en with equal thanks. (III.2.75–8)

By subduing his emotions, Horatio frees himself from the effects of fortune and becomes the stoics' wise and happy man. If Hamlet could do that, then he could cope with his father, mother and uncle. It is reluctance to tolerate life with the mind in chains that puts suicide on the stoic agenda:

> To be, or not to be – that is the question;
> Whether 'tis nobler in the mind to suffer
> The slings and arrows of outrageous fortune
> Or to take arms against a sea of troubles
> And by opposing end them. (III.1.56–60)

The Chorus in Seneca's *Trojan Women* engages in similar speculation. Again, Horatio, wanting to die with Hamlet, terms himself 'more an antique Roman than a Dane' (V.2.335).

For Seneca, in his *Moral Essays*, the man who achieves stoic mastery becomes godlike:

the wise man is next-door neighbour to the gods and like a god in all save his mortality. As he struggles and presses on towards those things that are lofty, well-ordered, undaunted, that flow on with even and harmonious current, that are untroubled, kindly, adapted to the public good, beneficial both to himself and to others, the wise man will covet nothing low, will never repine.

Hamlet is aware of this idealistic vision of man, but it no longer works for him:

> What a piece of work is a man, how noble in reason, how infinite in faculties, in form and moving how express and admirable, in action how like an angel, in apprehension how like a god: the beauty of the world, the paragon of animals! And yet to me what is this quintessence of dust? Man delights not me. (II.2.303–9)

Rottenness in the state of Denmark has undermined Hamlet's faith in humankind. The Ghost's demand that he set this right has drawn the optimistic humanist whom we associate with the Senecan essays into the worldview of the gruesome revenger of his plays.

GOD AND MAN

There is special providence in the fall of a sparrow. (V.2.213–14)

Placing Hamlet within the available concepts of revenge helps us to think about the familiar question about his 'character'. The strategy followed here is not to speculate about his personality, in the way we might gossip about a friend, or a celebrity or a character in a soap opera. Rather, it is to reconstruct aspects of contemporary thought which make *Hamlet* possible. For the Prince's speeches cannot exist outside the prevailing social arrangements (if they did, they would have been incomprehensible to contemporary audiences). They are a highly distinctive selection of the things that might be said in Shakespeare's time.

If the Ghost's talk of purgatory plants Roman Catholic imagery in *Hamlet*, there are also distinct traces of Reformation theology. Briefly, the Protestantism that was instituted and preached in the Church of England in Shakespeare's lifetime was Calvinistic: it emphasized the inability of the Christian individual to procure his or her own salvation, and its corollary, divine predestination. The Thirty-nine Articles were ordered to be read in church several times a year and repeated by the faithful as a condition of participation at the communion service. They are still printed at the back of *The Book of Common Prayer*. Article 10 asserts: 'Man . . . cannot turn and prepare himself, by his own natural strength and good works, to faith, and calling upon God.' Article 17 adds: 'Predestination to Life is the everlasting purpose of God, whereby (before the foundations of the world were laid) he hath constantly decreed by his counsel secret to us, to deliver from curse and damnation those whom he hath chosen.' So whether you are saved or not depends on the will of God. Such a belief may seem insupportable to many readers today, but it has a certain logic, and arguably suited the violent and punitive social system which it purported to explain and justify. The task for the theologian was to make it persuasive, for the playwright to explore its complications.

Hamlet sounds like a Calvinist in his conversations with Horatio after his return to Denmark. Horatio warns him to take care over the duel with Laertes. Hamlet replies that there is no point in attempting to anticipate the future; whatever he does, God has it all decided:

We defy augury. There is special providence in the fall of
a sparrow. If it be now, 'tis not to come. If it be not to
come, it will be now. If it be not now, yet it will come. The
readiness is all. Since no man knows of aught he leaves,
what is't to leave betimes? Let be. (V.2.213–18)

Jesus's remark about God's care for the sparrow (Matthew
10:29–31; Luke 12:6–7) was often quoted as evidence of
divine beneficence; 'special' providence is a Calvinistic
phrase, denoting that God's concern is detailed, not just
general. God, John Calvin writes, is 'a Governor and
Preserver, and that, not by producing a kind of general
motion in the machine of the globe as well as in each of
its parts, but by a special Providence sustaining, cher-
ishing, superintending, all the things which he has made,
to the very minutest, even to a sparrow' (*Calvin's
Institutes*, I.xvi.1). In fact, in the first version of the play
to be printed, the Quarto of 1603, Hamlet says at this
point 'there's a predestinate providence in the fall of a
sparrow'. The first Quarto is usually taken to be a faulty
reconstruction, perhaps by an actor from memory (see
An Account of the Text), but it shows how one well-
placed contemporary read the Prince's thought: it sounds
Calvinist.

This development seems to be prompted by Hamlet's
awareness of the extraordinary turns events have taken
– the appearance of the Ghost when Claudius seemed
secure, the arrival of the Players prompting the test of
the King, Hamlet's inspired discovery on the boat of
the plot against his life, and then his amazing delivery
through the pirates. When describing how he found the
King's letter and changed it, Hamlet credits it to 'a divinity
that shapes our ends, | Rough-hew them how we will';
when explaining how he was able to seal the altered

instructions, he says 'even in that was heaven ordinant' (i.e. 'in control'; V.2.10–11, 48). The shaping of events seems to require an extra-terrestrial explanation; so the Prince recognizes the folly and pretension of humanistic aspiration, and acknowledges the controlling power of God.

This doesn't make Hamlet a Calvinist. While predestination means, logically, that one's actions can make no difference to the destiny of one's soul, Protestant sermonizers, fearful that people would believe themselves released from social and political deference, urged that the believer should show his or her delight in God's will by cooperating as far and as eagerly as possible. Now, that is not how Hamlet appears. His version of predestination sounds more like an indifferent fate than providential care. He is not making a reverent statement about the rightness of God's control of the world but washing his hands of the whole business. So he plays with Osrick (this scene seems purposefully desultory) and competes recklessly with Laertes (V.2), makes no plan against the King. The final killing occurs in a burst of passionate inspiration, and when Hamlet himself is, in effect, slain.

There is no speech saying that Hamlet refuses to co-operate with the Calvinist deity because he is not persuaded of its goodness; probably that could have been said on a stage only by a manifest villain. But as members of an audience try to make sense of events in the play and Hamlet's responses to them, it may appear that the divine system revealed in the action is not as comfortable and delightful as Protestants proclaimed. It makes Hamlet wonder and admire; temporarily, when he is sending Rosencrantz and Guildenstern to their deaths, it exhilarates him; but ultimately it does not command his respect. In this view Hamlet's 'delay' is philosophical, not personal; the universe is not worth his collaboration.

It may seem that we have taken *Hamlet* into eccentric regions of theology. However, we have, in effect, been exploring the central dilemmas of tragedy. As Hamlet puts it, a man may be either 'the beauty of the world, the paragon of animals!' or 'this quintessence of dust' (II.2.306–8). The potential for affirmation in an exceptional human being; the countervailing pressure of something recalcitrant in the very nature of things: these have been the coordinates of Shakespearian tragedy in the dominant critical vision of modern times. Arguably Horatio's account of the action is about right:

> So shall you hear
> Of carnal, bloody, and unnatural acts,
> Of accidental judgements, casual slaughters,
> Of deaths put on by cunning and forced cause,
> And, in this upshot, purposes mistook
> Fallen on th'inventors' heads. (V.2.374–9)

If all this is divinely sanctioned, it is by the violent and punitive Calvinist deity. Whether or not you think the quality of Hamlet's engagement with such a universe constitutes a significant compensation for its brutality is a measure of whether you are an optimist or a pessimist.

IN CHARACTER

Let's follow, Gertrude. (IV.7.191)

In pursuit of these tragic themes I have offered some interpretation of Hamlet's motives – even while casting doubt upon the legitimacy of speculations about his personality. I began with the sense that he is a problem (meaning difficult to interpret), and attributed to him ideas and emotions that change in response to circumstances. However, I have tried to present Hamlet's situation and response in terms of the dramatic, philosophical and religious ideas that were available to Shakespeare – not treating the characters as if they were persons, and not presenting character as if it were the main factor in the play.

Hamlet is informed by a different sense of personhood from that we suppose today; one that tends towards convention, stereotyping and allegory. Identity is mainly to do with social positioning; the speech-prefixes in the original texts are 'King' and 'Queen', not 'Claudius' and 'Gertrude'. Being a prince and nephew to the King ('my lord', the others call him) is more important in the identity of Hamlet than being melancholy and misogynist – though he shows signs of both. Anyway, melancholy and misogyny are familiar stances for the malcontent at court, and not individual to Hamlet. The fate of Ophelia, Laertes and Polonius is determined more by their status at court than by any feelings between them. Perhaps Hamlet loves Horatio, but their relationship can hardly bloom when Horatio must observe such deference that he can speak only in response to Hamlet's approaches. The traditional character questions – why does Hamlet delay? is he mad? does he love Ophelia? is he obsessed with his mother? – are plainly not going to be answered. They have engaged some of the best minds of the western critical tradition, and we have to conclude at last that the play does not supply the evidence to resolve them.

Placing too much emphasis on character, many commentators have said, is to expect an early modern play to answer to a critical approach that would suit a nineteenth-century novel or the naturalistic plays of

Henrik Ibsen and August Strindberg. Unlike such modern writers, Shakespeare and his contemporaries perceived no *inauthenticity* when they borrowed stories from other writers and followed conventions and genres of speech and action (a Senecan Ghost, for instance). Scenery was minimal, and many scenes are set nowhere in particular. Ophelia and Gertrude were played by boy actors – Hamlet draws attention to this by remarking how the boy who is to play the Player Queen has grown; he hopes his voice has not broken (II.2.423–7). In this kind of theatre the immediate movement of a particular scene is more important than continuity between scenes. Hence the uncertainty about Hamlet's age (the initial impression is of a young man around eighteen, whereas his conversation with the First Clown indicates that he is thirty – see V.1.145–6, 159–60). When the narrative wants him to be a student, a lover, subject to his father and uncle, inexperienced and impetuous he appears to be eighteen; when it is required that he be reflective, wise and experienced he appears to be thirty. The ultimate issue is the kinds of subjectivity that may be discovered in early modern culture.

The assumption that a Shakespearian play should be approached mainly through analysis of its characters was championed in A. C. Bradley's classic account, *Shakespearean Tragedy* (1904). A hundred years later, despite much critical dispute, Bradley's study still typifies the commonsense notion of our culture: you will get to the truth of the play through imaginative critical insight into the characters, as you might do when pondering a living person whom you know, and this is the way to appreciate Shakespeare's art. However, Shakespeare's play itself calls Bradleyan character criticism into question, and invites the reader to envisage a more complex understanding. Hamlet himself prompts a distinctive awareness of subjectivity, one that hovers on the threshold of postmodernity.

Consider the representation in the play of the love between Hamlet and Ophelia. She says he has given her tokens of his love, he says not, so there is an uncertainty in the text. Bradley is dissatisfied with the most popular view of his time, which is that Hamlet's love for Ophelia remains constant, but the task of executing the Ghost's command makes him put aside all such thoughts. When he speaks harshly to her (III.1.96–150) it is to convince her that their love is impossible; at her graveside the truth bursts from him (V.1.265–80). This romantic interpretation won't do, according to Bradley. The thesis that Ophelia is central in Hamlet's life is belied by the fact that he says nothing about her in his soliloquies, or to Horatio. Further, Bradley says, Hamlet doesn't break with Ophelia in response to the Ghost; she breaks with him later, on her father's instruction. Her joining in the plot against him seems the likely reason for Hamlet's hostility towards her. Bradley concludes that 'Hamlet's love, though never lost, was, after Ophelia's apparent rejection of him, mingled with suspicion and resentment, and that his treatment of her was due in part to this cause'. The main evidence to the contrary is Hamlet jumping into the grave of Ophelia. Bradley seeks to explain it thus: 'when he declared that it was such a love as forty thousand brothers could not equal, he spoke sincerely indeed but not truly. What he said was true, if I may put it thus, of the inner healthy self which doubtless in time would have fully reasserted itself.'

There are two ways, then, of thinking about Hamlet's character in his relations with Ophelia. In one he is the constant lover; in the other he becomes suspicious and resentful of her. To secure his preferred view, Bradley strives to unearth clues that may paste together a consistent personality, while setting aside inconvenient aspects. But how is an actor to indicate that Hamlet is being sincere but untruthful when he says he loves Ophelia more than forty thousand brothers? How would a reader deduce this from the text? And what can we know about Hamlet's 'inner healthy self', when the signs of it are in an indefinitely remote future? Bradley is driven into over-elaborate arguments because the text does not resolve the question. There is either insufficient evidence or too much. The reason, I will argue shortly, is that Shakespeare's interests are engaged with other matters.

We should note first another kind of attempt to deal with the failure of Shakespearian characters to add up: the appeal to Freudian depth analysis. The most notorious instance is Ernest Jones's nomination of Hamlet as subject to an 'Oedipus Complex' (in an essay first published in the *American Journal of Psychology* in 1910; Jones benefits from a brief suggestion in Freud's *Interpretation of Dreams* (1900)). Doubt about the status of the Ghost, laziness, cowardice, a sensitive conscience, a wish to make sure Claudius goes to hell, a wish not to harm his mother, an open and generous disposition, a cautious and crafty disposition – all these are plausible motives for Hamlet, Jones observes, but, in the text, none of them is compelling, and they may even be contradictory. Perhaps, then, Hamlet is unconscious of what is inhibiting him; perhaps he is repressing it. In his Freudian reading of the play Jones stresses that Hamlet's malaise precedes his knowledge of the murder of his father: it is to do with his mother (hence his divided response to Ophelia). Like other little boys, the Prince is presumed to have regarded his father as a rival for the love of his mother. When Claudius murders King Hamlet, then, he is carrying out Hamlet's own, long-repressed desire. 'O my prophetic soul! | My uncle?' (I.5.40–41): in his unconscious Hamlet already knew it. And it is because Claudius incorporates Hamlet's deepest wishes that Hamlet cannot kill him. Perhaps; a great deal of the play seems to be left out. Notice also that, although depth analysis aims to go beyond Bradleyan common sense, it in fact relies on a Bradleyan expectation that the character will ultimately cohere.

Freudian critics throw emphasis onto Hamlet's relations with his mother, whereas Bradley, the Victorian, is embarrassed when the topic is female sexuality. The Queen is not usually regarded as a problematic figure, but in fact she illustrates Shakespeare's lack of interest in characterization for itself. Observe Hamlet's reiterated demand, that she should not continue in sexual relations with Claudius:

> Confess yourself to heaven.
> Repent what's past. Avoid what is to come;
> And do not spread the compost on the weeds
> To make them ranker. (III.4.150–53)

What she must *not* do is

> Let the bloat King tempt you again to bed,
> Pinch wanton on your cheek, call you his mouse,
> And let him, for a pair of reechy kisses,
> Or paddling in your neck with his damned fingers,
> Make you to ravel all this matter out . . . (III.4.183–7)

Gertrude doesn't reveal to the King what Hamlet has said to her, but does she allow Claudius to make love to her? He appeals to her in the ensuing scenes, in which the death of Polonius is investigated and Hamlet ordered to England: 'O Gertrude, come away!', 'Come, Gertrude', 'O, come away' (IV.1.28, 38, 44). Is he insisting because she is so complicit with his desires, or because she is showing reluctance? Does she respond supportively, or shrink away (perhaps she has a headache)? He invokes her support over the madness of Ophelia: 'O Gertrude, Gertrude', 'O my dear Gertrude' (IV.5.78, 95); the text gives her no reply. When Laertes arrives with riotous supporters she tries to protect the King; as she says, he is not responsible for the death of Polonius. She reports the death of Ophelia to Laertes, not to her husband. 'Let's follow, Gertrude', he exhorts (IV.7.191). In the last scene there is still ample opportunity to resolve the question of Gertrude's attitude to the King, but there is no indication, one way or the other, in the dialogue or the stage directions.

Of course, in performance the question has to be settled; the actor and director will decide. But the significant point is that Shakespeare wasn't sufficiently interested in the Queen to write any more dialogue for her. Her interiority – the state of her sex life and her eternal soul – is of interest only while it concerns Hamlet. In fact, this is one of a number of instances where Shakespeare briskly discards characters who are no longer required for the story. The Fool in *King Lear*, Adam in *As You Like It*, Christopher Sly in *The Taming of the Shrew* and the Nurse in *Romeo and Juliet* are prominent examples; Shakespeare doesn't even write them out, as in a soap opera, he just drops them. Other characters, such as Celia and Oliver in *As You Like It*, Olivia and Sebastian in *Twelfth Night* and Angelo and Mariana in *Measure for Measure*, are married off abruptly to people with whom they have no apparent affinity, with no opportunity to indicate how this might contribute to the development of their character. Minor characters are especially disposable. Barnardo is needed in the first scene of *Hamlet* to talk first with Francisco, then with Marcellus and Horatio, and he visits Hamlet to confirm the story of the Ghost. It seems that he will be with the others when they watch again for the Ghost (I.4), but he disappears. To be sure, this may be good dramatic economy, but it sits uneasily with an expectation that the characters will manifest consistent and developing personalities.

SUBJECTIVITIES

> *But I have that within which passes show –*
> *These but the trappings and the suits of woe.* (I.2.85–6)

There are two problems with character criticism. One, I have shown, is that it doesn't fit *Hamlet* very well; the other is that it doesn't fit postmodern ideas about subjectivity. None of us really has a consistent inner core of being, which could be captured in a thumbnail sketch (Hamlet as constant lover versus Hamlet as suspicious and resentful). For many thinkers today, *any* identity is, and should be, decentred – unstable, provisional, occupied only through processes of anxious repetition. Individuals may experience diverse identities and desires in diverse circumstances; we are all situated at points of intersection of diverse social pressures and limits. Belief in our individual selfhoods is a strategy that we need to survive in our atomized kind of society (though in actuality, market researchers find, we are remarkably similar).

Although *Hamlet* is remote from us it is not entirely foreign; we may well find in certain early modern texts

intimations of how the expectation of interiority and
consistency is going to develop in modern societies. These
glimpses may be sufficient to prompt character-oriented
questions – it is understandable that Bradley, Freud and
very many of Shakespeare's readers should attempt
them – but not sufficient to produce persuasive answers.
Without supposing that these dramatic contrivances are
unified personalities, or independent of the multiple
shaping assumptions of the culture, we may still observe
indications, at least intermittently, that the characters
experience themselves as continuous subjectivities. If
Hamlet is not written in a way that will entirely accommodate the character critic, nor is it conceived like a medieval
allegory, out of stock components (such as Everyman, Vice
and Revenge). While early modern culture was different
from ours, it was not altogether different.

An instance of the partial development of interiority is
when Polonius observes

> that with devotion's visage
> And pious action we do sugar o'er
> The devil himself. (III.1.47–9)

With the appearance of prayer and virtuous behaviour
we disguise devilish practices. The King picks this up in
an aside:

> How smart a lash that speech doth give my conscience!
> The harlot's cheek, beautied with plastering art,
> Is not more ugly to the thing that helps it
> Than is my deed to my most painted word. (III.1.50–53)

The capacity to appropriate and redirect the speech of
another, in accord with his own preoccupations, signals the

King's interiority. His conscience is not a static possession but may be stimulated by a casual remark. However, the idea is developed not in a way personal to Claudius but as a conventional jibe at female sexuality. The Bradleyan critic, bent upon discovering a psychological justification of every line, might find here a sign of Claudius's tendency to deflect his guilt onto others; however, that would be a far-fetched interpretation – one that contradicts the impression that a truth is being revealed. It seems safer to acknowledge that the King's subjectivity gives way to a conventional motif.

Of course, it is Hamlet who gives the strongest impression of subjectivity. Soliloquies signify interiority, even if they are somewhat stylized; Hamlet's are replete with self-reference, self-questioning, indecision and reviews of the action so far. In dialogue with the other characters he is teasing, deceitful, mercurial and politic – all indications of an adaptable, interior project beyond the immediate exchange. He obliges others to take account of his subjectivity; his opening gambit is to insist on a distinction between interior emotion and external expression. There may be customary manifestations of grief; they are

> actions that a man might play.
> But I have that within which passes show –
> These but the trappings and the suits of woe. (I.2.84–6)

Claudius accepts this distinction when he briefs Rosencrantz and Guildenstern:

> Something have you heard
> Of Hamlet's transformation – so call it,
> Sith nor th'exterior nor the inward man
> Resembles that it was. (II.2.4–7)

Guildenstern, reporting back, recognizes that Hamlet's self-presentation is concealing his true state of mind:

> Nor do we find him forward to be sounded,
> But with a crafty madness keeps aloof
> When we would bring him on to some confession
> Of his true state. (III.1.7–10)

Centrally, one might argue, *Hamlet* is *about* the realization of interiority. The issue is not the nature of Hamlet's subjectivity but what it might mean to have a subjectivity. If the Prince has appeared a notably 'modern' figure, then, it is not because he spontaneously expresses a nineteenth- or twentieth-century sensibility but because, by arriving at modernity in an incomplete way, he draws attention to its historical development.

On this analysis, it is understandable that Hamlet has proved an intriguing figure for the character critic. He gives us glimpses of subjectivity all the time in his dialogue, but some of them are provocatively discontinuous. They effect a sequence of loosely linked interiorities, not a coherent identity. Consider Hamlet's warning to Horatio and Marcellus that he may 'put an antic disposition on' (I.5.172). This would account for his erratic behaviour, but is all his madness contrived? The vigorous abuse of Ophelia and Gertrude, for instance? After all, the melancholy and misogyny precede the Ghost's revelation. The case is not conclusive either way. Leaping into Ophelia's grave with Laertes might be attributed to a contrived antic disposition, but Hamlet says otherwise: 'But I am very sorry, good Horatio, | That to Laertes I forgot myself' (V.2.75–6). It is not that there are insufficient signs of subjectivity in the text for character criticism to work on; there are too many.

THE INDIVIDUAL AND THE STATE

Something is rotten in the state of Denmark. (I.4.90)

Shakespeare, we may conclude, was more interested in something else; perhaps public affairs were more important than private. He has articulated, in *Hamlet*, a whole system of authority and rule undergoing corruption and disintegration. In comparison with this, whether Hamlet is mad all the time or just some of the time might be a minor matter. Focusing on the individual character, exceptional though he or she may be, is not the most promising way to understand human societies in general and the world of early modern drama in particular.

The appearance of the Ghost at the start of the play is not just about Hamlet: it 'bodes some strange eruption to our state', Horatio declares (I.1.69). Already strict watch is being kept, brass cannon are being cast and shipwrights impressed. The business between old Hamlet and old Fortinbras is not finished: young Fortinbras is trying to regain by conquest the territories that his father lost. The second scene shows Claudius dealing with this, while consolidating his rule by marrying the Queen and by managing powerful court figures. In Act II, scene 2 Voltemand and Cornelius return from their embassy to Norway; young Fortinbras is being reined in by his uncle, and seeks permission merely to cross Danish territory to attack the Poles. However, Hamlet's demeanour is already undermining the royal pragmatism; the King, Queen and Polonius become more concerned about Hamlet's state of mind.

Increasingly, the business of the court is narrowed and diverted; relations with England are contaminated.

Hamlet's manic presence entangles everyone, destroying the Polonius and Hamlet families. The Prince, meanwhile, applies all occasions to himself. He encounters Fortinbras's army, and draws from it not considerations of state but fuel for his own obsessions. He takes the death of Ophelia and the distress of Laertes as entirely personal affairs, whereas the King at least tries to deal with them as disturbances in the body politic. Hamlet is not bothered about whether the people become 'muddied, | Thick and unwholesome in their thoughts and whispers' (IV.5.82–3). His final endorsement of Fortinbras perhaps represents his dawning recognition that the Danish ruling elite are not able to govern themselves, let alone the country.

If you believe in order at any price, you may celebrate the restoration of state power when Fortinbras takes over at the end. Alternatively, we might observe that, while the Danes are engaged in internecine wrangling, the longstanding project of the Fortinbras family – the conquest of Denmark – is achieved. This may be taken as accidental: despite all the scheming of the play, closure comes quite by chance; it is a tragic irony. Kenneth Branagh offers another interpretation in his film *Hamlet* (1996). He shows Fortinbras's arrival as neither incidental nor innocent. During Act V the Norwegian soldiers stealthily storm the castle, disarming the sentries and occupying strategic sites. Already before the death of Claudius there has been effective regime change; we see soldiers hauling down a giant statue of King Hamlet. The noise of drums, trumpets and guns (see the stage directions at V.2.275 and V.2.343) may seem to be part of the King's carousing, but they turn out to be the commotion of an invasion. This is not the only way to read the scene, but it does develop an emphasis that is in the text. The intense familial struggles prove to have been a catastrophic distraction; the Danes should have attended to state affairs.

Yet it would not be altogether correct to say that they attend to private life at the expense of public matters; in effect, these characters have no privacy. First, Polonius and the King cultivate a regime of decoys, agents provocateurs, spies, informers and assassins, such that many private conversations are open to the state regulatory system. Polonius, Ophelia, the King, Rosencrantz and Guildenstern and the Queen are all deployed to spy on Hamlet; Polonius recruits Reynaldo to watch Laertes, and Laertes plots with the King. When Ophelia calls Hamlet 'Th'observed of all observers' (III.1.155) she means he has been admired and imitated; in fact, he is becoming the object of a comprehensive surveillance. Hamlet reacts by setting his own watch upon the King (at the mousetrap play) and opening confidential letters. We may find here a reminder of the surveillance practices of the Elizabethan government, under the regime of Sir Francis Walsingham, and of the government of James I, which foiled the famous plot of Guy Fawkes to blow up Parliament in 1605 through infiltration and torture.

To be sure, the Danish state is under threat; as in our own times this is taken as a reason to rescind the civil rights that are proclaimed as inscribing the justness of the system. Polonius knows that it is a sensitive moment when he proposes eavesdropping on the Queen and Prince to the King:

> And, as you said, and wisely was it said,
> 'Tis meet that some more audience than a mother,
> Since nature makes them partial, should o'erhear
> The speech, of vantage. (III.3.30–33)

In fact this was Polonius's own idea (III.1.185–6). In defending itself, the state forfeits its own justification. So Claudius claims privileges that he has himself violated: 'There's such divinity doth hedge a king | That treason can but peep to what it would' (IV.5.125–6). Notice, though, that the ruling elite closes ranks in the face of a threat from the lower orders. Gertrude's most specific moment of solidarity with Claudius occurs when Laertes encourages 'a riotous head' to threaten their dominance; 'you false Danish dogs' she calls them (IV.5.103, 112). In fact Laertes is easily drawn away from his popular constituency and reincorporated into the state apparatus.

PATRIARCHY AND MADNESS

Frailty, thy name is woman. (I.2.146)

Private life is public in Denmark, then, partly because of state surveillance. Also, the family, which we may think of as a private matter, is the institution through which sexuality and gender are channelled into directions that suit the state. The institution of marriage is supposed to ensure that suitable and fit human beings will combine to secure the continuation of the social unit, maintaining not only the gene pool but also the class structure, racial hierarchy and above all the legitimate transmission of property from one generation to the next. Males are expected to engage in rivalry for women of an appropriate class, who are expected to make themselves available. Other relations are forbidden or stigmatized, though extramarital liaisons may be permitted, unofficially, to the male. There are legitimate paths for securing these arrangements; *Hamlet* is about what happens when illegal means are adopted.

The state's interest in gender and sexuality is more obvious in respect of upper-class people. During the lifetime of King Hamlet the liaison between Gertrude and Claudius is 'traitorous' as well as 'incestuous' and 'adulterate' (I.5.42–3); when they marry it is a ratification of their entitlement to rule. We have seen that subjective motivation scarcely explains the actions of the Queen. Rather, she is the object upon which two powerful brothers have fixated, establishing their authority and territory by capturing her. Hamlet seeks her collaboration in his campaign against Claudius, while fighting with Laertes for possession of Ophelia.

The operations of patriarchal authority are evident in the Polonius family. Laertes's wish to return to France is granted readily by his father and the King; when we first see Ophelia she is being told, by Laertes at length, to forsake her wishes in respect of her affair with Hamlet. She replies submissively. Perhaps intending to lighten the mood, she warns Laertes to observe his own advice, but he brushes the idea aside: 'O, fear me not' (I.3.51). This discrepancy in the scope allowed to sons and daughters is repeated when Polonius gives Laertes advice on how to move in an independent, adult way through the world, then castigates Ophelia about Hamlet. She reports the Prince's 'many tenders | Of his affection', the 'honourable fashion' he has maintained and his 'holy vows of heaven' (I.3.99–100, 111, 114), but her father places a sceptical construction on all that: 'In few, Ophelia, | Do not believe his vows'; they are 'like sanctified and pious bawds, | The better to beguile' (I.3.126–7, 130–31). He slides from the precautionary injunction, 'Tender yourself more dearly' (I.3.107), to commanding her to break off the affair altogether.

At least Laertes did not belittle the lovers' feelings; he

was just trying to be practical about the Prince: 'For on his choice depends | The safety and health of this whole state' (I.3.20–21). Her father, however, systematically disconfirms Ophelia's perceptions; no wonder she goes mad. She has apprehended Hamlet as honourable and sincere, but at each step Polonius insists that she is misinterpreting. So her trust in her own feelings and perceptions is undermined. (King Lear's daughters similarly confuse him.)

OPHELIA

My lord, he hath importuned me with love
In honourable fashion.

POLONIUS

Ay, 'fashion' you may call it. Go to, go to.

OPHELIA

And hath given countenance to his speech, my lord,
With almost all the holy vows of heaven.

POLONIUS

Ay, springes to catch woodcocks. (I.3.110–15)

Ophelia's predicament is exacerbated by Hamlet. She knows he gave her tokens, but he says, 'I never gave you aught' (III.1.96). This means: I never really *gave you myself*; or: The *I* and the *you* that exchanged tokens are no longer the same people. When Hamlet insults her before the whole court – 'Lady, shall I lie in your lap?' (III.2.121) – he constitutes himself as the lascivious philanderer whom Polonius has alleged him to be. Further, he denies a bawdy intention, so that the offence appears to be hers: 'Do you think I meant country matters?' (III.2.125). No wonder this innocent maiden ends up singing bawdy songs. When Ophelia's love story becomes unsustainable she falls back on a tale of exploitation and betrayal:

> Quoth she, 'Before you tumbled me,
>   You promised me to wed.'

He answers:

> 'So would I ha' done, by yonder sun,
>   An thou hadst not come to my bed.' (IV.5.63–7)

Meanwhile a double standard is again manifest when Polonius contrives to check up on Laertes. He wants Reynaldo to gain confidences about his son's behaviour by attributing to him 'wanton, wild, and usual slips' (II.1.22). Reynaldo is anxious about bringing Laertes into disrepute, but Polonius is happy to countenance drinking, fighting, swearing, quarrelling and consorting with prostitutes. Such faults

>   may seem the taints of liberty,
> The flash and outbreak of a fiery mind,
> A savageness in unreclaimèd blood,
> Of general assault. (II.1.32–5)

Polonius really wants Laertes to be a red-blooded male, presumably because this means he will be well equipped to continue the family line. Actually, this kind of masculinity often goes along with a degree of stupidity; Laertes's impetuosity makes him available to the King's manipulation, leading to dishonour and death.

The attainment of a manhood that will sustain the state is not a straightforward matter. Consider Hamlet's repeated accusation that Claudius is not the man his brother was. The Ghost himself disparages Claudius as 'a wretch whose natural gifts were poor | [compared] To those of mine!' (I.5.51–2). The situation is similar in Norway: the brother of the slain king is unable to control young Fortinbras. One might infer a validation of primogeniture: older sons offer the best stock.

The confusions in sexuality and gender are not specified in the play. Instead, we are offered misogyny. What is rotten in the state of Denmark? The persistent answer is: female sexuality. 'Frailty, thy name is woman', Hamlet asserts, even before he gets the message of the Ghost (I.2.146). Ophelia comes in for some standard abuse: 'I have heard of your paintings too, well enough. God hath given you one face, and you make yourselves another. You jig and amble, and you lisp' (III.1.143–5). The address to the Queen is notoriously over-elaborate and over-intense.

> Nay, but to live
> In the rank sweat of an enseamèd bed,
> Stewed in corruption, honeying and making love
> Over the nasty sty – (III.4.92–5)

This may sound obsessive, but Gertrude is made to acknowledge its justice. Again, when Hamlet looks at Yorick's skull he thinks of cosmetics: 'Now get you to my lady's table and tell her, let her paint an inch thick, to this favour she must come' (V.1.189–91). When he dismisses Horatio's misgivings about the duel Hamlet calls it 'Such a kind of gaingiving as would perhaps trouble a woman' (V.2.209–10).

Such misogyny might be attributed to the Prince's character, but it is not his vision alone. I have remarked how the King evokes female sexuality when the focus for his conscience ought to be his own adultery and murder. Laertes, enjoined to be calm, asserts that if he has a calm drop of blood, it

> proclaims me bastard,
> Cries cuckold to my father, brands the harlot
> Even here between the chaste, unsmirchèd brows
> Of my true mother. (IV.5.119–22)

If Laertes is less than totally turbulent, he says, it signals
that he is not the son of his father, and that his mother
must have been unfaithful. Once again, female sexuality
carries an excessive freight. Misogyny is routine, reiterated, and active in the plot, as though the play were
designed to persuade us of it as a fact. Indeed, Gertrude
is made to accept the blame:

> O Hamlet, speak no more.
> Thou turnest mine eyes into my very soul,
> And there I see such black and grainèd spots
> As will not leave their tinct. (III.4.89–92)

Actually, little of the rottenness in Denmark derives
from the women; rather, they are pretexts in the attempts
of the men to gain advantage and control within a corrupt
political elite. Diverse social disturbances are displaced
onto gender and sexuality, obscuring the contradictions
and injustices in the social and political system.

TELLING *HAMLET*

All this can I
Truly deliver. (V.2.379–80)

Our exploration of some of the problems of *Hamlet* has
not resolved them; writing about the play produces not

an end to writing but more writing. By validating this or that interpretation of the play, the critic sets his or her agenda – on honour, revenge and the law; Christianity and paganism; trust or suspicion of the ruling elite; sensitivity, dissidence and militarism; man – his individual character, suffering, mastery and fate; gender roles, misogyny and the double standard; the historicity, coherence and universality of the Shakespearian text. The telling and retelling of stories is our main means for getting some insight into and control over our circumstances.

The desire to tell the story begins with Hamlet himself. 'Absent thee from felicity awhile', he asks Horatio, meaning from the happiness of death; 'And in this harsh world draw thy breath in pain, | To tell my story' (V.2.341–3). Horatio takes his task seriously:

> . . . give order that these bodies
> High on a stage be placèd to the view.
> And let me speak to th'yet unknowing world
> How these things came about. (V.2.371–4)

Fortinbras is pleased: 'Let us haste to hear it, | And call the noblest to the audience' (V.2.380–81).

Such commitment to the story may not rest altogether in an abstract desire for the truth. The ruling elite, including both Fortinbras and Horatio, wants a peaceful transition to the new regime. They want to establish their account of what has happened; uncertainty is dangerous.

> But let this same be presently performed,
> Even while men's minds are wild, lest more mischance
> On plots and errors happen. (V.2.387–9)

Fortinbras cannot wait for Horatio's report before embarking on his own analysis of Hamlet's character: 'For he was likely, had he been put on, | To have proved most royal' (V.2.391–2). Is this true? Is Fortinbras well placed to judge? Is he claiming Hamlet as forerunner to enhance his own position? Attempts to control the story of Hamlet start here, within the play. The rest is not silence.

Alan Sinfield

The Play in Performance

As you read this it is safe to assume that someone, somewhere is performing *Hamlet*. At this moment, perhaps in a park, a village hall or a national theatre, a group of actors are embodying Shakespeare's characters, speaking his words in new ways, breathing fresh life into this inexhaustible play. From the raw material you have in your hands, a book of 'words, words, words' (II.2.193), theatrical practitioners must conjure up and populate a three-dimensional world. In the 400 years since its premiere *Hamlet* has probably been the most frequently performed of all Shakespeare's plays. Those centuries of performance have thrown up a dizzying array of interpretations, acting styles, scenic and costume designs, adaptations, parodies and translations in an astonishing variety of locations across the world. What started at the Globe theatre in or around 1600 has since become the most global of plays. What every production of *Hamlet*, whether in Stratford-upon-Avon or Singapore, has in common is the need to negotiate a set of challenges that Shakespeare's texts present to the director, designer and actor.

'THIS IS TOO LONG'

Hamlet is Shakespeare's longest play. One of the first challenges any director faces is whether to take the play, in Hamlet's image, 'to the barber's' (II.2.497). 'Full-text' productions of *Hamlet*, meaning an all-inclusive conflation of the second Quarto (Q2) and first Folio (F) texts (like this edition; see An Account of the Text), have been the exception not the rule. To speak every line of the full text, even at galloping pace, takes about four hours. Perhaps the lesson we can learn from the existence of the first or 'bad' Quarto of 1603 (Q1), by far the shortest of the three versions of the play, is that theatre practitioners have always been challenged by the length of *Hamlet*, and have devised their own solutions accordingly. There is also good reason to believe that the practice of cutting and reworking began with the playwright's approval, the Folio text being a revised and slightly abbreviated version of the earlier Q2. Throughout stage history certain passages have been repeatedly cut from performance: Hamlet's meditation on 'the stamp of one defect' (I.4.13–38); his final, self-lacerating soliloquy ('How all occasions do inform against me', IV.4.9–66; passage in Q2 only); his thoughts on the skulls of the members of various professions (V.1.75–115); and the once theatrically topical discussion of boy actors, 'the little eyases' passage (II.2.329–67). Most pre-twentieth-century productions found no room for such characters as Cornelius and Voltemand, Reynaldo and the lord who repeats Osrick's invitation to the fencing match. Remarkably, Fortinbras was largely absent from performance until the late nineteenth century. The advantage of heavy cutting of the play is to increase the momentum of the action, the excitement of events unfolding without apparent pause. The drawback has traditionally been a loss of *Hamlet*'s political dimensions, the diplomatic and military manoeuvrings in the public sphere that counter-balance the more domestic tragedies of two families. Peter Hall's production for the RSC in 1965 was notable, at the time, for its marked retention of the political and inter-national context.

Scenes and passages, if not taken to the barber's, can be rearranged and relocated. In Q1 Hamlet's 'To be or not to be' speech and his subsequent traumatic encounter with Ophelia occur before the arrival of the Players (at II.2.419 in this edition), rather than after it (III.1) as in Q2 and F. Structurally, this creates a strong arc of action, from the despair and indecision of 'To be or not to be' through the energy and emotion of the scenes with Ophelia, and Rosencrantz and Guildenstern, then climaxing with the arrival of the Players and Hamlet's excited, upbeat resolution to use theatre 'to catch the conscience of the king'. Although relatively rare, this rearrangement has proved successful in a number of stage productions and, as in Franco Zeffirelli's 1990 film version, on screen.

Similarly, Claudius's tempting of Laertes (IV.7) has sometimes (as in the films of Laurence Olivier (1948), Grigori Kosintzev (1964) and Zeffirelli (1990)) been placed after rather than before Ophelia's funeral (V.1), in order to imbue Laertes with a stronger, grief-stricken motive to agree to Claudius's dishonourable enterprise. Some directors have cut and pasted scenes to such a radical extent that the result is disorienting, a bracing re-imagination of what can seem to be over-familiar material. Peter Brook in his 2001 production at the Bouffes du Nord in Paris ended the play with Horatio once more greeting 'the morn in russet mantle clad' (I.1.167) before anxiously inquiring 'Who's there?', as if the play were destined to repeat itself infinitely. Charles Marowitz in his *Hamlet Collage* (1965) condensed and reordered the action to produce a breathless critique of Hamlet's character, 'the conscience-stricken but paralyzed liberal', as Marowitz saw him. The *Collage* concludes with Hamlet vowing 'From this time forth, | My thoughts be bloody, or be nothing worth' (IV.4.65–6) only to be met with a chorus of derisive laughter and heckles from the rest of the cast.

Hamlet might also be cut in view of the number of actors available. The process of doubling roles can lead to intriguing new layers of meaning in performance that are unavailable in a reading of the play. To have the same actor play both the ghost of Hamlet's father and his brother and murderer, Claudius, is not only plausible physically but also raises the question of whether Hamlet's assertion that his father was Hyperion to his uncle's satyr (I.2.140) is an example of hero-worship that reality might complicate. 'Look here upon this picture, and on this' (III.4.54) Hamlet demands of Gertrude, but what if there is little to choose between the two outward forms? Doubling Polonius and the first gravedigger can also resonate in performance. There is something intrinsically unnerving about this comic 'Clown' (as both Q2 and F call him), and this quality can be enhanced if we in some sense see Polonius 'underneath': the father digging his own daughter's grave, riddling, punning, getting the upper hand with Hamlet in an inversion of their earlier talk of 'fishmongers' and of crabs going backwards (II.2.171–219) in which the young man ran rings around the older. Polonius is the first person Hamlet has ever killed; in Act V, scene 1, with the right doubling, we can see him face to face not only with the mortality of Yorick but also with that of his victim.

Whatever decisions are taken with doubling, and with the order or the length of scenes, the *Hamlet* director must attempt to balance the linear drive of the narrative, the excitement and suspense of a revenge tragedy, and the more expansive, lateral moments of reflection and digression, the scenes and passages which give us such a powerful sense both of the 'reality' of the characters and of the military-political context in which they exist.

'DENMARK'S A PRISON'

What and where is 'Elsinore'? Is it the brooding, sea-beaten Nordic castle of Olivier and Kozintsev's films or the hypermodern corporate New York of soft-drinks dispensers and hand-held digital cameras in which Michael Almerayda set his 2001 film? Peter Brook once famously asserted that the basic definition of a stage is an 'empty space': 'A man walks across this empty space while someone else is watching him, and that is all that is needed for an act of theatre to be engaged' (*The Empty Space* (1968)). *Hamlet* can be performed anywhere. Empty spaces as diverse as a boat off the coast of Sierra Leone (the first clearly recorded performance of the play in 1607), the original Globe theatre (and also the one that stands on the South Bank of the Thames today), Richard Nixon's White House and Elsinore castle itself have all hosted versions of *Hamlet*.

The geographical location of performance is part of its meaning. Lines such as 'But break, my heart, for I must hold my tongue' (I.2.159) and Claudius's anxious inquiry about the political content of *The Mousetrap*

(III.2.242–3) have and will continue to resonate in societies in which the individual and the artist are pitched against state censorship. The senseless loss of life involved in battling over 'a little patch of ground' (IV.4.18) can have a heartbreaking immediacy depending on the location and timing of a performance. But directors and designers must also decide how to fill the empty space in which these lines are spoken. Should Elsinore appear exotic or familiar? Barry Jackson, in his production at the Birmingham Repertory theatre in 1925, bravely chose the latter, turning his back on centuries of stage tradition by placing *Hamlet* squarely in a contemporary setting. Costume is one of our first means of orientation when watching Shakespeare. Jackson had his cast wear the fashions of his audience: flapper dresses, lounge suits and, notoriously, plus-fours (leisured-class golf wear). Hamlet smoked while considering the ways in which all occasions informed against him; Ophelia improvised the latest jazz dance steps whilst singing her songs of madness. In Germany a year later, in 1926, Leopold Jessner presented Elsinore as the military court of Kaiser Wilhelm II, thus holding the mirror up to an arrogant and corrupt regime.

Directors and designers concerned with anachronisms (i.e. why does a twenty-first-century soldier carry a 'partisan', a cumbersome weapon, when he could carry a machine gun?) are unlikely to set the play in the present, but will look to a number of past eras for the visual and social backdrop to their *Hamlet*. Thus the play has been set in the Renaissance, the Regency, the Edwardian and the Victorian eras, to name but four. Another popular option is to create a more abstract setting that apparently transcends social history. Edward Gordon Craig's radical designs for the Moscow Arts Theatre production of 1912 were more concerned with space and monolithic shapes as metaphors for psychological experience than with settings as realistic, recognizable backdrop to action. How Elsinore looks has an enormous effect on our experience of the play and will do much to elaborate, complement or complicate the work of the actors.

'THE PURPOSE OF PLAYING'

More than any other Shakespeare play, *Hamlet* self-consciously explores the medium of theatre and the nature of performance. With the exception of the Induction to *The Taming of the Shrew*, no other play in the canon asks professional actors to impersonate professional actors. Shakespeare's earlier comedies, *A Midsummer Night's Dream* and *Love's Labour's Lost*, both contain plays-within-the-play performed at the conclusion by amateur (customarily incompetent) 'actors'. But it is a sign of the importance of acting in *Hamlet* that *The Mousetrap* stands at the centre of the piece.

In the lead-up to *The Mousetrap* we see Hamlet as director, perhaps presumptuously instructing the actors on their own profession. His advice seems clear enough: 'Suit the action to the word, the word to the action, with this special observance, that you o'erstep not the modesty of nature' (III.2.17–19). The 'purpose of playing', he tells them, 'is to hold, as 'twere, the mirror up to nature, to show virtue her own feature, scorn her own image, and the very age and body of the time his form and pressure' (III.2.21–4). This has repeatedly been invoked as Shakespeare's own advice to his company of actors, as if it were a straightforward, unambiguous set of instructions, a miracle cure for bad acting. Like most things

Hamlet says, though, it is open to interpretation. Holding the mirror up to nature is a complex injunction, as it is not at all clear that human nature is stable or knowable. What is 'natural' behaviour? The play is interested in the question. Is it natural bloodily to revenge your father's murder? Is it natural to marry your dead husband's brother? Is it natural to lose your sanity on the death of a parent? Just as these questions admit no simple answers, so the question of what constitutes natural theatrical behaviour is more complicated than Hamlet's advice implies. Acting naturally has meant vastly different things for different actors and actresses over the last 400 years. What was thought a natural mode of behaviour in one period will not necessarily satisfy or convince in the next.

The stage history of Hamlet's early meetings with the ghost of his father (I.4, I.5) illustrates the imperative for each theatrical era to find a new way of suiting 'the action to the word'. When the Ghost of Hamlet's father first appeared to David Garrick's Prince in the 1740s the German critic-tourist Georg Lichtenberg reported that the actor gave a 'start', then a retreat of two or three paces. Garrick was rooted to the spot, his mouth ajar and his legs apart, but, as Lichtenberg reassures us, 'with no loss of dignity'. Such a response was perfectly attuned to an age of sensibility, in which much artistic representation was based on the notion that inner feelings always had external symptoms. According to some reports, Garrick, with mechanical assistance, caused his hair to stand on end, 'like quills upon the fretful porpentine' (I.5.20). But as social beliefs about the existence of ghosts have changed in the centuries since Garrick so directors have been challenged to reimagine both the Ghost and Hamlet's reaction to it. The Ghost can still appear in modern productions as otherworldly, intimidating, but he is just as likely now to be less supernatural in appearance, a sad father telling a pitiful story to his son. Some productions, holding the mirror up to an age sceptical of the metaphysical, have chosen not to embody the Ghost at all. In Richard Eyre's 1980 production at the Royal Court Jonathan Pryce's Hamlet spoke his father's lines as if possessed. The relationship between Shakespeare's words and 'natural' theatrical action is dynamic and unpredictable, always responsive to and constituted by the wider cultural contexts in which performance takes place.

'BY INDIRECTIONS FIND DIRECTION OUT'

We cannot know for sure if or how Shakespeare directed the first performance of *Hamlet*. Furthermore, he never committed to print the lengthy stage directions or detailed, novelistic character descriptions that later playwrights, such as George Bernard Shaw or Henrik Ibsen, included in their texts to help guide readers and theatre practitioners towards the author's ideal staging. It is partly this openness to interpretation that has kept Shakespeare's plays on the stage. *Hamlet*, of course, contains some strong hints about how it might be staged: it seems clear that in the first performance at the Globe the Ghost must have descended beneath the stage after his exit at I.5.91, or why else would Hamlet joke about the fellow in the cellarage, or the old mole (I.5.151, 162)? But there are many other moments when the modern director has no definitive textual authority for a performance decision but, in collaboration with the cast, will mix judgement and instinct to make a choice.

Should Hamlet, for example, know that Claudius and Polonius are spying on his conversation with Ophelia? In the 1820s the American actor J. B. Booth was possibly the first Hamlet to catch sight of the eavesdroppers, and many Hamlets have since followed suit. If Hamlet knows he's being spied on and that Ophelia is lying when she tells him that her father is 'at home', his subsequent anger and misogyny can, to some extent, be excused. Nevertheless, the brave actor might not make the whole scene pivot on 'Where's your father?', would not sense the presence of the spies. In doing so, he would risk losing or, at the very least, complicating audience sympathy.

Performance choices like this abound in *Hamlet*. If the dumb show before *The Mousetrap* is retained – it is often cut – at what point should Claudius visibly react, at what moment will the actor show us the catching of his conscience? Should Hamlet, as some actors have done, speak 'To be or not to be' to Ophelia? Should she over-hear his 'soliloquy'? How should Ophelia's eventual descent into 'madness' be represented? What combination of costume, gesture and vocal pitch will convince the audience? Compare, for examples, the hushed self-possession of Anastasia Vertinskaya in Kozintsev's film with the strait-jacketed fury of Kate Winslet in Branagh's (1996).

In the long scene between Hamlet and Gertrude (III.4, commonly referred to as 'the closet scene') should the action of the scene, as is now common, revolve around a bed, even though neither the stage directions nor the dialogue refer to this complexly symbolic prop? How 'Freudian', if at all, is this charged encounter between mother and son? When the Ghost re-enters, does Gertrude see, half-sense or not see at all the spirit of her dead

husband? How does Gertrude end the scene? Has she
effectively switched loyalty from Claudius to Hamlet?
Does she exit at the end of the scene, or does she remain
onstage before Claudius enters with Rosencrantz and
Guildenstern? If so, what does the actress convey to us
in that moment of solitude? For much of the play's stage
history this scene ended with Hamlet exiting on 'I must
be cruel only to be kind' (III.4.179), thus cutting off not
only Hamlet's obsessive return to the image of his mother
and step-father's love-making but also Gertrude's apparently unambiguous guarantee of loyalty (198–200).

Each scene and every individual performance is a
mosaic of such decisions. Although now unfashionable in
literary studies (see Introduction), the idea of character
criticism, of treating the characters as if they were real
people, is indispensable to the actor. What sort of person,
for example, is Polonius? Where will the actor place him
on the spectrum between incompetent buffoon and
capable, wily politician? What kind of father is he? Distant
and patriarchal or tender and affectionate? Polonius's lines
and actions support any of these readings or a complex
combination of them all. According to Hamlet's improvised epitaph, he was 'a foolish prating knave' (III.4.216),
but why should we believe Hamlet? It is often rewarding
for actor and audience alike if the supporting character is
played not according to what Hamlet says of them but
from the character's own point of view. Claudius, for
example, can be played as a more complicated man than
the 'Remorseless, treacherous, lecherous, kindless villain'
(II.2.578) of Hamlet's description.

At the centre of any performance of the play stands
Hamlet himself. Hamlet is the most coveted role in world
drama, a challenge that every actor wants to face at some
point in his or her career. 'Her' because there is a long

tradition of female Hamlets, the most celebrated of which was the great French tragedienne Sarah Bernhardt, who first played the part in 1899. Some fortunate actors have had the chance to revisit and re-evaluate Hamlet throughout their career: John Gielgud, synonymous with the role in the mid twentieth century, played the part hundreds of times over the course of sixteen years (1930–46). The role was in all probability first played by Richard Burbage at the Globe, since which time many very different actors have donned the inky cloak. J. B. Booth told his teenage son and future actor Edwin, 'You look like Hamlet.' But Hamlets have come in all shapes and sizes since Burbage. Although the great aesthetic cliché is that Hamlet should be blond (see Olivier and Branagh's peroxide crops), there is nothing in the text that demands this. What the text does demand of the actor is a combination of any number of qualities: stamina, vulnerability, charm, lunacy, wit, anger, vocal technique and variety, arrogance, melancholy, classicism, colloquialism, irony, generosity and cruelty. Hamlet has all these and much more. The actor's race and nationality is irrelevant: what counts is the ability to embody at least some of the character's myriad emotional and intellectual life, to revel in the excessive subjectivity of the part, its inconsistencies, discontinuities and mercurial shifts.

Hamlet will continue to be remade through performance for decades and presumably centuries to come. No production, no individual performance can hope to be definitive. We should be suspicious of directors who talk of letting the play 'speak for itself', because no one knows what that would sound like. A performance may capture the 'form and pressure' of its time but cannot anticipate the concerns of future generations of artists and audiences to whom the play will speak in new accents. The processes of casting, cutting, choosing a venue and re-imagining sets and costumes will generate, through the pragmatic alchemy of theatre, interpretations and images that are unthinkable today. Seconds away from death, Hamlet implores Horatio: 'Absent thee from felicity awhile, | And in this harsh world draw thy breath in pain, | To tell my story' (V.2.341–3). It is an inexhaustible story and one that is most thrillingly and movingly told through the act of live performance.

Paul Prescott

Further Reading

It's hardly surprising that recent major editions of *Hamlet* should give so much attention in their introductory material to a proper understanding of the play's extraordinarily complicated textual situation where three quasi-independent editions – the first Quarto (Q1; 1603), the second (Q2; 1604–5), the Folio (F; 1623) – vie for editorial consideration. Even the hitherto much despised Q1 has its advocates in Brian Loughrey and Graham Holderness in their treatment of it in the Shakespearean Originals series (1992) as an authentic and surprisingly powerful 'performance text' in which 'the problems of the play became less psychological, more circumstantial and contingent'. They argue with some justice that these first three editions of *Hamlet* are so different that they should be regarded 'not simply as variants of a single work, but as discrete textualizations independently framed within a complex and diversified product of cultural production'. The same year (1992) produced a differently focused view of Q1 in Thomas Clayton's volume *The 'Hamlet' First Published (Q1, 1603): Origins, Form, Intertextualities*. Is the enigmatic Q1 an honest ghost or goblin damned? Defenders of Q1, Clayton argues, are motivated by political and/or theatrical reasons, not literary ones: 'perhaps another manifestation of the antiliterary decanonizing temper of our time'. The 'more literary' editors of the Arden *Hamlet* (1982), the New Cambridge Shakespeare (1985) and the Oxford Shakespeare (1987) continue to argue for the desperate inferiority of Q1. G. R. Hibbard, the Oxford editor, makes an impressive case for Q2 as Shakespeare's first draft, with the 1623 Folio a revision of this first draft and Q1 a reported version of an abridgement of this revised text. There are, it seems, as many indirections in the history of the play's printing career as in the play's plot. Paul Bertram and Bernice W. Kliman provide a means for the reader to understand what all the fuss is about with their *Three-Text 'Hamlet': Parallel Texts of the First and Second Quartos and First Folio* (1991). At all events it is important for students of the play to buttress their reading of this edition's Account of the Text with the above-mentioned works.

Before leaving them, a mention should also be made of their contributions to our understanding of the play in other important areas – its theatrical history, its sources, date, and its linguistic, theological, political and psychological cruxes. In particular, the three editions from the 1980s shed much light on some old controversies. Even the 'To be' soliloquy gets a refurbishing from Harold Jenkins, the Arden editor, in one of his densely argued 'Longer Notes'. His dogmatic acuteness is apparent in his contention that in this, the most famous of all soliloquies, Hamlet cannot mean what so many readers have taken him to mean, namely that by opposing a sea of troubles he can overcome them – what Hamlet means is that the troubles will only end by the opposer's death (presumably by drowning) in his inevitably futile struggle against the overwhelming numbers implied in 'a sea of troubles'.

Given the mountains of commentary on *Hamlet*, Ossas piled on Pelions, a rewarding initial approach might well take advantage of the metacritical times we live in by looking at works that purport to explain just why so much has been written on the play. One such is Cedric Watts's fine Harvester New Critical Introduction (1988), which maintains that 'the play's pregnancy breeds midwives': 'it is the veering seismograph which registers the earth-tremors and landslides of ideology.' We should not shrink, he says, from acknowledging (and enjoying) in the play the 'fruitful friction between muddle and complexity, the improvised and the orchestrated, the traditional and the innovatory'. Another perspicacious combination of book about *Hamlet* and book about books about *Hamlet* is Michael Hattaway's in the Critics Debate Series (1987), while Paul Cantor's 'wide-angled approach' in the Landmarks of World Literature Series (1989) helps us to see *Hamlet* in the boundless reaches of the inter-textuality of world literature. Cantor is particularly good on the importance for an understanding of *Hamlet* of the traditional ambivalence in world literature – especially Christian world literature – towards heroism. To change the angle of approach slightly, Martin Scofield's *The Ghosts of 'Hamlet': The Play and Modern Writers* (1980) looks at what modern writers like Eliot and Kafka have made of the play – modern not Romantic (no Yeats or Pasternak here) – and his own reading of *Hamlet* reflects their fascination with the play's indeterminacy. What Scofield does with modern writers, Michael Cohen attempts to do with nine modern productions in his *'Hamlet' in My Mind's Eye* (1989), which offers 'a kind of bedlam *Hamlet* with a multiple personality disorder'. James L. Calderwood's *To Be and Not To Be: Negation and Metadrama in 'Hamlet'* (1983) focuses on the pursuit of motes with Blakeian infinities in a play that 'seems dedicated to its own deconstruction'. These points of view owe a debt, I would say, to Harry Levin's masterly little book *The Question of 'Hamlet'* (1959), which examines the play in terms of its obsession with interrogation, doubt and irony. All these works celebrate rather than scold the play's intractability.

It was not always so (and often still isn't). T. S. Eliot's famous essay on the play (1919) – reprinted in David Bevington's *Twentieth-Century Interpretations* (1968) along with other cavillers' and aspiring integrators' – found Hamlet's emotion about his parents excessive and disproportionate. G. W. Knight's equally famous essay in *The Wheel of Fire* (1930) judged Hamlet a villain. Ernest Jones in *Hamlet and Oedipus* (1949) pronounced Hamlet a victim of the Oedipus Complex. A. C. Bradley in his highly influential *Shakespearean Tragedy* (1904) diagnosed him as suffering from melancholy induced by the moral shock on a noble and idealistic nature of his mother's o'erhasty remarriage. Two very readable works by L. C. Knights are Bradleyan in approach but far more censorious of the prince than Bradley is: *An Approach to 'Hamlet'* (1961) and 'Prince Hamlet' (1940). These are some of the huge number of attempts to pluck out the heart of Hamlet's mystery in response to what Watts calls 'a quality of opacity in his nature'. The hectic pursuit continues. C. L. Barber and Richard P. Wheeler in *The Whole Journey: Shakespeare's Power of Development* (1986) see a connection between the play and Shakespeare's home life – John Shakespeare, for instance, as a possible alcoholic Claudius. Indeed, the 'whole tragic period can be seen as a reckoning with the problem of inheritance from one generation to the next'. This book might be read in conjunction with Janet Adelman's feminist

Suffocating Mothers: Fantasies of Maternal Origin in Shakespeare's Plays, 'Hamlet' to 'The Tempest' (1992), in which the 'buried fantasy of *Hamlet*' is the subjection of the male to the female. The queen, the queen's to blame. An instructive contrast is Linda Bamber's equally feminist *Comic Women, Tragic Men: A Study of Gender and Genre in Shakespeare* (1982), which emphasizes – credibly I think – how *Hamlet* deflects our impulse to criticize Gertrude. Gertrude and Ophelia are, as it were, attendant lords, 'psychologically and morally neutral characters who take on the coloration of the play's mood'. H. R. Coursen concentrates on representations of Ophelia in *Shakespearean Performance as Interpretation* (1992).

Much was – and still is – made of the incompatibility of the play's, rather than the main character's, parents. That is, there are frequent attempts to explain the play's opacities in terms of a confluence in it of different and jarring dramatic and narrative traditions with Shakespeare's own complicating additions. A. J. A. Waldock's *'Hamlet': A Study in Critical Method* (1931) follows Schücking and Stoll, among others, in this pursuit. Peter Mercer continues this tradition in *'Hamlet' and the Acting of Revenge* (1987), in which – in the context of Kyd's *Spanish Tragedy* (1587–9), Marston's *Antonio's Revenge* (1599?), and Middleton's *Revenger's Tragedy* (1607) – he argues that the peculiarity of *Hamlet* may come from the convergence of two different expressive modes: the dramatic mode of revenge tragedy and the rhetorical mode of satire and complaint. As we might imagine, such an enigmatic play as *Hamlet* is a frequent candidate for parabolically minded critics, particularly religious ones. Arthur McGee, for example, in *The Elizabethan 'Hamlet'* (1987), in the rather strident tradition of Eleanor Prosser's *'Hamlet' and Revenge* (1967), argues for a Protestant Hamlet in a Catholic court possessed by the devil, whose emissary is Hamlet's father. Walter N. King's *Hamlet's Search for Meaning* (1982) finds its meaning – as do other works – in the notion that providence finally governs the play, though the carnage at the play's end might suggest otherwise. And Linda Kay Hoff's *Hamlet's Choice: A Reformation Allegory* (1988) thinks of the play as a '"typal" allegory of the Reformation itself'. The play, that is, as a king of infinite space.

Books on the play in the theatre are numerous and often helpful, given the succulent difficulties of its acting roles. Besides Coursen's and Michael Cohen's, John A. Mills in *Hamlet on Stage: The Great Tradition* (1985) deals with Hamlets from the Restoration to Albert Finney in 1975. Mary Maher's *Modern Hamlets and Their Soliloquies* (1992) interviews a number of late-twentieth-century Hamlets. Bernice W. Kliman's *'Hamlet': Film, Television and Audio Performance* (1988) looks at *Hamlet* on stage and television, in silent film and sound recordings. Maurice Charney's two books on the play – *Style in 'Hamlet'* (1969) and *Hamlet's Fictions* (1988) – are written with due awareness of the theatre and theatrical convention. And Marvin Rosenberg's *The Masks of 'Hamlet'* (1992) is a vast account of stage business associated with the play.

In his edition of Modern Critical Interpretations of *Hamlet* (1986) Harold Bloom maintains that these essays 'tell us again that Hamlet's consciousness remains the largest and most comprehensive of all Western representations of human character and personality'. What also tells us this again – and again – is the inexhaustibility of any of the topics of the play that have been chewed over by critics for decades. Despairing of these post-modern times, William Kerrigan in *Hamlet's Perfection* (1994) responds to the 'shocking decadence' of the *Hamlet* criticism of the 1980s by pleading for a return to the Romantic Hamlet, even the Bradleyan one. In *'Hamlet' and the Concept of Character* (1992) Bert States obliges with a stunning re-examination of Bradley's subject in the belief that 'old questions, like old soldiers and dead metaphors, never die . . . it is only the answers that change or get expressed in different language'. There is, he says, 'a combinatory logic in character-formation' and his brilliant, quotable book persuades us that he was right 'to give in to the seductive power of mimesis' once again.

Michael Taylor

The theme of the Prince's interiority is also pursued by John Lee in *Hamlet and the Controversies of the Self* (2000).

Hamlet studies took on an unworldly air at the millennium. Stephen Greenblatt in *Hamlet in Purgatory* (2001) combines a scholarly investigation of ghosts and purgatory with a meditation on remembering the dead. Jacques Derrida uses the play as a starting point for ideas of ghostliness in political philosophy in *Specters of Marx: The State of the Debt, the Work of Mourning, and the New International* (1994; not for beginners). Michael Neill discovers in *Hamlet*, centrally, a disturbing combination of narrative closure and dread of ending, in his *Issues of Death: Mortality and Identity in English Renaissance Tragedy* (1998).

Many books seek to illuminate large questions by focusing on particular aspects. *'Hamlet' versus 'Lear': Cultural Politics and Shakespeare's Art* by R. A. Foakes (1993) charts the changes in the status of *Hamlet* and

Lear. *Stage Directions in 'Hamlet'* is the theme of a collection of essays edited by Hardin L. Aasand (2003). Robert S. Miola, in *Shakespeare and Classical Tragedy: The Influence of Seneca* (1992), offers a careful examination of the place of *Hamlet* in the Senecan tradition. *'Hamlet' and the Visual Arts, 1709–1900* by Alan R. Young (2003) explores representations in paintings and books. Collections of essays on new approaches are edited by Mark Thornton Burnett and John Manning, *New Essays on 'Hamlet'* (1994); and Arthur Kinney, *'Hamlet': Critical Essays* (2001).

Books designed to help students to catch up with debates around the play include a New Casebook on *Hamlet*, compiled by Martin Coyle (1992); and *Understanding 'Hamlet': A Student Casebook to Issues, Sources, and Historical Documents*, edited by Richard Corum (1998). Ann Thompson and Neil Taylor give a crisp account of the main issues in *William Shakespeare: 'Hamlet'* (1996). Huw Griffiths traces the history of criticism in an accessible way in *Shakespeare – 'Hamlet'* (2004).

Alan Sinfield

PERFORMANCE

Anyone interested in the stage history of *Hamlet* should consult the excellent overviews provided by Anthony B. Dawson's *Shakespeare in Performance: 'Hamlet'* (1995) and Robert Hapgood's *Shakespeare in Production: 'Hamlet'* (1999). Whilst the titles are nearly indistinguishable, the historical approach is distinct. Dawson offers a series of incisive and perceptive essays while Hapgood, after an extensive introduction, annotates a text of the play with examples of how particular lines and moments have been interpreted over the last four centuries. Harley Granville Barker's *Preface to Hamlet* (1937, repr. 1993) and Michael Pennington's *'Hamlet': A User's Guide* (1996) are invaluable (and highly readable) accounts of how the play works in performance as experienced by two great theatrical practitioners. Actors' eye-witness accounts and reminiscences can also be found in Carol Carlisle Jones's *Shakespeare from the Greenroom: Actors' Criticisms of Four Major Tragedies* (1969). The visual history of *Hamlet* production is the subject of Raymond Mander and Joe Mitchenson's *'Hamlet' Through the Ages: A Pictorial Record from 1709* (1952), and of *Hamlet on the Ramparts* (http://shea.mit.edu/ramparts), an innovative website which aims to provide free access to an evolving collection of texts, images and film relevant to Hamlet's first encounter with the Ghost. Charles Marowitz's adaptation, *Hamlet Collage*, is reprinted in *The Marowitz Shakespeare* (1978), while Andy Lavender's *'Hamlet' in Pieces: Shakespeare Reworked: Peter Brook, Robert Lepage, Robert Wilson* (2001) offers a detailed appraisal of three radical appropriations of *Hamlet* from the end of the twentieth century.

Paul Prescott

THE TRAGEDY OF HAMLET,
PRINCE OF DENMARK

The Characters in the Play

GHOST of Hamlet, lately King of Denmark
Claudius, his brother, now KING of Denmark
Gertrude, QUEEN of Denmark, widow of the late King
   and now wife of his brother Claudius
HAMLET, son of the late King Hamlet and of Gertrude

POLONIUS, counsellor to the King
LAERTES, son of Polonius
OPHELIA, daughter of Polonius
REYNALDO, servant of Polonius
FOLLOWERS of Laertes

HORATIO, friend of Prince Hamlet

VOLTEMAND
CORNELIUS
ROSENCRANTZ
GUILDENSTERN } members of the Danish court
OSRICK
LORD
GENTLEMEN

FRANCISCO
BARNARDO } soldiers
MARCELLUS

Two MESSENGERS
SAILOR
FIRST CLOWN, a gravedigger
SECOND CLOWN, his companion
PRIEST

FORTINBRAS, Prince of Norway
CAPTAIN, a Norwegian

English AMBASSADORS

FIRST PLAYER, who leads the troupe and takes the part of
    a king
SECOND PLAYER, who takes the part of a queen
THIRD PLAYER, who takes the part of Lucianus, nephew
    of the king
FOURTH PLAYER, who speaks a Prologue

Lords, attendants, players, guards, soldiers, sailors

Enter Francisco and Barnardo, two Sentinels

BARNARDO Who's there?

FRANCISCO Nay, answer me. Stand and unfold yourself.

BARNARDO Long live the King!

FRANCISCO Barnardo?

BARNARDO He.

FRANCISCO
You come most carefully upon your hour.

BARNARDO
'Tis now struck twelve. Get thee to bed, Francisco.

FRANCISCO
For this relief much thanks. 'Tis bitter cold,
And I am sick at heart.

BARNARDO
Have you had quiet guard?

FRANCISCO   Not a mouse stirring.

BARNARDO
Well, good night.
If you do meet Horatio and Marcellus,
The rivals of my watch, bid them make haste.
    Enter Horatio and Marcellus

FRANCISCO
I think I hear them. Stand ho! Who is there?

HORATIO
  Friends to this ground.
MARCELLUS   And liegemen to the Dane.
FRANCISCO
  Give you good night.
MARCELLUS   O, farewell, honest soldier.
  Who hath relieved you?
FRANCISCO   Barnardo hath my place.
  Give you good night.   *Exit*
MARCELLUS   Holla, Barnardo!
BARNARDO   Say —
  What, is Horatio there?
HORATIO   A piece of him.
BARNARDO
20 Welcome, Horatio. Welcome, good Marcellus.
MARCELLUS
  What, has this thing appeared again tonight?
BARNARDO
  I have seen nothing.
MARCELLUS
  Horatio says 'tis but our fantasy,
  And will not let belief take hold of him
  Touching this dreaded sight twice seen of us.
  Therefore I have entreated him along
  With us to watch the minutes of this night,
  That, if again this apparition come,
  He may approve our eyes and speak to it.
HORATIO
30 Tush, tush, 'twill not appear.
BARNARDO   Sit down awhile,
  And let us once again assail your ears,
  That are so fortified against our story,
  What we have two nights seen.

HORATIO   Well, sit we down,
And let us hear Barnardo speak of this.

BARNARDO
Last night of all,
When yond same star that's westward from the pole
Had made his course t'illume that part of heaven
Where now it burns, Marcellus and myself,
The bell then beating one —
    Enter the Ghost

MARCELLUS
Peace, break thee off. Look where it comes again.   40

BARNARDO
In the same figure like the King that's dead.

MARCELLUS
Thou art a scholar. Speak to it, Horatio.

BARNARDO
Looks 'a not like the King? Mark it, Horatio.

HORATIO
Most like. It harrows me with fear and wonder.

BARNARDO
It would be spoke to.

MARCELLUS   Speak to it, Horatio.

HORATIO
What art thou that usurpest this time of night,
Together with that fair and warlike form
In which the majesty of buried Denmark
Did sometimes march? By heaven I charge thee, speak.

MARCELLUS
It is offended.

BARNARDO   See, it stalks away.   50

HORATIO
Stay. Speak, speak. I charge thee, speak.
                              Exit the Ghost

MARCELLUS
  'Tis gone and will not answer.

BARNARDO
  How now, Horatio? You tremble and look pale.
  Is not this something more than fantasy?
  What think you on't?

HORATIO
  Before my God, I might not this believe
  Without the sensible and true avouch
  Of mine own eyes.

MARCELLUS   Is it not like the King?

HORATIO
  As thou art to thyself.

60 Such was the very armour he had on
  When he the ambitious Norway combated.
  So frowned he once when, in an angry parle,
  He smote the sledded poleaxe on the ice.
  'Tis strange.

MARCELLUS
  Thus twice before, and jump at this dead hour,
  With martial stalk hath he gone by our watch.

HORATIO
  In what particular thought to work I know not.
  But, in the gross and scope of mine opinion,
  This bodes some strange eruption to our state.

MARCELLUS
70 Good now, sit down, and tell me he that knows
  Why this same strict and most observant watch
  So nightly toils the subject of the land,
  And why such daily cast of brazen cannon
  And foreign mart for implements of war,
  Why such impress of shipwrights, whose sore task
  Does not divide the Sunday from the week.
  What might be toward that this sweaty haste

Doth make the night joint-labourer with the day?
Who is't that can inform me?

HORATIO   That can I.
At least the whisper goes so. Our last King,   80
Whose image even but now appeared to us,
Was, as you know, by Fortinbras of Norway,
Thereto pricked on by a most emulate pride,
Dared to the combat; in which our valiant Hamlet –
For so this side of our known world esteemed him –
Did slay this Fortinbras; who, by a sealed compact
Well ratified by law and heraldy,
Did forfeit, with his life, all these his lands
Which he stood seised of, to the conqueror;
Against the which a moiety competent   90
Was gagèd by our King, which had returned
To the inheritance of Fortinbras,
Had he been vanquisher, as, by the same covenant
And carriage of the article designed,
His fell to Hamlet. Now, sir, young Fortinbras,
Of unimprovèd mettle hot and full,
Hath in the skirts of Norway here and there
Sharked up a list of lawless resolutes
For food and diet to some enterprise
That hath a stomach in't; which is no other,   100
As it doth well appear unto our state,
But to recover of us by strong hand
And terms compulsatory those foresaid lands
So by his father lost. And this, I take it,
Is the main motive of our preparations,
The source of this our watch, and the chief head
Of this posthaste and romage in the land.

BARNARDO
I think it be no other but e'en so.
Well may it sort that this portentous figure

110   Comes armèd through our watch so like the King
        That was and is the question of these wars.
    HORATIO
        A mote it is to trouble the mind's eye.
        In the most high and palmy state of Rome,
        A little ere the mightiest Julius fell,
        The graves stood tenantless and the sheeted dead
        Did squeak and gibber in the Roman streets –
        As stars with trains of fire and dews of blood,
        Disasters in the sun; and the moist star
        Upon whose influence Neptune's empire stands
120   Was sick almost to Doomsday with eclipse.
        And even the like precurse of feared events,
        As harbingers preceding still the fates
        And prologue to the omen coming on,
        Have heaven and earth together demonstrated
        Unto our climatures and countrymen.
            Enter the Ghost
        But soft, behold, lo where it comes again!
        I'll cross it, though it blast me.
            He spreads his arms
        Stay, illusion.
        If thou hast any sound or use of voice,
130   Speak to me.
        If there be any good thing to be done
        That may to thee do ease and grace to me,
        Speak to me.
        If thou art privy to thy country's fate,
        Which happily foreknowing may avoid,
        O, speak!
        Or if thou hast uphoarded in thy life
        Extorted treasure in the womb of earth,
        For which, they say, you spirits oft walk in death,
140   Speak of it.

The cock crows
>   Stay and speak. Stop it, Marcellus.

MARCELLUS
  Shall I strike it with my partisan?

HORATIO
  Do, if it will not stand.

BARNARDO   'Tis here.

HORATIO   'Tis here.
>   *Exit the Ghost*

MARCELLUS
  'Tis gone.
  We do it wrong, being so majestical,
  To offer it the show of violence,
  For it is as the air invulnerable,
  And our vain blows malicious mockery.

BARNARDO
  It was about to speak when the cock crew.

HORATIO
  And then it started, like a guilty thing
  Upon a fearful summons. I have heard   150
  The cock, that is the trumpet to the morn,
  Doth with his lofty and shrill-sounding throat
  Awake the god of day, and at his warning,
  Whether in sea or fire, in earth or air,
  Th'extravagant and erring spirit hies
  To his confine. And of the truth herein
  This present object made probation.

MARCELLUS
  It faded on the crowing of the cock.
  Some say that ever 'gainst that season comes
  Wherein our Saviour's birth is celebrated,   160
  This bird of dawning singeth all night long.
  And then, they say, no spirit dare stir abroad;
  The nights are wholesome; then no planets strike;

No fairy takes; nor witch hath power to charm.
So hallowed and so gracious is that time.

HORATIO

So have I heard and do in part believe it.
But look, the morn in russet mantle clad
Walks o'er the dew of yon high eastward hill.
Break we our watch up. And by my advice
170   Let us impart what we have seen tonight
Unto young Hamlet. For, upon my life,
This spirit, dumb to us, will speak to him.
Do you consent we shall acquaint him with it,
As needful in our loves, fitting our duty?

MARCELLUS

Let's do't, I pray. And I this morning know
Where we shall find him most conveniently.   *Exeunt*

I.2   *Flourish*
           Enter Claudius, King of Denmark, Gertrude the
           Queen, and the council, including Polonius with his
           son Laertes, Hamlet, Voltemand, Cornelius, and
           attendants

KING

Though yet of Hamlet our dear brother's death
The memory be green, and that it us befitted
To bear our hearts in grief, and our whole kingdom
To be contracted in one brow of woe,
Yet so far hath discretion fought with nature
That we with wisest sorrow think on him
Together with remembrance of ourselves.
Therefore our sometime sister, now our Queen,
Th'imperial jointress to this warlike state,
10   Have we, as 'twere with a defeated joy,
With an auspicious and a dropping eye,

With mirth in funeral and with dirge in marriage,
In equal scale weighing delight and dole,
Taken to wife. Nor have we herein barred
Your better wisdoms, which have freely gone
With this affair along. For all, our thanks.
Now follows that you know. Young Fortinbras,
Holding a weak supposal of our worth,
Or thinking by our late dear brother's death
Our state to be disjoint and out of frame,   20
Colleaguèd with this dream of his advantage,
He hath not failed to pester us with message
Importing the surrender of those lands
Lost by his father, with all bands of law,
To our most valiant brother. So much for him.
Now for ourself and for this time of meeting.
Thus much the business is: we have here writ
To Norway, uncle of young Fortinbras –
Who, impotent and bedrid, scarcely hears
Of this his nephew's purpose – to suppress   30
His further gait herein, in that the levies,
The lists, and full proportions are all made
Out of his subject. And we here dispatch
You, good Cornelius, and you, Voltemand,
For bearers of this greeting to old Norway,
Giving to you no further personal power
To business with the King, more than the scope
Of these delated articles allow.
Farewell; and let your haste commend your duty.

VOLTEMAND *and* CORNELIUS
   In that, and all things, will we show our duty.   40
KING
   We doubt it nothing. Heartily farewell.
                        Exeunt Voltemand and Cornelius

And now, Laertes, what's the news with you?
You told us of some suit. What is't, Laertes?
You cannot speak of reason to the Dane
And lose your voice. What wouldst thou beg, Laertes,
That shall not be my offer, not thy asking?
The head is not more native to the heart,
The hand more instrumental to the mouth,
Than is the throne of Denmark to thy father.
What wouldst thou have, Laertes?

LAERTES   My dread lord,
Your leave and favour to return to France,
From whence though willingly I came to Denmark
To show my duty in your coronation,
Yet now I must confess, that duty done,
My thoughts and wishes bend again toward France
And bow them to your gracious leave and pardon.

KING
Have you your father's leave? What says Polonius?

POLONIUS
He hath, my lord, wrung from me my slow leave
By laboursome petition, and at last
Upon his will I sealed my hard consent.
I do beseech you give him leave to go.

KING
Take thy fair hour, Laertes. Time be thine;
And thy best graces spend it at thy will.
But now, my cousin Hamlet, and my son –

HAMLET (*aside*)
A little more than kin, and less than kind!

KING
How is it that the clouds still hang on you?

HAMLET
Not so, my lord. I am too much in the sun.

QUEEN

Good Hamlet, cast thy nighted colour off,
And let thine eye look like a friend on Denmark.
Do not for ever with thy vailèd lids   70
Seek for thy noble father in the dust.
Thou knowest 'tis common. All that lives must die,
Passing through nature to eternity.

HAMLET

Ay, madam, it is common.

QUEEN   If it be,
Why seems it so particular with thee?

HAMLET

'Seems', madam? Nay, it is. I know not 'seems'.
'Tis not alone my inky cloak, good mother,
Nor customary suits of solemn black,
Nor windy suspiration of forced breath,
No, nor the fruitful river in the eye,   80
Nor the dejected 'haviour of the visage,
Together with all forms, moods, shapes of grief,
That can denote me truly. These indeed 'seem';
For they are actions that a man might play.
But I have that within which passes show –
These but the trappings and the suits of woe.

KING

'Tis sweet and commendable in your nature, Hamlet,
To give these mourning duties to your father.
But you must know your father lost a father;
That father lost, lost his; and the survivor bound   90
In filial obligation for some term
To do obsequious sorrow. But to persever
In obstinate condolement is a course
Of impious stubbornness. 'Tis unmanly grief.
It shows a will most incorrect to heaven,
A heart unfortified, a mind impatient,

An understanding simple and unschooled.
For what we know must be, and is as common
As any the most vulgar thing to sense,
Why should we in our peevish opposition
Take it to heart? Fie, 'tis a fault to heaven,
A fault against the dead, a fault to nature,
To reason most absurd, whose common theme
Is death of fathers, and who still hath cried,
From the first corse till he that died today,
'This must be so.' We pray you throw to earth
This unprevailing woe, and think of us
As of a father. For, let the world take note,
You are the most immediate to our throne;
And with no less nobility of love
Than that which dearest father bears his son
Do I impart toward you. For your intent
In going back to school in Wittenberg,
It is most retrograde to our desire;
And, we beseech you, bend you to remain
Here in the cheer and comfort of our eye,
Our chiefest courtier, cousin, and our son.

QUEEN
Let not thy mother lose her prayers, Hamlet.
I pray thee stay with us. Go not to Wittenberg.

HAMLET
I shall in all my best obey you, madam.

KING
Why, 'tis a loving and a fair reply.
Be as ourself in Denmark. Madam, come.
This gentle and unforced accord of Hamlet
Sits smiling to my heart; in grace whereof
No jocund health that Denmark drinks today
But the great cannon to the clouds shall tell,
And the King's rouse the heaven shall bruit again,

Re-speaking earthly thunder. Come away.

Flourish   *Exeunt all but Hamlet*

HAMLET

O that this too too sullied flesh would melt,
Thaw, and resolve itself into a dew;   130
Or that the Everlasting had not fixed
His canon 'gainst self-slaughter. O God, God,
How weary, stale, flat, and unprofitable
Seem to me all the uses of this world!
Fie on't, ah, fie, 'tis an unweeded garden
That grows to seed. Things rank and gross in nature
Possess it merely. That it should come to this –
But two months dead, nay, not so much, not two!
So excellent a king, that was to this
Hyperion to a satyr; so loving to my mother   140
That he might not beteem the winds of heaven
Visit her face too roughly. Heaven and earth,
Must I remember? Why, she would hang on him
As if increase of appetite had grown
By what it fed on. And yet within a month –
Let me not think on't. Frailty, thy name is woman.
A little month, or e'er those shoes were old
With which she followed my poor father's body
Like Niobe, all tears, why she, even she –
O God, a beast that wants discourse of reason   150
Would have mourned longer – married with my uncle,
My father's brother, but no more like my father
Than I to Hercules. Within a month,
Ere yet the salt of most unrighteous tears
Had left the flushing in her gallèd eyes,
She married. O, most wicked speed, to post
With such dexterity to incestuous sheets!
It is not, nor it cannot come to good.
But break, my heart, for I must hold my tongue.

Enter Horatio, Marcellus, and Barnardo

HORATIO

160 Hail to your lordship!

HAMLET   I am glad to see you well.
   Horatio – or I do forget myself.

HORATIO
   The same, my lord, and your poor servant ever.

HAMLET
   Sir, my good friend. I'll change that name with you.
   And what make you from Wittenberg, Horatio?
   Marcellus?

MARCELLUS
   My good lord!

HAMLET
   I am very glad to see you. (*To Barnardo*) Good even, sir.
   (*To Horatio*)
   But what, in faith, make you from Wittenberg?

HORATIO
   A truant disposition, good my lord.

HAMLET

170 I would not hear your enemy say so,
   Nor shall you do my ear that violence
   To make it truster of your own report
   Against yourself. I know you are no truant.
   But what is your affair in Elsinore?
   We'll teach you to drink deep ere you depart.

HORATIO
   My lord, I came to see your father's funeral.

HAMLET
   I prithee do not mock me, fellow-student.
   I think it was to see my mother's wedding.

HORATIO
   Indeed, my lord, it followed hard upon.

HAMLET

    Thrift, thrift, Horatio. The funeral baked meats   180
    Did coldly furnish forth the marriage tables.
    Would I had met my dearest foe in heaven
    Or ever I had seen that day, Horatio!
    My father – methinks I see my father.

HORATIO

    Where, my lord?

HAMLET   In my mind's eye, Horatio.

HORATIO

    I saw him once. 'A was a goodly king.

HAMLET

    'A was a man. Take him for all in all,
    I shall not look upon his like again.

HORATIO

    My lord, I think I saw him yesternight.

HAMLET

    Saw? Who?   190

HORATIO

    My lord, the King your father.

HAMLET   The King my father?

HORATIO

    Season your admiration for a while
    With an attent ear till I may deliver
    Upon the witness of these gentlemen
    This marvel to you.

HAMLET   For God's love, let me hear!

HORATIO

    Two nights together had these gentlemen,
    Marcellus and Barnardo, on their watch
    In the dead waste and middle of the night
    Been thus encountered: a figure like your father,
    Armèd at point exactly, cap-a-pe,   200

Appears before them and with solemn march
Goes slow and stately by them. Thrice he walked
By their oppressed and fear-surprisèd eyes
Within his truncheon's length, whilst they, distilled
Almost to jelly with the act of fear,
Stand dumb and speak not to him. This to me
In dreadful secrecy impart they did,
And I with them the third night kept the watch,
Where, as they had delivered, both in time,
210   Form of the thing, each word made true and good,
The apparition comes. I knew your father.
These hands are not more like.

HAMLET   But where was this?

MARCELLUS
My lord, upon the platform where we watch.

HAMLET
Did you not speak to it?

HORATIO   My lord, I did,
But answer made it none. Yet once methought
It lifted up it head and did address
Itself to motion like as it would speak.
But even then the morning cock crew loud,
And at the sound it shrunk in haste away
220   And vanished from our sight.

HAMLET   'Tis very strange.

HORATIO
As I do live, my honoured lord, 'tis true.
And we did think it writ down in our duty
To let you know of it.

HAMLET
Indeed, indeed, sirs. But this troubles me.
Hold you the watch tonight?

ALL   We do, my lord.

HAMLET
  Armed, say you?
ALL
  Armed, my lord.
HAMLET
  From top to toe?
ALL   My lord, from head to foot.
HAMLET
  Then saw you not his face?
HORATIO
  O, yes, my lord. He wore his beaver up.   230
HAMLET
  What, looked he frowningly?
HORATIO
  A countenance more in sorrow than in anger.
HAMLET
  Pale or red?
HORATIO
  Nay, very pale.
HAMLET   And fixed his eyes upon you?
HORATIO
  Most constantly.
HAMLET   I would I had been there.
HORATIO
  It would have much amazed you.
HAMLET
  Very like, very like. Stayed it long?
HORATIO
  While one with moderate haste might tell a hundred.
MARCELLUS *and* BARNARDO
  Longer, longer.
HORATIO
  Not when I saw't.
HAMLET   His beard was grizzled, no?   240

HORATIO
    It was as I have seen it in his life,
    A sable silvered.

HAMLET   I will watch tonight.
    Perchance 'twill walk again.

HORATIO   I warrant it will.

HAMLET
    If it assume my noble father's person,
    I'll speak to it though hell itself should gape
    And bid me hold my peace. I pray you all,
    If you have hitherto concealed this sight,
    Let it be tenable in your silence still.
    And whatsomever else shall hap tonight,
250   Give it an understanding but no tongue.
    I will requite your loves. So fare you well.
    Upon the platform 'twixt eleven and twelve
    I'll visit you.

ALL   Our duty to your honour.

HAMLET
    Your loves, as mine to you. Farewell.

                     Exeunt all but Hamlet

    My father's spirit! In arms! All is not well.
    I doubt some foul play. Would the night were come!
    Till then sit still, my soul. Foul deeds will rise,
    Though all the earth o'erwhelm them, to men's eyes.

                              Exit

I.3   *Enter Laertes and Ophelia*

LAERTES
    My necessaries are embarked. Farewell.
    And, sister, as the winds give benefit
    And convoy is assistant, do not sleep
    But let me hear from you.

OPHELIA   Do you doubt that?

LAERTES

    For Hamlet, and the trifling of his favour,
    Hold it a fashion and a toy in blood,
    A violet in the youth of primy nature,
    Forward, not permanent, sweet, not lasting,
    The perfume and suppliance of a minute,
    No more.

OPHELIA   No more but so?

LAERTES   Think it no more.   10

    For nature crescent does not grow alone
    In thews and bulk, but as this temple waxes
    The inward service of the mind and soul
    Grows wide withal. Perhaps he loves you now,
    And now no soil nor cautel doth besmirch
    The virtue of his will. But you must fear,
    His greatness weighed, his will is not his own.
    For he himself is subject to his birth.
    He may not, as unvalued persons do,
    Carve for himself. For on his choice depends   20
    The safety and health of this whole state.
    And therefore must his choice be circumscribed
    Unto the voice and yielding of that body
    Whereof he is the head. Then, if he says he loves you,
    It fits your wisdom so far to believe it
    As he in his particular act and place
    May give his saying deed; which is no further
    Than the main voice of Denmark goes withal.
    Then weigh what loss your honour may sustain
    If with too credent ear you list his songs,   30
    Or lose your heart, or your chaste treasure open
    To his unmastered importunity.
    Fear it, Ophelia, fear it, my dear sister.
    And keep you in the rear of your affection,

Out of the shot and danger of desire.
The chariest maid is prodigal enough
If she unmask her beauty to the moon.
Virtue itself 'scapes not calumnious strokes.
The canker galls the infants of the spring
40   Too oft before their buttons be disclosed;
And in the morn and liquid dew of youth
Contagious blastments are most imminent.
Be wary then. Best safety lies in fear.
Youth to itself rebels, though none else near.

OPHELIA
I shall the effect of this good lesson keep
As watchman to my heart. But, good my brother,
Do not, as some ungracious pastors do,
Show me the steep and thorny way to heaven
Whiles like a puffed and reckless libertine
50   Himself the primrose path of dalliance treads
And recks not his own rede.

LAERTES   O, fear me not.
I stay too long.
      Enter Polonius
                  But here my father comes.
A double blessing is a double grace.
Occasion smiles upon a second leave.

POLONIUS
Yet here, Laertes? Aboard, aboard, for shame!
The wind sits in the shoulder of your sail,
And you are stayed for. There – my blessing with thee.
And these few precepts in thy memory
Look thou character. Give thy thoughts no tongue,
60   Nor any unproportioned thought his act.
Be thou familiar, but by no means vulgar.
Those friends thou hast, and their adoption tried,
Grapple them unto thy soul with hoops of steel.

But do not dull thy palm with entertainment
Of each new-hatched, unfledged courage. Beware
Of entrance to a quarrel. But, being in,
Bear't that th'opposèd may beware of thee.
Give every man thine ear, but few thy voice.
Take each man's censure, but reserve thy judgement.
Costly thy habit as thy purse can buy,   70
But not expressed in fancy; rich, not gaudy;
For the apparel oft proclaims the man,
And they in France of the best rank and station
Are of a most select and generous chief in that.
Neither a borrower nor a lender be,
For loan oft loses both itself and friend,
And borrowing dulleth edge of husbandry.
This above all: to thine own self be true,
And it must follow, as the night the day,
Thou canst not then be false to any man.   80
Farewell. My blessing season this in thee!

LAERTES
Most humbly do I take my leave, my lord.

POLONIUS
The time invites you. Go. Your servants tend.

LAERTES
Farewell, Ophelia; and remember well
What I have said to you.

OPHELIA   'Tis in my memory locked,
And you yourself shall keep the key of it.

LAERTES
Farewell.   *Exit*

POLONIUS
What is't, Ophelia, he hath said to you?

OPHELIA
So please you, something touching the Lord Hamlet.

POLONIUS

90   Marry, well bethought.
'Tis told me he hath very oft of late
Given private time to you, and you yourself
Have of your audience been most free and bounteous.
If it be so – as so 'tis put on me,
And that in way of caution – I must tell you
You do not understand yourself so clearly
As it behoves my daughter and your honour.
What is between you? Give me up the truth.

OPHELIA

He hath, my lord, of late made many tenders
100 Of his affection to me.

POLONIUS

Affection? Pooh! You speak like a green girl,
Unsifted in such perilous circumstance.
Do you believe his tenders, as you call them?

OPHELIA

I do not know, my lord, what I should think.

POLONIUS

Marry, I will teach you. Think yourself a baby
That you have ta'en these tenders for true pay
Which are not sterling. Tender yourself more dearly,
Or – not to crack the wind of the poor phrase,
Running it thus – you'll tender me a fool.

OPHELIA

110 My lord, he hath importuned me with love
In honourable fashion.

POLONIUS

Ay, 'fashion' you may call it. Go to, go to.

OPHELIA

And hath given countenance to his speech, my lord,
With almost all the holy vows of heaven.

POLONIUS

Ay, springes to catch woodcocks. I do know,
When the blood burns, how prodigal the soul
Lends the tongue vows. These blazes, daughter,
Giving more light than heat, extinct in both
Even in their promise, as it is a-making,
You must not take for fire. From this time   120
Be something scanter of your maiden presence.
Set your entreatments at a higher rate
Than a command to parle. For Lord Hamlet,
Believe so much in him that he is young,
And with a larger tether may he walk
Than may be given you. In few, Ophelia,
Do not believe his vows. For they are brokers,
Not of that dye which their investments show,
But mere implorators of unholy suits,
Breathing like sanctified and pious bawds,   130
The better to beguile. This is for all:
I would not, in plain terms, from this time forth
Have you so slander any moment leisure
As to give words or talk with the Lord Hamlet.
Look to't, I charge you. Come your ways.

OPHELIA

I shall obey, my lord.   *Exeunt*

Enter Hamlet, Horatio, and Marcellus   I.4

HAMLET

The air bites shrewdly. It is very cold.

HORATIO

It is a nipping and an eager air.

HAMLET

What hour now?

HORATIO   I think it lacks of twelve.

MARCELLUS
  No, it is struck.

HORATIO
  Indeed? I heard it not. It then draws near the season
  Wherein the spirit held his wont to walk.
    A flourish of trumpets, and two pieces of ordnance go
    off
  What does this mean, my lord?

HAMLET
  The King doth wake tonight and takes his rouse,
  Keeps wassail, and the swaggering upspring reels.
  And as he drains his draughts of Rhenish down
  The kettledrum and trumpet thus bray out
  The triumph of his pledge.

HORATIO   Is it a custom?

HAMLET
  Ay, marry, is't.
  But to my mind, though I am native here
  And to the manner born, it is a custom
  More honoured in the breach than the observance.
  This heavy-headed revel east and west
  Makes us traduced and taxed of other nations.
  They clepe us drunkards and with swinish phrase
  Soil our addition; and indeed it takes
  From our achievements, though performed at height,
  The pith and marrow of our attribute.
  So oft it chances in particular men
  That — for some vicious mole of nature in them,
  As in their birth, wherein they are not guilty,
  Since nature cannot choose his origin —
  By the o'ergrowth of some complexion,
  Oft breaking down the pales and forts of reason,
  Or by some habit that too much o'er-leavens
  The form of plausive manners — that these men,

Carrying, I say, the stamp of one defect,
Being nature's livery or fortune's star,
His virtues else, be they as pure as grace,
As infinite as man may undergo,
Shall in the general censure take corruption
From that particular fault. The dram of evil
Doth all the noble substance of a doubt,
To his own scandal —

Enter the Ghost

HORATIO   Look, my lord, it comes.

HAMLET

Angels and ministers of grace defend us!
Be thou a spirit of health or goblin damned,   40
Bring with thee airs from heaven or blasts from hell,
Be thy intents wicked or charitable,
Thou comest in such a questionable shape
That I will speak to thee. I'll call thee Hamlet,
King, father, royal Dane. O, answer me!
Let me not burst in ignorance. But tell
Why thy canonized bones, hearsèd in death,
Have burst their cerements; why the sepulchre
Wherein we saw thee quietly interred
Hath oped his ponderous and marble jaws   50
To cast thee up again. What may this mean
That thou, dead corse, again in complete steel,
Revisits thus the glimpses of the moon,
Making night hideous, and we fools of nature
So horridly to shake our disposition
With thoughts beyond the reaches of our souls?
Say, why is this? Wherefore? What should we do?

The Ghost beckons him

HORATIO

It beckons you to go away with it,
As if it some impartment did desire

60   To you alone.

MARCELLUS   Look with what courteous action
It waves you to a more removèd ground.
But do not go with it.

HORATIO   No, by no means.

HAMLET
It will not speak. Then I will follow it.

HORATIO
Do not, my lord.

HAMLET   Why, what should be the fear?
I do not set my life at a pin's fee.
And for my soul, what can it do to that,
Being a thing immortal as itself?
It waves me forth again. I'll follow it.

HORATIO
What if it tempt you toward the flood, my lord,
70   Or to the dreadful summit of the cliff
That beetles o'er his base into the sea,
And there assume some other, horrible form,
Which might deprive your sovereignty of reason
And draw you into madness? Think of it.
The very place puts toys of desperation,
Without more motive, into every brain
That looks so many fathoms to the sea
And hears it roar beneath.

HAMLET   It waves me still. —
Go on. I'll follow thee.

MARCELLUS
80   You shall not go, my lord.

HAMLET   Hold off your hands.

HORATIO
Be ruled. You shall not go.

HAMLET   My fate cries out

And makes each petty artere in this body
As hardy as the Nemean lion's nerve.
Still am I called. Unhand me, gentlemen.
By heaven, I'll make a ghost of him that lets me!
I say, away! Go on. I'll follow thee.

Exeunt the Ghost and Hamlet

HORATIO

He waxes desperate with imagination.

MARCELLUS

Let's follow. 'Tis not fit thus to obey him.

HORATIO

Have after. To what issue will this come?

MARCELLUS

Something is rotten in the state of Denmark.   90

HORATIO

Heaven will direct it.

MARCELLUS   Nay, let's follow him.   *Exeunt*

Enter the Ghost and Hamlet   I.5

HAMLET

Whither wilt thou lead me? Speak. I'll go no further.

GHOST

Mark me.

HAMLET   I will.

GHOST   My hour is almost come,
When I to sulphurous and tormenting flames
Must render up myself.

HAMLET   Alas, poor ghost!

GHOST

Pity me not, but lend thy serious hearing
To what I shall unfold.

HAMLET   Speak. I am bound to hear.

GHOST
   So art thou to revenge, when thou shalt hear.

HAMLET
   What?

GHOST
   I am thy father's spirit,
10   Doomed for a certain term to walk the night,
   And for the day confined to fast in fires,
   Till the foul crimes done in my days of nature
   Are burnt and purged away. But that I am forbid
   To tell the secrets of my prison house,
   I could a tale unfold whose lightest word
   Would harrow up thy soul, freeze thy young blood,
   Make thy two eyes like stars start from their spheres,
   Thy knotted and combinèd locks to part,
   And each particular hair to stand an end
20   Like quills upon the fretful porpentine.
   But this eternal blazon must not be
   To ears of flesh and blood. List, list, O, list!
   If thou didst ever thy dear father love –

HAMLET
   O God!

GHOST
   Revenge his foul and most unnatural murder.

HAMLET
   Murder?

GHOST
   Murder most foul, as in the best it is,
   But this most foul, strange, and unnatural.

HAMLET
   Haste me to know't, that I, with wings as swift
30   As meditation or the thoughts of love,
   May sweep to my revenge.

GHOST   I find thee apt,

And duller shouldst thou be than the fat weed
That roots itself in ease on Lethe wharf,
Wouldst thou not stir in this. Now, Hamlet, hear.
'Tis given out that, sleeping in my orchard,
A serpent stung me. So the whole ear of Denmark
Is by a forgèd process of my death
Rankly abused. But know, thou noble youth,
The serpent that did sting thy father's life
Now wears his crown.

HAMLET   O my prophetic soul!   40
  My uncle?

GHOST
  Ay, that incestuous, that adulterate beast,
  With witchcraft of his wit, with traitorous gifts —
  O wicked wit and gifts, that have the power
  So to seduce! — won to his shameful lust
  The will of my most seeming-virtuous Queen.
  O Hamlet, what a falling off was there,
  From me, whose love was of that dignity
  That it went hand in hand even with the vow
  I made to her in marriage; and to decline   50
  Upon a wretch whose natural gifts were poor
  To those of mine!
  But virtue as it never will be moved,
  Though lewdness court it in a shape of heaven,
  So lust, though to a radiant angel linked,
  Will sate itself in a celestial bed
  And prey on garbage.
  But soft, methinks I scent the morning air.
  Brief let me be. Sleeping within my orchard,
  My custom always of the afternoon,
  Upon my secure hour thy uncle stole   60
  With juice of cursèd hebona in a vial,
  And in the porches of my ears did pour

The leperous distilment; whose effect
Holds such an enmity with blood of man
That swift as quicksilver it courses through
The natural gates and alleys of the body,
And with a sudden vigour it doth posset
And curd, like eager droppings into milk,
70 The thin and wholesome blood. So did it mine.
And a most instant tetter barked about,
Most lazar-like, with vile and loathsome crust
All my smooth body.
      Thus was I sleeping by a brother's hand
Of life, of crown, of queen at once dispatched,
Cut off even in the blossoms of my sin,
Unhouseled, disappointed, unaneled,
No reckoning made, but sent to my account
With all my imperfections on my head.
80 O, horrible! O, horrible! Most horrible!
If thou hast nature in thee, bear it not.
Let not the royal bed of Denmark be
A couch for luxury and damned incest.
But howsomever thou pursues this act,
Taint not thy mind, nor let thy soul contrive
Against thy mother aught. Leave her to heaven
And to those thorns that in her bosom lodge
To prick and sting her. Fare thee well at once.
The glow-worm shows the matin to be near
90 And 'gins to pale his uneffectual fire.
Adieu, adieu, adieu. Remember me.   *Exit*

HAMLET
O all you host of heaven! O earth! What else?
And shall I couple hell? O, fie! Hold, hold, my heart.
And you, my sinews, grow not instant old,
But bear me stiffly up. Remember thee?
Ay, thou poor ghost, whiles memory holds a seat

In this distracted globe. Remember thee?
Yea, from the table of my memory
I'll wipe away all trivial fond records,
All saws of books, all forms, all pressures past   100
That youth and observation copied there,
And thy commandment all alone shall live
Within the book and volume of my brain,
Unmixed with baser matter. Yes, by heaven!
O most pernicious woman!
O villain, villain, smiling, damnèd villain!
My tables – meet it is I set it down
That one may smile, and smile, and be a villain.
At least I am sure it may be so in Denmark.
    He writes
So, uncle, there you are. Now to my word: 110
It is 'Adieu, adieu, remember me.'
I have sworn't.
    Enter Horatio and Marcellus

HORATIO
My lord, my lord!
MARCELLUS   Lord Hamlet!
HORATIO   Heavens secure him!
HAMLET
So be it!
MARCELLUS
Illo, ho, ho, my lord!
HAMLET
Hillo, ho, ho, boy! Come, bird, come.
MARCELLUS
How is't, my noble lord?
HORATIO   What news, my lord?
HAMLET
O, wonderful!

HORATIO
　Good my lord, tell it.

HAMLET　　　　　　　　No, you will reveal it.

HORATIO
120　Not I, my lord, by heaven.

MARCELLUS　　　　　　　Nor I, my lord.

HAMLET
　How say you then? Would heart of man once think it?
　But you'll be secret?

HORATIO *and* MARCELLUS Ay, by heaven, my lord.

HAMLET
　There's never a villain dwelling in all Denmark —
　But he's an arrant knave.

HORATIO
　There needs no ghost, my lord, come from the grave
　To tell us this.

HAMLET　　　　　Why, right, you are in the right,
　And so, without more circumstance at all,
　I hold it fit that we shake hands and part:
　You, as your business and desire shall point you,
130　For every man hath business and desire,
　Such as it is; and for my own poor part
　I will go pray.

HORATIO
　These are but wild and whirling words, my lord.

HAMLET
　I am sorry they offend you, heartily.
　Yes, faith, heartily.

HORATIO　　　　　　There's no offence, my lord.

HAMLET
　Yes, by Saint Patrick, but there is, Horatio,
　And much offence too. Touching this vision here,
　It is an honest ghost, that let me tell you.
　For your desire to know what is between us,

O'ermaster't as you may. And now, good friends,   140
As you are friends, scholars, and soldiers,
Give me one poor request.

HORATIO
What is't, my lord? We will.

HAMLET
Never make known what you have seen tonight.

HORATIO *and* MARCELLUS
My lord, we will not.

HAMLET   Nay, but swear't.

HORATIO   In faith,
My lord, not I.

MARCELLUS   Nor I, my lord – in faith.

HAMLET
Upon my sword.

MARCELLUS   We have sworn, my lord, already.

HAMLET
Indeed, upon my sword, indeed.
       The Ghost cries under the stage

GHOST
Swear.

HAMLET
Ha, ha, boy, sayst thou so? Art thou there, truepenny?   150
Come on. You hear this fellow in the cellarage.
Consent to swear.

HORATIO   Propose the oath, my lord.

HAMLET
Never to speak of this that you have seen,
Swear by my sword.

GHOST (*beneath*)
Swear.

HAMLET
Hic et ubique? Then we'll shift our ground.
Come hither, gentlemen,

And lay your hands again upon my sword.
Swear by my sword
160   Never to speak of this that you have heard.

GHOST (*beneath*)
Swear by his sword.

HAMLET
Well said, old mole! Canst work i'th'earth so fast?
A worthy pioneer! Once more remove, good friends.

HORATIO
O day and night, but this is wondrous strange!

HAMLET
And therefore as a stranger give it welcome.
There are more things in heaven and earth, Horatio,
Than are dreamt of in your philosophy.
But come.
Here as before, never, so help you mercy,
170   How strange or odd some'er I bear myself –
As I perchance hereafter shall think meet
To put an antic disposition on –
That you, at such times seeing me, never shall,
With arms encumbered thus, or this head-shake,
Or by pronouncing of some doubtful phrase,
As 'Well, well, we know', or 'We could, an if we would',
Or 'If we list to speak', or 'There be, an if they might',
Or such ambiguous giving out, to note
That you know aught of me – this do swear,
180   So grace and mercy at your most need help you.

GHOST (*beneath*)
Swear.

HAMLET
Rest, rest, perturbèd spirit! So, gentlemen,
With all my love I do commend me to you,
And what so poor a man as Hamlet is

May do t'express his love and friending to you,
God willing, shall not lack. Let us go in together,
And still your fingers on your lips, I pray.
The time is out of joint. O, cursèd spite,
That ever I was born to set it right!
Nay, come, let's go together.   *Exeunt*   190

*

Enter Polonius, with his man Reynaldo   II.1

POLONIUS
   Give him this money and these notes, Reynaldo.
REYNALDO
   I will, my lord.
POLONIUS
   You shall do marvellous wisely, good Reynaldo,
   Before you visit him, to make inquire
   Of his behaviour.
REYNALDO   My lord, I did intend it.
POLONIUS
   Marry, well said. Very well said. Look you, sir,
   Inquire me first what Danskers are in Paris,
   And how, and who, what means, and where they keep,
   What company, at what expense; and finding
   By this encompassment and drift of question   10
   That they do know my son, come you more nearer
   Than your particular demands will touch it.
   Take you as 'twere some distant knowledge of him,
   As thus, 'I know his father and his friends,
   And in part him' – do you mark this, Reynaldo?
REYNALDO
   Ay, very well, my lord.

POLONIUS
   'And in part him, but,' you may say, 'not well;
   But if 't be he I mean, he's very wild,
   Addicted so and so.' And there put on him
20   What forgeries you please – marry, none so rank
   As may dishonour him – take heed of that –
   But, sir, such wanton, wild, and usual slips
   As are companions noted and most known
   To youth and liberty.
REYNALDO   As gaming, my lord.
POLONIUS
   Ay, or drinking, fencing, swearing, quarrelling,
   Drabbing. You may go so far.
REYNALDO
   My lord, that would dishonour him.
POLONIUS
   Faith, no, as you may season it in the charge.
   You must not put another scandal on him,
30   That he is open to incontinency.
   That's not my meaning. But breathe his faults so
       quaintly
   That they may seem the taints of liberty,
   The flash and outbreak of a fiery mind,
   A savageness in unreclaimèd blood,
   Of general assault.
REYNALDO   But, my good lord –
POLONIUS
   Wherefore should you do this?
REYNALDO   Ay, my lord,
   I would know that.
POLONIUS   Marry, sir, here's my drift,
   And I believe it is a fetch of warrant.
   You laying these slight sullies on my son,

As 'twere a thing a little soiled i'th'working,   40
Mark you,
Your party in converse, him you would sound,
Having ever seen in the prenominate crimes
The youth you breathe of guilty, be assured
He closes with you in this consequence:
'Good sir', or so, or 'friend', or 'gentleman' —
According to the phrase or the addition
Of man and country —

REYNALDO   Very good, my lord.

POLONIUS And then, sir, does 'a this — 'a does — What
was I about to say? By the mass, I was about to say   50
something! Where did I leave?

REYNALDO At 'closes in the consequence', at 'friend',
'or so', and 'gentleman'.

POLONIUS At 'closes in the consequence' — Ay, marry!
He closes thus: 'I know the gentleman.
I saw him yesterday, or th'other day,
Or then, or then, with such or such, and, as you say,
There was 'a gaming; there o'ertook in's rouse;
There falling out at tennis'; or perchance
'I saw him enter such a house of sale',   60
Videlicet, a brothel, or so forth.
See you now —
Your bait of falsehood takes this carp of truth,
And thus do we of wisdom and of reach,
With windlasses and with assays of bias,
By indirections find directions out.
So, by my former lecture and advice,
Shall you my son. You have me, have you not?

REYNALDO
My lord, I have.

POLONIUS   God bye ye, fare ye well.

REYNALDO
70   Good my lord.

POLONIUS
Observe his inclination in yourself.

REYNALDO
I shall, my lord.

POLONIUS
And let him ply his music.

REYNALDO   Well, my lord.

POLONIUS
Farewell.   *Exit Reynaldo*
      Enter Ophelia
            How now, Ophelia, what's the matter?

OPHELIA
O my lord, my lord, I have been so affrighted!

POLONIUS
With what, i'th'name of God?

OPHELIA
My lord, as I was sewing in my closet,
Lord Hamlet, with his doublet all unbraced,
No hat upon his head, his stockings fouled,
80   Ungartered, and down-gyvèd to his ankle,
Pale as his shirt, his knees knocking each other,
And with a look so piteous in purport
As if he had been loosèd out of hell
To speak of horrors – he comes before me.

POLONIUS
Mad for thy love?

OPHELIA   My lord, I do not know,
But truly I do fear it.

POLONIUS   What said he?

OPHELIA
He took me by the wrist and held me hard.
Then goes he to the length of all his arm,

And with his other hand thus o'er his brow
He falls to such perusal of my face   90
As 'a would draw it. Long stayed he so.
At last, a little shaking of mine arm
And thrice his head thus waving up and down,
He raised a sigh so piteous and profound
As it did seem to shatter all his bulk
And end his being. That done, he lets me go;
And, with his head over his shoulder turned,
He seemed to find his way without his eyes;
For out o'doors he went without their helps
And to the last bended their light on me.   100

POLONIUS
Come, go with me. I will go seek the King.
This is the very ecstasy of love,
Whose violent property fordoes itself
And leads the will to desperate undertakings
As oft as any passion under heaven
That does afflict our natures. I am sorry.
What, have you given him any hard words of late?

OPHELIA
No, my good lord. But, as you did command,
I did repel his letters and denied
His access to me.

POLONIUS   That hath made him mad.   110
I am sorry that with better heed and judgement
I had not quoted him. I feared he did but trifle
And meant to wrack thee. But beshrew my jealousy.
By heaven, it is as proper to our age
To cast beyond ourselves in our opinions
As it is common for the younger sort
To lack discretion. Come, go we to the King.
This must be known, which, being kept close, might
      move.

More grief to hide than hate to utter love.
120   Come.   *Exeunt*

II.2   *Flourish*
            Enter the King and Queen, Rosencrantʒ and Guilden-
            stern, with attendants

KING
      Welcome, dear Rosencrantz and Guildenstern.
      Moreover that we much did long to see you,
      The need we have to use you did provoke
      Our hasty sending. Something have you heard
      Of Hamlet's transformation – so call it,
      Sith nor th'exterior nor the inward man
      Resembles that it was. What it should be,
      More than his father's death, that thus hath put him
      So much from th'understanding of himself
10   I cannot dream of. I entreat you both
      That, being of so young days brought up with him,
      And sith so neighboured to his youth and 'haviour,
      That you vouchsafe your rest here in our court
      Some little time, so by your companies
      To draw him on to pleasures, and to gather
      So much as from occasion you may glean,
      Whether aught to us unknown afflicts him thus,
      That, opened, lies within our remedy.

QUEEN
      Good gentlemen, he hath much talked of you,
20   And sure I am two men there is not living
      To whom he more adheres. If it will please you
      To show us so much gentry and good will
      As to expend your time with us awhile
      For the supply and profit of our hope,
      Your visitation shall receive such thanks

As fits a king's remembrance.

ROSENCRANTZ   Both your majesties
Might, by the sovereign power you have of us,
Put your dread pleasures more into command
Than to entreaty.

GUILDENSTERN   But we both obey,
And here give up ourselves in the full bent   30
To lay our service freely at your feet,
To be commanded.

KING
Thanks, Rosencrantz and gentle Guildenstern.

QUEEN
Thanks, Guildenstern and gentle Rosencrantz.
And I beseech you instantly to visit
My too much changèd son. – Go, some of you,
And bring these gentlemen where Hamlet is.

GUILDENSTERN
Heavens make our presence and our practices
Pleasant and helpful to him!

QUEEN   Ay, amen!

                              Exeunt Rosencrantz and
                              Guildenstern with attendants

    Enter Polonius

POLONIUS
The ambassadors from Norway, my good lord,   40
Are joyfully returned.

KING
Thou still hast been the father of good news.

POLONIUS
Have I, my lord? Assure you, my good liege,
I hold my duty as I hold my soul,
Both to my God and to my gracious King.
And I do think – or else this brain of mine
Hunts not the trail of policy so sure

As it hath used to do – that I have found
The very cause of Hamlet's lunacy.

KING

50   O, speak of that! That do I long to hear.

POLONIUS

Give first admittance to th'ambassadors.
My news shall be the fruit to that great feast.

KING

Thyself do grace to them and bring them in.

                                        Exit Polonius

He tells me, my dear Gertrude, he hath found
The head and source of all your son's distemper.

QUEEN

I doubt it is no other but the main,
His father's death and our o'erhasty marriage.

KING

Well, we shall sift him.

        Enter Voltemand and Cornelius, the ambassadors,
        with Polonius

                                Welcome, my good friends.
Say, Voltemand, what from our brother Norway?

VOLTEMAND

60   Most fair return of greetings and desires.
Upon our first, he sent out to suppress
His nephew's levies, which to him appeared
To be a preparation 'gainst the Polack,
But, better looked into, he truly found
It was against your highness; whereat grieved,
That so his sickness, age, and impotence
Was falsely borne in hand, sends out arrests
On Fortinbras; which he in brief obeys,
Receives rebuke from Norway, and in fine
70   Makes vow before his uncle never more
To give th'assay of arms against your majesty.

Whereon old Norway, overcome with joy,
Gives him three thousand crowns in annual fee
And his commission to employ those soldiers,
So levied as before, against the Polack,
With an entreaty, herein further shown,
　　(*He gives a paper to the King*)
That it might please you to give quiet pass
Through your dominions for this enterprise,
On such regards of safety and allowance
As therein are set down.

KING　　　　　　　　　　It likes us well.　　　　　　　80
And at our more considered time we'll read,
Answer, and think upon this business.
Meantime we thank you for your well-took labour.
Go to your rest. At night we'll feast together.
Most welcome home!　　　　*Exeunt the ambassadors*

POLONIUS　　　　　　　This business is well ended.
My liege and madam, to expostulate
What majesty should be, what duty is,
Why day is day, night night, and time is time,
Were nothing but to waste night, day, and time.
Therefore, since brevity is the soul of wit,　　　　90
And tediousness the limbs and outward flourishes,
I will be brief. Your noble son is mad.
Mad call I it. For, to define true madness,
What is't but to be nothing else but mad?
But let that go.

QUEEN　　　　　　More matter, with less art.

POLONIUS
Madam, I swear I use no art at all.
That he's mad, 'tis true. 'Tis true, 'tis pity,
And pity 'tis 'tis true – a foolish figure.
But farewell it; for I will use no art.
Mad let us grant him then. And now remains　　　　100

Hamlet's poem to Ophelia

That we find out the cause of this effect –
Or rather say, the cause of this defect,
For this effect defective comes by cause.
Thus it remains, and the remainder thus.
Perpend.
I have a daughter – have while she is mine –
Who in her duty and obedience, mark,
Hath given me this. Now gather, and surmise.
    (*He reads the letter*)
To the celestial, and my soul's idol, the most beautified
Ophelia – That's an ill phrase, a vile phrase; 'beautified'
is a vile phrase. But you shall hear. Thus:
    (*He reads*)
In her excellent white bosom, these, et cetera.

QUEEN
Came this from Hamlet to her?

POLONIUS
Good madam, stay awhile. I will be faithful.
    (*He reads*)
Doubt thou the stars are fire.
    Doubt that the sun doth move.
Doubt truth to be a liar.
    But never doubt I love.
O dear Ophelia, I am ill at these numbers. I have not art
to reckon my groans. But that I love thee best, O most best,
believe it. Adieu.
        Thine evermore, most dear lady, whilst
        this machine is to him,

                                    Hamlet
This in obedience hath my daughter shown me,
And more above hath his solicitings,
As they fell out by time, by means, and place,
All given to mine ear.

KING   But how hath she

Received his love?

POLONIUS   What do you think of me?

KING

As of a man faithful and honourable.   130

POLONIUS

I would fain prove so. But what might you think
When I had seen this hot love on the wing –
As I perceived it, I must tell you that,
Before my daughter told me – what might you,
Or my dear majesty your Queen here, think
If I had played the desk or table-book,
Or given my heart a winking, mute and dumb,
Or looked upon this love with idle sight?
What might you think? No, I went round to work,
And my young mistress thus I did bespeak: 140
'Lord Hamlet is a prince, out of thy star.
This must not be.' And then I prescripts gave her,
That she should lock herself from his resort,
Admit no messengers, receive no tokens.
Which done, she took the fruits of my advice,
And he, repellèd, a short tale to make,
Fell into a sadness, then into a fast,
Thence to a watch, thence into a weakness,
Thence to a lightness, and, by this declension,
Into the madness wherein now he raves   150
And all we mourn for.

KING   Do you think 'tis this?

QUEEN

It may be, very like.

POLONIUS

Hath there been such a time – I would fain know that –
That I have positively said ''Tis so'
When it proved otherwise?

KING   Not that I know.

POLONIUS

    Take this from this, if this be otherwise.

    If circumstances lead me, I will find

    Where truth is hid, though it were hid indeed

    Within the centre.

KING   How may we try it further?

POLONIUS

160   You know sometimes he walks four hours together

    Here in the lobby.

QUEEN   So he does indeed.

POLONIUS

    At such a time I'll loose my daughter to him.

    Be you and I behind an arras then.

    Mark the encounter. If he love her not,

    And be not from his reason fallen thereon,

    Let me be no assistant for a state,

    But keep a farm and carters.

KING   We will try it.

    Enter Hamlet

QUEEN

    But look where sadly the poor wretch comes reading.

POLONIUS

    Away, I do beseech you both, away.

170   I'll board him presently. O, give me leave.

                     Exeunt the King and Queen

    How does my good Lord Hamlet?

HAMLET Well, God-a-mercy.

POLONIUS Do you know me, my lord?

HAMLET Excellent well. You are a fishmonger.

POLONIUS Not I, my lord.

HAMLET Then I would you were so honest a man.

POLONIUS Honest, my lord?

HAMLET Ay, sir. To be honest, as this world goes, is to be

    one man picked out of ten thousand.

madness — method.

POLONIUS That's very true, my lord.

HAMLET For if the sun breed maggots in a dead dog,
  being a good kissing carrion – have you a daughter?

POLONIUS I have, my lord.

HAMLET Let her not walk i'th'sun. Conception is a blessing. But as your daughter may conceive, friend, look
  to't.

POLONIUS (*aside*) How say you by that? Still harping on
  my daughter. Yet he knew me not at first. 'A said I was
  a fishmonger. 'A is far gone, far gone. And truly in my
  youth I suffered much extremity for love, very near   190
  this. I'll speak to him again. – What do you read, my
  lord?

HAMLET Words, words, words.

POLONIUS What is the matter, my lord?

HAMLET Between who?

POLONIUS I mean the matter that you read, my lord.

HAMLET Slanders, sir. For the satirical rogue says here
  that old men have grey beards, that their faces are
  wrinkled, their eyes purging thick amber and plum-tree
  gum, and that they have a plentiful lack of wit, together   200
  with most weak hams; all which, sir, though I most
  powerfully and potently believe, yet I hold it not
  honesty to have it thus set down. For yourself, sir, shall
  grow old as I am – if, like a crab, you could go backward.

POLONIUS (*aside*) Though this be madness, yet there is
  method in't. – Will you walk out of the air, my lord?

HAMLET Into my grave?

POLONIUS Indeed, that's out of the air. (*Aside*) How
  pregnant sometimes his replies are! A happiness that
  often madness hits on, which reason and sanity could   210
  not so prosperously be delivered of. I will leave him
  and suddenly contrive the means of meeting between
  him and my daughter. – My honourable lord, I will

most humbly take my leave of you.

HAMLET You cannot, sir, take from me anything that I
will not more willingly part withal — except my life,
except my life, except my life.

POLONIUS Fare you well, my lord.

HAMLET These tedious old fools!

Enter Guildenstern and Rosencrantz

220 POLONIUS You go to seek the Lord Hamlet. There he is.

ROSENCRANTZ (*to Polonius*) God save you, sir!

Exit Polonius

GUILDENSTERN My honoured lord!

ROSENCRANTZ My most dear lord!

HAMLET
My excellent good friends.
How dost thou, Guildenstern? Ah, Rosencrantz!
Good lads, how do you both?

ROSENCRANTZ
As the indifferent children of the earth.

GUILDENSTERN
Happy in that we are not over-happy.
On Fortune's cap we are not the very button.

HAMLET
230 Nor the soles of her shoe?

ROSENCRANTZ   Neither, my lord.

HAMLET Then you live about her waist, or in the middle
of her favours?

GUILDENSTERN Faith, her privates we.

HAMLET In the secret parts of Fortune? O, most true!
She is a strumpet. What news?

ROSENCRANTZ None, my lord, but that the world's
grown honest.

HAMLET Then is Doomsday near. But your news is not
true. Let me question more in particular. What have
240 you, my good friends, deserved at the hands of Fortune

that she sends you to prison hither?

GUILDENSTERN Prison, my lord?

HAMLET Denmark's a prison.

ROSENCRANTZ Then is the world one.

HAMLET A goodly one; in which there are many confines,
wards, and dungeons, Denmark being one o'th'worst.

ROSENCRANTZ We think not so, my lord.

HAMLET Why, then 'tis none to you. For there is nothing
either good or bad but thinking makes it so. To me it is
a prison.   250

ROSENCRANTZ Why, then your ambition makes it one.
'Tis too narrow for your mind.

HAMLET O God, I could be bounded in a nutshell and
count myself a king of infinite space, were it not that I
have bad dreams.

GUILDENSTERN Which dreams indeed are ambition.
For the very substance of the ambitious is merely the
shadow of a dream.

HAMLET A dream itself is but a shadow.

ROSENCRANTZ Truly; and I hold ambition of so airy and   260
light a quality that it is but a shadow's shadow.

HAMLET Then are our beggars bodies, and our monarchs
and outstretched heroes the beggars' shadows. Shall
we to th'court? For, by my fay, I cannot reason.

ROSENCRANTZ *and* GUILDENSTERN We'll wait upon
you.

HAMLET No such matter. I will not sort you with the rest
of my servants. For, to speak to you like an honest man,
I am most dreadfully attended. But in the beaten way
of friendship, what make you at Elsinore?   270

ROSENCRANTZ To visit you, my lord. No other occasion.

HAMLET Beggar that I am, I am even poor in thanks.
But I thank you. And sure, dear friends, my thanks are
too dear a halfpenny. Were you not sent for? Is it your

own inclining? Is it a free visitation? Come, come, deal justly with me. Come, come. Nay, speak.

GUILDENSTERN What should we say, my lord?

HAMLET Why, anything but to th'purpose. You were sent for. And there is a kind of confession in your looks, which your modesties have not craft enough to colour. I know the good King and Queen have sent for you.

ROSENCRANTZ To what end, my lord?

HAMLET That you must teach me. But let me conjure you by the rights of our fellowship, by the consonancy of our youth, by the obligation of our ever-preserved love, and by what more dear a better proposer can charge you withal, be even and direct with me whether you were sent for or no.

ROSENCRANTZ (*aside to Guildenstern*) What say you?

HAMLET (*aside*) Nay then, I have an eye of you. — If you love me, hold not off.

GUILDENSTERN My lord, we were sent for.

HAMLET I will tell you why. So shall my anticipation prevent your discovery, and your secrecy to the King and Queen moult no feather. I have of late — but wherefore I know not — lost all my mirth, forgone all custom of exercises. And indeed it goes so heavily with my disposition that this goodly frame the earth seems to me a sterile promontory. This most excellent canopy, the air, look you, this brave o'erhanging firmament, this majestical roof fretted with golden fire — why, it appeareth nothing to me but a foul and pestilent congregation of vapours. What a piece of work is a man, how noble in reason, how infinite in faculties, in form and moving how express and admirable, in action how like an angel, in apprehension how like a god: the beauty of the world, the paragon of animals! And yet to me what is this quintessence of dust? Man delights

not me — nor woman neither, though by your smiling
you seem to say so.   310

ROSENCRANTZ My lord, there was no such stuff in my
thoughts.

HAMLET Why did ye laugh then, when I said 'Man
delights not me'?

ROSENCRANTZ To think, my lord, if you delight not in
man, what lenten entertainment the players shall
receive from you. We coted them on the way. And
hither are they coming to offer you service.

HAMLET He that plays the king shall be welcome — his
majesty shall have tribute of me; the adventurous   320
knight shall use his foil and target; the lover shall not
sigh gratis; the humorous man shall end his part in
peace; the clown shall make those laugh whose lungs
are tickle o'th'sere; and the lady shall say her mind
freely, or the blank verse shall halt for't. What players
are they?

ROSENCRANTZ Even those you were wont to take such
delight in, the tragedians of the city.

HAMLET How chances it they travel? Their residence,
both in reputation and profit, was better both ways.   330

ROSENCRANTZ I think their inhibition comes by the
means of the late innovation.

HAMLET Do they hold the same estimation they did when
I was in the city? Are they so followed?

ROSENCRANTZ No, indeed are they not.

HAMLET How comes it? Do they grow rusty?

ROSENCRANTZ Nay, their endeavour keeps in the wonted
pace. But there is, sir, an eyrie of children, little eyases,
that cry out on the top of question and are most tyrannically clapped for't. These are now the fashion, and so   340
berattle the common stages — so they call them — that
many wearing rapiers are afraid of goosequills and dare

scarce come thither.

HAMLET What, are they children? Who maintains 'em? How are they escoted? Will they pursue the quality no longer than they can sing? Will they not say afterwards, if they should grow themselves to common players – as it is most like, if their means are not better – their writers do them wrong to make them exclaim against
350   their own succession?

ROSENCRANTZ Faith, there has been much to-do on both sides, and the nation holds it no sin to tarre them to controversy. There was, for a while, no money bid for argument unless the poet and the player went to cuffs in the question.

HAMLET Is't possible?

GUILDENSTERN O, there has been much throwing about of brains.

HAMLET Do the boys carry it away?

360 ROSENCRANTZ Ay, that they do, my lord – Hercules and his load too.

HAMLET It is not very strange. For my uncle is King of Denmark, and those that would make mows at him while my father lived give twenty, forty, fifty, a hundred ducats apiece for his picture in little. 'Sblood, there is something in this more than natural, if philosophy could find it out.

    A flourish

GUILDENSTERN There are the players.

HAMLET Gentlemen, you are welcome to Elsinore. Your
370   hands. Come then. Th'appurtenance of welcome is fashion and ceremony. Let me comply with you in this garb, lest my extent to the players, which I tell you must show fairly outwards, should more appear like entertainment than yours. You are welcome. But my uncle-father and aunt-mother are deceived.

GUILDENSTERN In what, my dear lord?

HAMLET I am but mad north-north-west. When the wind is southerly, I know a hawk from a handsaw.

Enter Polonius

POLONIUS Well be with you, gentlemen.

HAMLET Hark you, Guildenstern – and you too – at each   380
ear a hearer. That great baby you see there is not yet
out of his swaddling clouts.

ROSENCRANTZ Happily he is the second time come to
them. For they say an old man is twice a child.

HAMLET I will prophesy he comes to tell me of the
players. Mark it. – You say right, sir. 'A Monday morning, 'twas then, indeed.

POLONIUS My lord, I have news to tell you.

HAMLET My lord, I have news to tell you. When Roscius
was an actor in Rome –   390

POLONIUS The actors are come hither, my lord.

HAMLET Buzz, buzz.

POLONIUS Upon my honour –

HAMLET Then came each actor on his ass –

POLONIUS The best actors in the world, either for
tragedy, comedy, history, pastoral, pastoral-comical,
historical-pastoral, tragical-historical, tragical-comical-
historical-pastoral, scene individable, or poem unlimited. Seneca cannot be too heavy, nor Plautus too
light. For the law of writ and the liberty, these are the   400
only men.

HAMLET O Jephthah, judge of Israel, what a treasure
hadst thou!

POLONIUS What a treasure had he, my lord?

HAMLET Why,

        'One fair daughter, and no more,
            The which he lovèd passing well.'

POLONIUS (*aside*) Still on my daughter.

HAMLET Am I not i'th'right, old Jephthah?

410 POLONIUS If you call me Jephthah, my lord, I have a
daughter that I love passing well.

HAMLET Nay, that follows not.

POLONIUS What follows then, my lord?

HAMLET Why,

       'As by lot, God wot,'

and then you know,

       'It came to pass, as most like it was.'

The first row of the pious chanson will show you more.
For look where my abridgement comes.

   Enter the Players

420 You are welcome, masters, welcome, all. – I am glad
to see thee well. – Welcome, good friends. – O old friend,
why, thy face is valanced since I saw thee last. Comest
thou to beard me in Denmark? – What, my young lady
and mistress? By'r Lady, your ladyship is nearer to
heaven than when I saw you last by the altitude of a
chopine. Pray God your voice, like a piece of uncurrent
gold, be not cracked within the ring. – Masters, you are
all welcome. We'll e'en to't like French falconers: fly
at anything we see. We'll have a speech straight. Come,
430 give us a taste of your quality. Come, a passionate
speech.

FIRST PLAYER What speech, my good lord?

HAMLET I heard thee speak me a speech once, but it was
never acted, or if it was, not above once. For the play, I
remember, pleased not the million. 'Twas caviary to the
general. But it was – as I received it, and others, whose
judgements in such matters cried in the top of mine –
an excellent play, well digested in the scenes, set down
with as much modesty as cunning. I remember one said
440 there were no sallets in the lines to make the matter
savoury, nor no matter in the phrase that might indict

the author of affectation, but called it an honest method,
as wholesome as sweet, and by very much more handsome than fine. One speech in't I chiefly loved. 'Twas
Aeneas' tale to Dido; and thereabout of it especially
when he speaks of Priam's slaughter. If it live in your
memory, begin at this line – let me see, let me see.

   'The rugged Pyrrhus, like th'Hyrcanian beast –'
'Tis not so. It begins with Pyrrhus.

   'The rugged Pyrrhus, he whose sable arms,   450
   Black as his purpose, did the night resemble
   When he lay couchèd in th'ominous horse,
   Hath now this dread and black complexion smeared
   With heraldy more dismal. Head to foot
   Now is he total gules, horridly tricked
   With blood of fathers, mothers, daughters, sons,
   Baked and impasted with the parching streets,
   That lend a tyrannous and a damnèd light
   To their lord's murder; roasted in wrath and fire,
   And thus o'er-sizèd with coagulate gore,   460
   With eyes like carbuncles, the hellish Pyrrhus
   Old grandsire Priam seeks.'

So, proceed you.

POLONIUS 'Fore God, my lord, well spoken, with good
   accent and good discretion.

FIRST PLAYER   'Anon he finds him,
   Striking too short at Greeks. His antique sword,
   Rebellious to his arm, lies where it falls,
   Repugnant to command. Unequal matched,
   Pyrrhus at Priam drives, in rage strikes wide,   470
   But with the whiff and wind of his fell sword
   Th'unnervèd father falls. Then senseless Ilium,
   Seeming to feel this blow, with flaming top
   Stoops to his base, and with a hideous crash
   Takes prisoner Pyrrhus' ear. For lo! his sword,

Which was declining on the milky head
Of reverend Priam, seemed i'th'air to stick.
So as a painted tyrant Pyrrhus stood,
And like a neutral to his will and matter
Did nothing.
But as we often see, against some storm,
A silence in the heavens, the rack stand still,
The bold winds speechless, and the orb below
As hush as death; anon the dreadful thunder
Doth rend the region; so after Pyrrhus' pause,
A rousèd vengeance sets him new a-work,
And never did the Cyclops' hammers fall
On Mars's armour, forged for proof eterne,
With less remorse than Pyrrhus' bleeding sword
Now falls on Priam.
Out, out, thou strumpet Fortune! All you gods,
In general synod, take away her power!
Break all the spokes and fellies from her wheel,
And bowl the round nave down the hill of heaven,
As low as to the fiends!'

POLONIUS This is too long.

HAMLET It shall to the barber's, with your beard. –
Prithee say on. He's for a jig or a tale of bawdry, or he
sleeps. Say on. Come to Hecuba.

FIRST PLAYER
        'But who, ah woe!, had seen the mobled Queen –'

HAMLET 'The mobled Queen'?

POLONIUS That's good. 'Mobled Queen' is good.

FIRST PLAYER
        'Run barefoot up and down, threatening the flames
With bisson rheum; a clout upon that head
Where late the diadem stood; and for a robe,
About her lank and all o'er-teemèd loins,
A blanket in the alarm of fear caught up –

Who this had seen, with tongue in venom steeped
'Gainst Fortune's state would treason have
          pronounced.
But if the gods themselves did see her then,   510
When she saw Pyrrhus make malicious sport
In mincing with his sword her husband's limbs,
The instant burst of clamour that she made,
Unless things mortal move them not at all,
Would have made milch the burning eyes of heaven
And passion in the gods.'

POLONIUS Look whe'er he has not turned his colour,
and has tears in's eyes. Prithee no more.

HAMLET 'Tis well. I'll have thee speak out the rest of this
soon. – Good my lord, will you see the players well   520
bestowed? Do you hear? Let them be well used, for
they are the abstract and brief chronicles of the time.
After your death you were better have a bad epitaph
than their ill report while you live.

POLONIUS My lord, I will use them according to their
desert.

HAMLET God's bodkin, man, much better! Use every
man after his desert, and who shall 'scape whipping?
Use them after your own honour and dignity. The less
they deserve, the more merit is in your bounty. Take   530
them in.

POLONIUS Come, sirs.

HAMLET Follow him, friends. We'll hear a play tomorrow. (*Aside to First Player*) Dost thou hear me, old
friend? Can you play *The Murder of Gonzago*?

FIRST PLAYER Ay, my lord.

HAMLET We'll ha't tomorrow night. You could for a
need study a speech of some dozen lines or sixteen lines,
which I would set down and insert in't, could you not?

FIRST PLAYER Ay, my lord.   540

HAMLET Very well. — Follow that lord, and look you mock him not.

Exeunt Polonius and Players

My good friends, I'll leave you till night. You are welcome to Elsinore.

ROSENCRANTZ Good my lord.

HAMLET Ay, so, God bye to you.

Exeunt Rosencrantz and Guildenstern

Now I am alone.
O, what a rogue and peasant slave am I!
Is it not monstrous that this player here,
But in a fiction, in a dream of passion,
550 Could force his soul so to his own conceit
That from her working all his visage wanned,
Tears in his eyes, distraction in his aspect,
A broken voice, and his whole function suiting
With forms to his conceit? And all for nothing.
For Hecuba!
What's Hecuba to him, or he to her,
That he should weep for her? What would he do
Had he the motive and the cue for passion
That I have? He would drown the stage with tears
560 And cleave the general ear with horrid speech,
Make mad the guilty and appal the free,
Confound the ignorant, and amaze indeed
The very faculties of eyes and ears. Yet I,
A dull and muddy-mettled rascal, peak
Like John-a-dreams, unpregnant of my cause,
And can say nothing, no, not for a king
Upon whose property and most dear life
A damned defeat was made. Am I a coward?
Who calls me villain? Breaks my pate across?
570 Plucks off my beard and blows it in my face?
Tweaks me by the nose? Gives me the lie i'th'throat

As deep as to the lungs? Who does me this?
Ha, 'swounds, I should take it. For it cannot be
But I am pigeon-livered and lack gall
To make oppression bitter, or ere this
I should ha' fatted all the region kites
With this slave's offal. Bloody, bawdy villain!
Remorseless, treacherous, lecherous, kindless villain!
O, vengeance!
Why, what an ass am I! This is most brave,   580
That I, the son of a dear father murdered,
Prompted to my revenge by heaven and hell,
Must like a whore unpack my heart with words
And fall a-cursing like a very drab,
A stallion! Fie upon't, foh!
About, my brains. Hum — I have heard
That guilty creatures sitting at a play
Have by the very cunning of the scene
Been struck so to the soul that presently
They have proclaimed their malefactions.   590
For murder, though it have no tongue, will speak
With most miraculous organ. I'll have these players
Play something like the murder of my father
Before mine uncle. I'll observe his looks.
I'll tent him to the quick. If 'a do blench,
I know my course. The spirit that I have seen
May be a devil, and the devil hath power
T'assume a pleasing shape, yea, and perhaps
Out of my weakness and my melancholy,
As he is very potent with such spirits,   600
Abuses me to damn me. I'll have grounds
More relative than this. The play's the thing
Wherein I'll catch the conscience of the King.   *Exit*

*

III.1   *Enter the King and Queen, Polonius, Ophelia,*
               Rosencrantz, Guildenstern, and lords

KING
       And can you by no drift of conference
       Get from him why he puts on this confusion,
       Grating so harshly all his days of quiet
       With turbulent and dangerous lunacy?

ROSENCRANTZ
       He does confess he feels himself distracted,
       But from what cause 'a will by no means speak.

GUILDENSTERN
       Nor do we find him forward to be sounded,
       But with a crafty madness keeps aloof
       When we would bring him on to some confession
10   Of his true state.

QUEEN   Did he receive you well?

ROSENCRANTZ
       Most like a gentleman.

GUILDENSTERN
       But with much forcing of his disposition.

ROSENCRANTZ
       Niggard of question, but of our demands
       Most free in his reply.

QUEEN   Did you assay him
       To any pastime?

ROSENCRANTZ
       Madam, it so fell out that certain players
       We o'er-raught on the way. Of these we told him,
       And there did seem in him a kind of joy
       To hear of it. They are here about the court,
20   And, as I think, they have already order
       This night to play before him.

POLONIUS   'Tis most true,
       And he beseeched me to entreat your majesties

To hear and see the matter.

KING

    With all my heart, and it doth much content me
    To hear him so inclined.
    Good gentlemen, give him a further edge
    And drive his purpose into these delights.

ROSENCRANTZ

    We shall, my lord.

              Exeunt Rosencrantz, Guildenstern, and lords

KING   Sweet Gertrude, leave us too.

    For we have closely sent for Hamlet hither,
    That he, as 'twere by accident, may here   30
    Affront Ophelia.
    Her father and myself, lawful espials,
    We'll so bestow ourselves that, seeing unseen,
    We may of their encounter frankly judge,
    And gather by him, as he is behaved,
    If 't be th'affliction of his love or no
    That thus he suffers for.

QUEEN   I shall obey you. –

    And for your part, Ophelia, I do wish
    That your good beauties be the happy cause
    Of Hamlet's wildness. So shall I hope your virtues   40
    Will bring him to his wonted way again,
    To both your honours.

OPHELIA   Madam, I wish it may.

                        Exit the Queen

POLONIUS

    Ophelia, walk you here. – Gracious, so please you,
    We will bestow ourselves. (*To Ophelia*) Read on this
        book,
    That show of such an exercise may colour
    Your loneliness. We are oft to blame in this,
    'Tis too much proved, that with devotion's visage

And pious action we do sugar o'er
The devil himself.

KING   O, 'tis too true.

50   (*Aside*) How smart a lash that speech doth give my
            conscience!
      The harlot's cheek, beautied with plastering art,
      Is not more ugly to the thing that helps it
      Than is my deed to my most painted word.
      O, heavy burden!

POLONIUS
      I hear him coming. Let's withdraw, my lord.

                              Exeunt the King and Polonius

      Enter Hamlet

HAMLET
      To be, or not to be – that is the question;
      Whether 'tis nobler in the mind to suffer
      The slings and arrows of outrageous fortune
      Or to take arms against a sea of troubles

60   And by opposing end them. To die, to sleep –
      No more – and by a sleep to say we end
      The heartache and the thousand natural shocks
      That flesh is heir to. 'Tis a consummation
      Devoutly to be wished. To die, to sleep –
      To sleep – perchance to dream. Ay, there's the rub.
      For in that sleep of death what dreams may come
      When we have shuffled off this mortal coil
      Must give us pause. There's the respect
      That makes calamity of so long life.

70   For who would bear the whips and scorns of time,
      Th'oppressor's wrong, the proud man's contumely,
      The pangs of despised love, the law's delay,
      The insolence of office, and the spurns
      That patient merit of th'unworthy takes,
      When he himself might his quietus make

With a bare bodkin? Who would fardels bear,
To grunt and sweat under a weary life,
But that the dread of something after death,
The undiscovered country, from whose bourn
No traveller returns, puzzles the will,   80
And makes us rather bear those ills we have
Than fly to others that we know not of?
Thus conscience does make cowards of us all;
And thus the native hue of resolution
Is sicklied o'er with the pale cast of thought,
And enterprises of great pitch and moment
With this regard their currents turn awry
And lose the name of action. Soft you now,
The fair Ophelia! – Nymph, in thy orisons
Be all my sins remembered.

OPHELIA   Good my lord,   90
How does your honour for this many a day?

HAMLET
I humbly thank you, well, well, well.

OPHELIA
My lord, I have remembrances of yours
That I have longèd long to re-deliver.
I pray you now receive them.

HAMLET   No, not I.
I never gave you aught.

OPHELIA
My honoured lord, you know right well you did,
And with them words of so sweet breath composed
As made the things more rich. Their perfume lost,
Take these again. For to the noble mind   100
Rich gifts wax poor when givers prove unkind.
There, my lord.

HAMLET Ha, ha! Are you honest?

OPHELIA My lord?

HAMLET Are you fair?

OPHELIA What means your lordship?

HAMLET That if you be honest and fair, your honesty
should admit no discourse to your beauty.

OPHELIA Could beauty, my lord, have better commerce
110   than with honesty?

HAMLET Ay, truly. For the power of beauty will sooner
transform honesty from what it is to a bawd than the
force of honesty can translate beauty into his likeness.
This was sometime a paradox, but now the time gives it
proof. I did love you once.

OPHELIA Indeed, my lord, you made me believe so.

HAMLET You should not have believed me. For virtue
cannot so inoculate our old stock but we shall relish of
it. I loved you not.

120 OPHELIA I was the more deceived.

HAMLET Get thee to a nunnery. Why wouldst thou be a
breeder of sinners? I am myself indifferent honest, but
yet I could accuse me of such things that it were better
my mother had not borne me. I am very proud, revengeful, ambitious, with more offences at my beck than I
have thoughts to put them in, imagination to give them
shape, or time to act them in. What should such fellows
as I do crawling between earth and heaven? We are
arrant knaves all. Believe none of us. Go thy ways to a
130   nunnery. Where's your father?

OPHELIA At home, my lord.

HAMLET Let the doors be shut upon him, that he may
play the fool nowhere but in's own house. Farewell.

OPHELIA O, help him, you sweet heavens!

HAMLET If thou dost marry, I'll give thee this plague for
thy dowry: be thou as chaste as ice, as pure as snow,
thou shalt not escape calumny. Get thee to a nunnery.
Go, farewell. Or if thou wilt needs marry, marry a fool.

For wise men know well enough what monsters you
make of them. To a nunnery, go, and quickly too. Fare-   140
well.

OPHELIA O heavenly powers, restore him!

HAMLET I have heard of your paintings too, well enough.
God hath given you one face, and you make yourselves
another. You jig and amble, and you lisp. You nickname God's creatures and make your wantonness your
ignorance. Go to, I'll no more on't. It hath made me
mad. I say we will have no more marriage. Those that
are married already – all but one – shall live. The rest
shall keep as they are. To a nunnery, go.   *Exit*   150

OPHELIA
O, what a noble mind is here o'erthrown!
The courtier's, soldier's, scholar's, eye, tongue, sword,
Th'expectancy and rose of the fair state,
The glass of fashion and the mould of form,
Th'observed of all observers, quite, quite down!
And I, of ladies most deject and wretched,
That sucked the honey of his music vows,
Now see that noble and most sovereign reason
Like sweet bells jangled, out of time and harsh,
That unmatched form and feature of blown youth   160
Blasted with ecstasy. O, woe is me
T'have seen what I have seen, see what I see!
    Enter the King and Polonius

KING
Love? His affections do not that way tend;
Nor what he spake, though it lacked form a little,
Was not like madness. There's something in his soul
O'er which his melancholy sits on brood,
And I do doubt the hatch and the disclose
Will be some danger; which for to prevent,
I have in quick determination

170 Thus set it down: he shall with speed to England
For the demand of our neglected tribute.
Haply the seas, and countries different,
With variable objects, shall expel
This something-settled matter in his heart,
Whereon his brains still beating puts him thus
From fashion of himself. What think you on't?

POLONIUS
It shall do well. But yet do I believe
The origin and commencement of his grief
Sprung from neglected love. — How now, Ophelia?
180 You need not tell us what Lord Hamlet said.
We heard it all. — My lord, do as you please,
But if you hold it fit, after the play
Let his Queen mother all alone entreat him
To show his grief. Let her be round with him,
And I'll be placed, so please you, in the ear
Of all their conference. If she find him not,
To England send him, or confine him where
Your wisdom best shall think.

KING   It shall be so.
Madness in great ones must not unwatched go.

Exeunt

III.2   *Enter Hamlet and the Players*

HAMLET Speak the speech, I pray you, as I pronounced
it to you, trippingly on the tongue. But if you mouth it
as many of our players do, I had as lief the town crier
spoke my lines. Nor do not saw the air too much with
your hand, thus. But use all gently. For in the very tor-
rent, tempest, and, as I may say, whirlwind of your
passion, you must acquire and beget a temperance that
may give it smoothness. O, it offends me to the soul to

hear a robustious periwig-pated fellow tear a passion to
tatters, to very rags, to split the ears of the groundlings,   10
who for the most part are capable of nothing but in-
explicable dumb shows and noise. I would have such a
fellow whipped for o'erdoing Termagant. It out-Herods
Herod. Pray you avoid it.

FIRST PLAYER I warrant your honour.

HAMLET Be not too tame neither. But let your own discretion be your tutor. Suit the action to the word, the
word to the action, with this special observance, that
you o'erstep not the modesty of nature. For anything so
o'erdone is from the purpose of playing, whose end,   20
both at the first and now, was and is to hold, as 'twere,
the mirror up to nature, to show virtue her own feature,
scorn her own image, and the very age and body of the
time his form and pressure. Now this overdone, or come
tardy off, though it make the unskilful laugh, cannot
but make the judicious grieve; the censure of the which
one must in your allowance o'erweigh a whole theatre
of others. O, there be players that I have seen play, and
heard others praise, and that highly, not to speak it
profanely, that, neither having th'accent of Christians   30
nor the gait of Christian, pagan, nor man, have so
strutted and bellowed that I have thought some of
Nature's journeymen had made men, and not made
them well, they imitated humanity so abominably.

FIRST PLAYER I hope we have reformed that indifferently with us, sir.

HAMLET O, reform it altogether! And let those that play
your clowns speak no more than is set down for them.
For there be of them that will themselves laugh to set on
some quantity of barren spectators to laugh too, though   40
in the meantime some necessary question of the play be
then to be considered. That's villainous, and shows a

most pitiful ambition in the fool that uses it. And then
you have some again that keeps one suit of jests, as a man
is known by one suit of apparel; and gentlemen quote
his jests down in their tables before they come to the
play; as thus, 'Cannot you stay till I eat my porridge?',
and 'You owe me a quarter's wages', and 'My coat
wants a cullison', and 'Your beer is sour', and blabbering with his lips, and thus keeping in his cinquepace of
jests, when, God knows, the warm clown cannot make a
jest unless by chance, as the blind man catcheth a hare.
Masters, tell him of it.

FIRST PLAYER We will, my lord.

HAMLET Well, go make you ready.   *Exeunt Players*
        Enter Polonius, Rosencrantz, and Guildenstern
How now, my lord? Will the King hear this piece of
work?

POLONIUS And the Queen too, and that presently.

HAMLET Bid the players make haste.   *Exit Polonius*
Will you two help to hasten them?

ROSENCRANTZ Ay, my lord.
                    Exeunt Rosencrantz and Guildenstern

HAMLET What, ho, Horatio!
        Enter Horatio

HORATIO
Here, sweet lord, at your service.

HAMLET
Horatio, thou art e'en as just a man
As e'er my conversation coped withal.

HORATIO
O my dear lord —

HAMLET   Nay, do not think I flatter.
For what advancement may I hope from thee,
That no revenue hast but thy good spirits
To feed and clothe thee? Why should the poor be
    flattered?

No, let the candied tongue lick absurd pomp,   70
And crook the pregnant hinges of the knee
Where thrift may follow fawning. Dost thou hear?
Since my dear soul was mistress of her choice
And could of men distinguish her election,
Sh'hath sealed thee for herself. For thou hast been
As one, in suffering all, that suffers nothing,
A man that Fortune's buffets and rewards
Hast ta'en with equal thanks. And blest are those
Whose blood and judgement are so well commeddled
That they are not a pipe for Fortune's finger   80
To sound what stop she please. Give me that man
That is not passion's slave, and I will wear him
In my heart's core, ay, in my heart of heart,
As I do thee. Something too much of this.
There is a play tonight before the King.
One scene of it comes near the circumstance,
Which I have told thee, of my father's death.
I prithee, when thou seest that act afoot,
Even with the very comment of thy soul
Observe my uncle. If his occulted guilt   90
Do not itself unkennel in one speech,
It is a damnèd ghost that we have seen,
And my imaginations are as foul
As Vulcan's stithy. Give him heedful note.
For I mine eyes will rivet to his face,
And after we will both our judgements join
In censure of his seeming.
HORATIO   Well, my lord.
If 'a steal aught the whilst this play is playing,
And 'scape detecting, I will pay the theft.
HAMLET They are coming to the play. I must be idle. Get   100
  you a place.

Danish march. Flourish
Trumpets and kettledrums
Enter the King and Queen, Polonius, Ophelia,
Rosencrantz, Guildenstern, and other Lords atten-
dant, with the guard carrying torches

KING How fares our cousin Hamlet?

HAMLET Excellent, i'faith; of the chameleon's dish. I eat
the air, promise-crammed. You cannot feed capons so.

KING I have nothing with this answer, Hamlet. These
words are not mine.

HAMLET No, nor mine now. (*To Polonius*) My lord, you
played once i'th'university, you say?

POLONIUS That did I, my lord, and was accounted a
110   good actor.

HAMLET What did you enact?

POLONIUS I did enact Julius Caesar. I was killed
i'th'Capitol. Brutus killed me.

HAMLET It was a brute part of him to kill so capital a calf
there. Be the players ready?

ROSENCRANTZ Ay, my lord. They stay upon your
patience.

QUEEN Come hither, my dear Hamlet, sit by me.

HAMLET No, good mother. Here's metal more attractive.

120 POLONIUS (*to the King*) O ho! Do you mark that?

HAMLET Lady, shall I lie in your lap?

OPHELIA No, my lord.

HAMLET I mean, my head upon your lap?

OPHELIA Ay, my lord.

HAMLET Do you think I meant country matters?

OPHELIA I think nothing, my lord.

HAMLET That's a fair thought — to lie between maids'
legs.

OPHELIA What is, my lord?

130 HAMLET Nothing.

OPHELIA You are merry, my lord.

HAMLET Who, I?

OPHELIA Ay, my lord.

HAMLET O God, your only jig-maker! What should a
man do but be merry? For look you how cheerfully my
mother looks, and my father died within's two hours.

OPHELIA Nay, 'tis twice two months, my lord.

HAMLET So long? Nay then, let the devil wear black, for
I'll have a suit of sables. O heavens! Die two months
ago, and not forgotten yet? Then there's hope a great   140
man's memory may outlive his life half a year. But, by'r
Lady, 'a must build churches then, or else shall 'a suffer
not thinking on, with the hobby-horse, whose epitaph
is 'For O, for O, the hobby-horse is forgot!'

The trumpets sound
Dumb show follows: Enter a King and a Queen very
lovingly, the Queen embracing him, and he her. She
kneels, and makes show of protestation unto him. He
takes her up, and declines his head upon her neck. He
lies him down upon a bank of flowers. She, seeing
him asleep, leaves him. Anon come in another man;
takes off his crown, kisses it, pours poison in the
sleeper's ears, and leaves him. The Queen returns,
finds the King dead, makes passionate action. The
poisoner, with some three or four, come in again,
seem to condole with her. The dead body is carried
away. The poisoner woos the Queen with gifts. She
seems harsh awhile, but in the end accepts love
                                          Exeunt dumb show

OPHELIA What means this, my lord?

HAMLET Marry, this is miching mallecho. It means mischief.

OPHELIA Belike this show imports the argument of the
play.

Enter the Fourth Player as Prologue

150 HAMLET We shall know by this fellow. The players cannot keep counsel. They'll tell all.

OPHELIA Will 'a tell us what this show meant?

HAMLET Ay, or any show that you will show him. Be not
you ashamed to show, he'll not shame to tell you what
it means.

OPHELIA You are naught, you are naught. I'll mark the
play.

FOURTH PLAYER (*as Prologue*)
    For us and for our tragedy,
    Here stooping to your clemency,
160   We beg your hearing patiently.

                                                    Exit

HAMLET Is this a prologue, or the posy of a ring?

OPHELIA 'Tis brief, my lord.

HAMLET As woman's love.

    Enter two Players as King and Queen

FIRST PLAYER (*as King*)
    Full thirty times hath Phoebus' cart gone round
    Neptune's salt wash and Tellus' orbèd ground,
    And thirty dozen moons with borrowed sheen
    About the world have times twelve thirties been
    Since love our hearts, and Hymen did our hands,
    Unite commutual in most sacred bands.

SECOND PLAYER (*as Queen*)
170   So many journeys may the sun and moon
    Make us again count o'er ere love be done!
    But woe is me, you are so sick of late,
    So far from cheer and from your former state
    That I distrust you. Yet, though I distrust,
    Discomfort you, my lord, it nothing must.
    For women fear too much, even as they love,
    And women's fear and love hold quantity,

In neither aught, or in extremity.
Now what my love is, proof hath made you know,
And as my love is sized, my fear is so.   180
Where love is great, the littlest doubts are fear.
Where little fears grow great, great love grows there.

FIRST PLAYER (*as King*)
Faith, I must leave thee, love, and shortly too.
My operant powers their functions leave to do.
And thou shalt live in this fair world behind,
Honoured, beloved; and haply one as kind
For husband shalt thou —

SECOND PLAYER (*as Queen*)
                              O, confound the rest!
Such love must needs be treason in my breast.
In second husband let me be accurst!
None wed the second but who killed the first.   190

HAMLET (*aside*)
That's wormwood.

SECOND PLAYER (*as Queen*)
The instances that second marriage move
Are base respects of thrift, but none of love.
A second time I kill my husband dead
When second husband kisses me in bed.

FIRST PLAYER (*as King*)
I do believe you think what now you speak,
But what we do determine oft we break.
Purpose is but the slave to memory,
Of violent birth, but poor validity,
Which now, like fruit unripe, sticks on the tree,   200
But fall unshaken when they mellow be.
Most necessary 'tis that we forget
To pay ourselves what to ourselves is debt.
What to ourselves in passion we propose,
The passion ending, doth the purpose lose.

The violence of either grief or joy
Their own enactures with themselves destroy.
Where joy most revels, grief doth most lament.
Grief joys, joy grieves, on slender accident.
210   This world is not for aye, nor 'tis not strange
That even our loves should with our fortunes change.
For 'tis a question left us yet to prove,
Whether love lead fortune, or else fortune love.
The great man down, you mark his favourite flies.
The poor advanced makes friends of enemies.
And hitherto doth love on fortune tend,
For who not needs shall never lack a friend,
And who in want a hollow friend doth try
Directly seasons him his enemy.
220   But, orderly to end where I begun,
Our wills and fates do so contrary run
That our devices still are overthrown.
Our thoughts are ours, their ends none of our own.
So think thou wilt no second husband wed,
But die thy thoughts when thy first lord is dead.

SECOND PLAYER (*as Queen*)
Nor earth to me give food, nor heaven light,
Sport and repose lock from me day and night,
To desperation turn my trust and hope,
An anchor's cheer in prison be my scope,
230   Each opposite that blanks the face of joy
Meet what I would have well, and it destroy,
Both here and hence pursue me lasting strife,
If, once a widow, ever I be wife!

HAMLET (*aside*)
If she should break it now!

FIRST PLAYER (*as King*)
'Tis deeply sworn. Sweet, leave me here awhile.
My spirits grow dull, and fain I would beguile

The tedious day with sleep.

SECOND PLAYER (*as Queen*)

                  Sleep rock thy brain,
And never come mischance between us twain!

      The Player-King sleeps. Exit the Player-Queen

HAMLET

Madam, how like you this play?

QUEEN

The lady doth protest too much, methinks.   240

HAMLET

O, but she'll keep her word.

KING Have you heard the argument? Is there no offence
in't?

HAMLET No, no, they do but jest, poison in jest. No
offence i'th'world.

KING What do you call the play?

HAMLET *The Mousetrap.* Marry, how? Tropically. This
play is the image of a murder done in Vienna. Gonzago
is the duke's name; his wife, Baptista. You shall see
anon. 'Tis a knavish piece of work. But what of that?   250
Your majesty, and we that have free souls, it touches us
not. Let the galled jade wince. Our withers are unwrung.

    Enter the Third Player, as Lucianus

This is one Lucianus, nephew to the King.

OPHELIA You are as good as a chorus, my lord.

HAMLET I could interpret between you and your love, if
I could see the puppets dallying.

OPHELIA You are keen, my lord, you are keen.

HAMLET It would cost you a groaning to take off mine
edge.

OPHELIA Still better, and worse.   260

HAMLET So you must take your husbands. – Begin, murderer. Pox, leave thy damnable faces and begin. Come;
the croaking raven doth bellow for revenge.

THIRD PLAYER (*as Lucianus*)
>   Thoughts black, hands apt, drugs fit, and time agreeing,
>   Confederate season, else no creature seeing,
>   Thou mixture rank, of midnight weeds collected,
>   With Hecat's ban thrice blasted, thrice infected,
>   Thy natural magic and dire property
>   On wholesome life usurps immediately.

>   *He pours the poison in the King's ears*

270   HAMLET 'A poisons him i'th'garden for his estate. His
>   name's Gonzago. The story is extant, and written in very
>   choice Italian. You shall see anon how the murderer
>   gets the love of Gonzago's wife.

OPHELIA The King rises.

HAMLET What, frighted with false fire?

QUEEN How fares my lord?

POLONIUS Give o'er the play.

KING Give me some light. Away!

POLONIUS Lights, lights, lights!

>   *Exeunt all but Hamlet and Horatio*

HAMLET
280   Why, let the strucken deer go weep,
>   The hart ungallèd play.
>   For some must watch, while some must sleep.
>   Thus runs the world away.
>   Would not this, sir, and a forest of feathers — if the rest
>   of my fortunes turn Turk with me — with two Provincial
>   roses on my razed shoes, get me a fellowship in a cry of
>   players, sir?

HORATIO Half a share.

HAMLET A whole one, I.
290   For thou dost know, O Damon dear
>   This realm dismantled was
>   Of Jove himself; and now reigns here
>   A very, very — peacock.

HORATIO You might have rhymed.

HAMLET O good Horatio, I'll take the ghost's word for a
   thousand pound. Didst perceive?

HORATIO Very well, my lord.

HAMLET Upon the talk of the poisoning?

HORATIO I did very well note him.

HAMLET Aha! Come, some music! Come, the recorders!   300
   For if the King like not the comedy,
      Why then, belike he likes it not, perdy.
   Come, some music!

   Enter Rosencrantz and Guildenstern

GUILDENSTERN Good my lord, vouchsafe me a word
   with you.

HAMLET Sir, a whole history.

GUILDENSTERN The King, sir –

HAMLET Ay, sir, what of him?

GUILDENSTERN Is in his retirement marvellous distempered.   310

HAMLET With drink, sir?

GUILDENSTERN No, my lord, with choler.

HAMLET Your wisdom should show itself more richer to
   signify this to the doctor. For for me to put him to his
   purgation would perhaps plunge him into more choler.

GUILDENSTERN Good my lord, put your discourse into
   some frame, and start not so wildly from my affair.

HAMLET I am tame, sir. Pronounce.

GUILDENSTERN The Queen your mother in most great
   affliction of spirit hath sent me to you.   320

HAMLET You are welcome.

GUILDENSTERN Nay, good my lord, this courtesy is not
   of the right breed. If it shall please you to make me a
   wholesome answer, I will do your mother's commandment. If not, your pardon and my return shall be the
   end of my business.

HAMLET Sir, I cannot.

ROSENCRANTZ What, my lord?

HAMLET Make you a wholesome answer. My wit's
330   diseased. But, sir, such answer as I can make, you shall
    command; or rather, as you say, my mother. Therefore
    no more, but to the matter. My mother, you say —

ROSENCRANTZ Then thus she says: your behaviour hath
    struck her into amazement and admiration.

HAMLET O wonderful son, that can so 'stonish a mother!
    But is there no sequel at the heels of this mother's ad-
    miration? Impart.

ROSENCRANTZ She desires to speak with you in her
    closet ere you go to bed.

340 HAMLET We shall obey, were she ten times our mother.
    Have you any further trade with us?

ROSENCRANTZ My lord, you once did love me.

HAMLET And do still, by these pickers and stealers.

ROSENCRANTZ Good my lord, what is your cause of dis-
    temper? You do surely bar the door upon your own
    liberty if you deny your griefs to your friend.

HAMLET Sir, I lack advancement.

ROSENCRANTZ How can that be, when you have the
    voice of the King himself for your succession in Den-
350   mark?

HAMLET Ay, sir, but 'while the grass grows' — the pro-
    verb is something musty.

      Enter a Player with recorders

    O, the recorders. Let me see one. — To withdraw with
    you — why do you go about to recover the wind of me, as
    if you would drive me into a toil?

GUILDENSTERN O my lord, if my duty be too bold, my
    love is too unmannerly.

HAMLET I do not well understand that. Will you play
    upon this pipe?

GUILDENSTERN My lord, I cannot.   360

HAMLET I pray you.

GUILDENSTERN Believe me, I cannot.

HAMLET I do beseech you.

GUILDENSTERN I know no touch of it, my lord.

HAMLET It is as easy as lying. Govern these ventages with
your fingers and thumb; give it breath with your mouth;
and it will discourse most eloquent music. Look you,
these are the stops.

GUILDENSTERN But these cannot I command to any
utterance of harmony. I have not the skill.   370

HAMLET Why, look you now, how unworthy a thing you
make of me! You would play upon me. You would seem
to know my stops. You would pluck out the heart of my
mystery. You would sound me from my lowest note to
the top of my compass. And there is much music, excellent voice, in this little organ. Yet cannot you make it
speak. 'Sblood, do you think I am easier to be played
on than a pipe? Call me what instrument you will,
though you can fret me, you cannot play upon me.

      Enter Polonius

God bless you, sir!   380

POLONIUS My lord, the Queen would speak with you,
and presently.

HAMLET Do you see yonder cloud that's almost in shape
of a camel?

POLONIUS By th'mass, and 'tis like a camel indeed.

HAMLET Methinks it is like a weasel.

POLONIUS It is backed like a weasel.

HAMLET Or like a whale.

POLONIUS Very like a whale.

HAMLET Then I will come to my mother by and by.   390
(*Aside*) They fool me to the top of my bent. – I will
come by and by.

POLONIUS I will say so.

HAMLET

    'By and by' is easily said.   *Exit Polonius*

        Leave me, friends.

                Exeunt all but Hamlet

    'Tis now the very witching time of night,

    When churchyards yawn, and hell itself breathes out

    Contagion to this world. Now could I drink hot blood

    And do such bitter business as the day

    Would quake to look on. Soft, now to my mother.

400   O heart, lose not thy nature. Let not ever

    The soul of Nero enter this firm bosom.

    Let me be cruel, not unnatural.

    I will speak daggers to her, but use none.

    My tongue and soul in this be hypocrites.

    How in my words somever she be shent,

    To give them seals never, my soul, consent!   *Exit*

III.3   *Enter the King, Rosencrantz, and Guildenstern*

KING

    I like him not; nor stands it safe with us

    To let his madness range. Therefore prepare you.

    I your commission will forthwith dispatch,

    And he to England shall along with you.

    The terms of our estate may not endure

    Hazard so near us as doth hourly grow

    Out of his brows.

GUILDENSTERN   We will ourselves provide.

    Most holy and religious fear it is

    To keep those many many bodies safe

10   That live and feed upon your majesty.

ROSENCRANTZ

    The single and peculiar life is bound

With all the strength and armour of the mind
To keep itself from noyance; but much more
That spirit upon whose weal depends and rests
The lives of many. The cess of majesty
Dies not alone, but like a gulf doth draw
What's near it with it; or 'tis a massy wheel
Fixed on the summit of the highest mount,
To whose huge spokes ten thousand lesser things
Are mortised and adjoined; which when it falls,   20
Each small annexment, petty consequence,
Attends the boisterous ruin. Never alone
Did the king sigh, but with a general groan.

KING

Arm you, I pray you, to this speedy voyage.
For we will fetters put about this fear,
Which now goes too free-footed.

ROSENCRANTZ   We will haste us.

Exeunt Rosencrantz and Guildenstern
    Enter Polonius

POLONIUS

My lord, he's going to his mother's closet.
Behind the arras I'll convey myself
To hear the process. I'll warrant she'll tax him home.
And, as you said, and wisely was it said,   30
'Tis meet that some more audience than a mother,
Since nature makes them partial, should o'erhear
The speech, of vantage. Fare you well, my liege.
I'll call upon you ere you go to bed
And tell you what I know.

KING   Thanks, dear my lord.
                                        Exit Polonius

O, my offence is rank. It smells to heaven.
It hath the primal eldest curse upon't,
A brother's murder. Pray can I not,

Though inclination be as sharp as will.
My stronger guilt defeats my strong intent,
And like a man to double business bound
I stand in pause where I shall first begin,
And both neglect. What if this cursèd hand
Were thicker than itself with brother's blood,
Is there not rain enough in the sweet heavens
To wash it white as snow? Whereto serves mercy
But to confront the visage of offence?
And what's in prayer but this twofold force,
To be forestallèd ere we come to fall
Or pardoned being down? Then I'll look up.
My fault is past. But, O, what form of prayer
Can serve my turn? 'Forgive me my foul murder'?
That cannot be, since I am still possessed
Of those effects for which I did the murder,
My crown, mine own ambition, and my Queen.
May one be pardoned and retain th'offence?
In the corrupted currents of this world
Offence's gilded hand may shove by justice;
And oft 'tis seen the wicked prize itself
Buys out the law. But 'tis not so above.
There is no shuffling. There the action lies
In his true nature, and we ourselves compelled,
Even to the teeth and forehead of our faults,
To give in evidence. What then? What rests?
Try what repentance can. What can it not?
Yet what can it when one cannot repent?
O, wretched state! O, bosom black as death!
O limèd soul, that struggling to be free
Art more engaged! Help, angels! Make assay.
Bow, stubborn knees, and, heart with strings of steel,
Be soft as sinews of the new-born babe.
All may be well.

The King kneels. Enter Hamlet

HAMLET

Now might I do it pat, now 'a is a-praying.
And now I'll do't. And so 'a goes to heaven.
And so am I revenged. That would be scanned.
A villain kills my father, and for that
I, his sole son, do this same villain send
To heaven.
Why, this is hire and salary, not revenge.
'A took my father grossly, full of bread,   80
With all his crimes broad blown, as flush as May;
And how his audit stands, who knows save heaven?
But in our circumstance and course of thought,
'Tis heavy with him. And am I then revenged,
To take him in the purging of his soul,
When he is fit and seasoned for his passage?
No.
Up, sword, and know thou a more horrid hent.
When he is drunk asleep, or in his rage,
Or in th'incestuous pleasure of his bed,   90
At game, a-swearing, or about some act
That has no relish of salvation in't –
Then trip him, that his heels may kick at heaven,
And that his soul may be as damned and black
As hell, whereto it goes. My mother stays.
This physic but prolongs thy sickly days.   *Exit*

KING (*rising*)

My words fly up, my thoughts remain below.
Words without thoughts never to heaven go.   *Exit*

Enter the Queen and Polonius   III.4

POLONIUS

'A will come straight. Look you lay home to him.

Tell him his pranks have been too broad to bear with,
And that your grace hath screened and stood between
Much heat and him. I'll silence me even here.
Pray you be round with him.

HAMLET (*within*) Mother, mother, mother!

QUEEN I'll warrant you. Fear me not. Withdraw. I hear
him coming.

    Polonius hides behind the arras
    Enter Hamlet

HAMLET
Now, mother, what's the matter?

QUEEN

10   Hamlet, thou hast thy father much offended.

HAMLET
Mother, you have my father much offended.

QUEEN
Come, come, you answer with an idle tongue.

HAMLET
Go, go, you question with a wicked tongue.

QUEEN
Why, how now, Hamlet?

HAMLET   What's the matter now?

QUEEN
Have you forgot me?

HAMLET   No, by the Rood, not so!
You are the Queen, your husband's brother's wife,
And, would it were not so, you are my mother.

QUEEN
Nay, then I'll set those to you that can speak.

HAMLET
Come, come, and sit you down. You shall not budge.

20   You go not till I set you up a glass
Where you may see the inmost part of you.

QUEEN

    What wilt thou do? Thou wilt not murder me?
    Help, ho!

POLONIUS (*behind*)

    What, ho! Help!

HAMLET (*drawing his sword*)

    How now? A rat? Dead for a ducat, dead!

    He makes a thrust through the arras and kills Polonius

POLONIUS

    O, I am slain!

QUEEN   O me, what hast thou done?

HAMLET

    Nay, I know not. Is it the King?

QUEEN

    O, what a rash and bloody deed is this!

HAMLET

    A bloody deed — almost as bad, good mother,
    As kill a king and marry with his brother.   30

QUEEN

    As kill a king!

HAMLET   Ay, lady, it was my word.

    He sees Polonius

    Thou wretched, rash, intruding fool, farewell!
    I took thee for thy better. Take thy fortune.
    Thou findest to be too busy is some danger. —
    Leave wringing of your hands. Peace, sit you down,
    And let me wring your heart. For so I shall,
    If it be made of penetrable stuff,
    If damnèd custom have not brassed it so
    That it be proof and bulwark against sense.

QUEEN

    What have I done that thou darest wag thy tongue   40
    In noise so rude against me?

HAMLET   Such an act

That blurs the grace and blush of modesty;
Calls virtue hypocrite; takes off the rose
From the fair forehead of an innocent love
And sets a blister there; makes marriage vows
As false as dicers' oaths; O, such a deed
As from the body of contraction plucks
The very soul, and sweet religion makes
A rhapsody of words! Heaven's face does glow,
Yea, this solidity and compound mass,
With heated visage, as against the Doom,
Is thought-sick at the act.

QUEEN   Ay me, what act,
That roars so loud and thunders in the index?

HAMLET
Look here upon this picture, and on this,
The counterfeit presentment of two brothers.
See what a grace was seated on this brow:
Hyperion's curls, the front of Jove himself,
An eye like Mars, to threaten and command,
A station like the herald Mercury
New lighted on a heaven-kissing hill –
A combination and a form indeed
Where every god did seem to set his seal
To give the world assurance of a man.
This was your husband. Look you now what follows.
Here is your husband; like a mildewed ear,
Blasting his wholesome brother. Have you eyes?
Could you on this fair mountain leave to feed,
And batten on this moor? Ha! Have you eyes?
You cannot call it love. For at your age
The heyday in the blood is tame; it's humble,
And waits upon the judgement; and what judgement
Would step from this to this? Sense sure you have,
Else could you not have motion. But sure that sense

Is apoplexed. For madness would not err,
Nor sense to ecstasy was ne'er so thralled
But it reserved some quantity of choice
To serve in such a difference. What devil was't
That thus hath cozened you at hoodman-blind?
Eyes without feeling, feeling without sight,
Ears without hands or eyes, smelling sans all,   80
Or but a sickly part of one true sense
Could not so mope.
O shame, where is thy blush? Rebellious hell,
If thou canst mutine in a matron's bones,
To flaming youth let virtue be as wax
And melt in her own fire. Proclaim no shame
When the compulsive ardour gives the charge,
Since frost itself as actively doth burn,
And reason panders will.
QUEEN   O Hamlet, speak no more.
Thou turnest mine eyes into my very soul,   90
And there I see such black and grainèd spots
As will not leave their tint.
HAMLET   Nay, but to live
In the rank sweat of an enseamèd bed,
Stewed in corruption, honeying and making love
Over the nasty sty —
QUEEN   O, speak to me no more.
These words like daggers enter in mine ears.
No more, sweet Hamlet.
HAMLET   A murderer and a villain,
A slave that is not twentieth part the tithe
Of your precedent lord, a vice of kings,
A cutpurse of the empire and the rule,   100
That from a shelf the precious diadem stole
And put it in his pocket —
QUEEN   No more.

HAMLET

A king of shreds and patches –
    (*Enter the Ghost*)
Save me and hover o'er me with your wings,
You heavenly guards! – What would your gracious
    figure?

QUEEN

Alas, he's mad.

HAMLET

Do you not come your tardy son to chide,
That, lapsed in time and passion, lets go by
Th'important acting of your dread command?
O, say!

GHOST

Do not forget. This visitation
Is but to whet thy almost blunted purpose.
But look, amazement on thy mother sits.
O, step between her and her fighting soul!
Conceit in weakest bodies strongest works.
Speak to her, Hamlet.

HAMLET   How is it with you, lady?

QUEEN

Alas, how is't with you,
That you do bend your eye on vacancy,
And with th'incorporal air do hold discourse?
Forth at your eyes your spirits wildly peep,
And, as the sleeping soldiers in th'alarm,
Your bedded hair like life in excrements
Start up and stand an end. O gentle son,
Upon the heat and flame of thy distemper
Sprinkle cool patience. Whereon do you look?

HAMLET

On him, on him! Look you, how pale he glares!
His form and cause conjoined, preaching to stones,

Would make them capable. – Do not look upon me,
Lest with this piteous action you convert
My stern effects. Then what I have to do   130
Will want true colour – tears perchance for blood.

QUEEN
To whom do you speak this?

HAMLET   Do you see nothing there?

QUEEN
Nothing at all. Yet all that is I see.

HAMLET
Nor did you nothing hear?

QUEEN   No, nothing but ourselves.

HAMLET
Why, look you there! Look how it steals away!
My father, in his habit as he lived!
Look where he goes, even now, out at the portal!

Exit the Ghost

QUEEN
This is the very coinage of your brain.
This bodiless creation ecstasy
Is very cunning in.

HAMLET   Ecstasy?   140
My pulse as yours doth temperately keep time
And makes as healthful music. It is not madness
That I have uttered. Bring me to the test,
And I the matter will re-word, which madness
Would gambol from. Mother, for love of grace,
Lay not that flattering unction to your soul,
That not your trespass but my madness speaks.
It will but skin and film the ulcerous place
Whiles rank corruption, mining all within,
Infects unseen. Confess yourself to heaven.   150
Repent what's past. Avoid what is to come;
And do not spread the compost on the weeds

To make them ranker. Forgive me this my virtue.
For in the fatness of these pursy times
Virtue itself of vice must pardon beg,
Yea, curb and woo for leave to do him good.

QUEEN

O Hamlet, thou hast cleft my heart in twain.

HAMLET

O, throw away the worser part of it,
And live the purer with the other half.
160   Good night. But go not to my uncle's bed.
Assume a virtue, if you have it not.
That monster custom, who all sense doth eat,
Of habits devil, is angel yet in this,
That to the use of actions fair and good
He likewise gives a frock or livery
That aptly is put on. Refrain tonight,
And that shall lend a kind of easiness
To the next abstinence; the next more easy;
For use almost can change the stamp of nature,
170   And either master the devil or throw him out
With wondrous potency. Once more, good night.
And when you are desirous to be blest,
I'll blessing beg of you. For this same lord,
I do repent. But heaven hath pleased it so,
To punish me with this, and this with me,
That I must be their scourge and minister.
I will bestow him and will answer well
The death I gave him. So again good night.
I must be cruel only to be kind.
180   This bad begins, and worse remains behind.
One word more, good lady.

QUEEN   What shall I do?

HAMLET

Not this, by no means, that I bid you do:

Let the bloat King tempt you again to bed,
Pinch wanton on your cheek, call you his mouse,
And let him, for a pair of reechy kisses,
Or paddling in your neck with his damned fingers,
Make you to ravel all this matter out,
That I essentially am not in madness,
But mad in craft. 'Twere good you let him know.
For who that's but a queen, fair, sober, wise,   190
Would from a paddock, from a bat, a gib,
Such dear concernings hide? Who would do so?
No, in despite of sense and secrecy,
Unpeg the basket on the house's top.
Let the birds fly, and like the famous ape,
To try conclusions, in the basket creep
And break your own neck down.

QUEEN
Be thou assured, if words be made of breath,
And breath of life, I have no life to breathe
What thou hast said to me.   200

HAMLET
I must to England. You know that?

QUEEN   Alack,
I had forgot. 'Tis so concluded on.

HAMLET
There's letters sealed, and my two schoolfellows,
Whom I will trust as I will adders fanged,
They bear the mandate. They must sweep my way
And marshal me to knavery. Let it work.
For 'tis the sport to have the enginer
Hoist with his own petar; and 't shall go hard
But I will delve one yard below their mines
And blow them at the moon. O, 'tis most sweet   210
When in one line two crafts directly meet.
This man shall set me packing.

I'll lug the guts into the neighbour room.
Mother, good night. Indeed, this counsellor
Is now most still, most secret, and most grave,
Who was in life a foolish prating knave.
Come, sir, to draw toward an end with you.
Good night, mother.

Exeunt Hamlet, tugging in Polonius, and the Queen

*

IV.I   *Enter the King and Queen, with Rosencrantz and
                Guildenstern*

KING

There's matter in these sighs. These profound heaves
You must translate. 'Tis fit we understand them.
Where is your son?

QUEEN

Bestow this place on us a little while.

Exeunt Rosencrantz and Guildenstern

Ah, mine own lord, what have I seen tonight!

KING

What, Gertrude? How does Hamlet?

QUEEN

Mad as the sea and wind when both contend
Which is the mightier. In his lawless fit,
Behind the arras hearing something stir,
Whips out his rapier, cries 'A rat, a rat!'
And in this brainish apprehension kills
The unseen good old man.

KING   O, heavy deed!

It had been so with us, had we been there.
His liberty is full of threats to all,
To you yourself, to us, to everyone.

Alas, how shall this bloody deed be answered?
It will be laid to us, whose providence
Should have kept short, restrained, and out of haunt
This mad young man. But so much was our love,
We would not understand what was most fit,   20
But, like the owner of a foul disease,
To keep it from divulging let it feed
Even on the pith of life. Where is he gone?

QUEEN

To draw apart the body he hath killed;
O'er whom his very madness, like some ore
Among a mineral of metals base,
Shows itself pure. 'A weeps for what is done.

KING

O Gertrude, come away!
The sun no sooner shall the mountains touch
But we will ship him hence; and this vile deed   30
We must with all our majesty and skill
Both countenance and excuse. Ho, Guildenstern!

     Enter Rosencrantz and Guildenstern

Friends both, go join you with some further aid.
Hamlet in madness hath Polonius slain,
And from his mother's closet hath he dragged him.
Go seek him out. Speak fair. And bring the body
Into the chapel. I pray you haste in this.

               Exeunt Rosencrantz and Guildenstern

Come, Gertrude, we'll call up our wisest friends
And let them know both what we mean to do
And what's untimely done. So haply slander,   40
Whose whisper o'er the world's diameter
As level as the cannon to his blank
Transports his poisoned shot, may miss our name
And hit the woundless air. O, come away!
My soul is full of discord and dismay.   *Exeunt*

IV.2   *Enter Hamlet*

HAMLET Safely stowed.

GENTLEMEN (*within*) Hamlet! Lord Hamlet!

HAMLET

But soft, what noise? Who calls on Hamlet?
O, here they come.

        Enter Rosencrantz, Guildenstern, and attendants

ROSENCRANTZ

What have you done, my lord, with the dead body?

HAMLET

Compounded it with dust, whereto 'tis kin.

ROSENCRANTZ

Tell us where 'tis, that we may take it thence
And bear it to the chapel.

HAMLET Do not believe it.

10   ROSENCRANTZ Believe what?

HAMLET That I can keep your counsel and not mine own.
Besides, to be demanded of a sponge, what replication
should be made by the son of a king?

ROSENCRANTZ Take you me for a sponge, my lord?

HAMLET Ay, sir, that soaks up the King's countenance,
his rewards, his authorities. But such officers do the
King best service in the end. He keeps them, like an ape
an apple, in the corner of his jaw, first mouthed, to be
last swallowed. When he needs what you have gleaned,
20   it is but squeezing you and, sponge, you shall be dry
again.

ROSENCRANTZ I understand you not, my lord.

HAMLET I am glad of it. A knavish speech sleeps in a
foolish ear.

ROSENCRANTZ My lord, you must tell us where the body
is, and go with us to the King.

HAMLET The body is with the King, but the King is not
with the body. The King is a thing –

GUILDENSTERN A thing, my lord?

HAMLET Of nothing. Bring me to him. Hide fox, and all   30
    after.   *Exeunt*

      Enter the King and two or three attendants   IV.3

KING

    I have sent to seek him and to find the body.
    How dangerous is it that this man goes loose!
    Yet must not we put the strong law on him.
    He's loved of the distracted multitude,
    Who like not in their judgement but their eyes;
    And where 'tis so, th'offender's scourge is weighed,
    But never the offence. To bear all smooth and even,
    This sudden sending him away must seem
    Deliberate pause. Diseases desperate grown
    By desperate appliance are relieved,   10
    Or not at all.

      Enter Rosencrantz, Guildenstern, and all the rest
             How now? What hath befallen?

ROSENCRANTZ

    Where the dead body is bestowed, my lord,
    We cannot get from him.

KING   But where is he?

ROSENCRANTZ

    Without, my lord; guarded, to know your pleasure.

KING

    Bring him before us.

ROSENCRANTZ   Ho! Bring in the lord.

      Enter attendants with Hamlet

KING Now, Hamlet, where's Polonius?

HAMLET At supper.

KING At supper? Where?

HAMLET Not where he eats, but where 'a is eaten. A cer-

20   tain convocation of politic worms are e'en at him. Your
worm is your only emperor for diet. We fat all creatures
else to fat us, and we fat ourselves for maggots. Your
fat king and your lean beggar is but variable service —
two dishes, but to one table. That's the end.

KING Alas, alas!

HAMLET A man may fish with the worm that hath eat of a
king, and eat of the fish that hath fed of that worm.

KING What dost thou mean by this?

HAMLET Nothing but to show you how a king may go a
30   progress through the guts of a beggar.

KING Where is Polonius?

HAMLET In heaven. Send thither to see. If your messenger find him not there, seek him i'th'other place
yourself. But if indeed you find him not within this
month, you shall nose him as you go up the stairs into
the lobby.

KING (*to attendants*) Go seek him there.

HAMLET 'A will stay till you come.   *Exeunt attendants*

KING

    Hamlet, this deed, for thine especial safety,
40   Which we do tender as we dearly grieve
    For that which thou hast done, must send thee hence
    With fiery quickness. Therefore prepare thyself.
    The bark is ready and the wind at help,
    Th'associates tend, and everything is bent
    For England.

HAMLET For England?

KING Ay, Hamlet.

HAMLET Good.

KING

    So is it, if thou knewest our purposes.

50 HAMLET I see a cherub that sees them. But come, for
England! Farewell, dear mother.

KING Thy loving father, Hamlet.

HAMLET My mother. Father and mother is man and wife;
man and wife is one flesh; and so, my mother. Come,
for England!   *Exit*

KING
Follow him at foot. Tempt him with speed aboard.
Delay it not. I'll have him hence tonight.
Away! For everything is sealed and done
That else leans on the affair. Pray you make haste.
                              Exeunt all but the King

And, England, if my love thou holdest at aught —   60
As my great power thereof may give thee sense,
Since yet thy cicatrice looks raw and red
After the Danish sword, and thy free awe
Pays homage to us — thou mayst not coldly set
Our sovereign process, which imports at full,
By letters congruing to that effect,
The present death of Hamlet. Do it, England.
For like the hectic in my blood he rages,
And thou must cure me. Till I know 'tis done,
Howe'er my haps, my joys were ne'er begun.   *Exit*   70

Enter Fortinbras with his army over the stage   IV.4
FORTINBRAS
Go, captain, from me greet the Danish King.
Tell him that by his licence Fortinbras
Craves the conveyance of a promised march
Over his kingdom. You know the rendezvous.
If that his majesty would aught with us,
We shall express our duty in his eye.
And let him know so.

CAPTAIN   I will do't, my lord.

FORTINBRAS Go softly on.   *Exeunt all but the Captain*

Enter Hamlet, Rosencrantz, Guildenstern, and
attendants

HAMLET Good sir, whose powers are these?

10 CAPTAIN They are of Norway, sir.

HAMLET How purposed, sir, I pray you?

CAPTAIN Against some part of Poland.

HAMLET Who commands them, sir?

CAPTAIN
The nephew to old Norway, Fortinbras.

HAMLET
Goes it against the main of Poland, sir,
Or for some frontier?

CAPTAIN
Truly to speak, and with no addition,
We go to gain a little patch of ground
That hath in it no profit but the name.

20 To pay five ducats, five, I would not farm it;
Nor will it yield to Norway or the Pole
A ranker rate, should it be sold in fee.

HAMLET
Why, then the Polack never will defend it.

CAPTAIN
Yes, it is already garrisoned.

HAMLET
Two thousand souls and twenty thousand ducats
Will not debate the question of this straw.
This is th'imposthume of much wealth and peace,
That inward breaks, and shows no cause without
Why the man dies. I humbly thank you, sir.

CAPTAIN
30 God bye you, sir.   *Exit*

ROSENCRANTZ   Will't please you go, my lord?

HAMLET
I'll be with you straight. Go a little before.

Exeunt all but Hamlet

How all occasions do inform against me
And spur my dull revenge! What is a man,
If his chief good and market of his time
Be but to sleep and feed? A beast, no more.
Sure He that made us with such large discourse,
Looking before and after, gave us not
That capability and godlike reason
To fust in us unused. Now, whether it be
Bestial oblivion, or some craven scruple   40
Of thinking too precisely on th'event –
A thought which, quartered, hath but one part wisdom
And ever three parts coward – I do not know
Why yet I live to say 'This thing's to do',
Sith I have cause, and will, and strength, and means
To do't. Examples gross as earth exhort me.
Witness this army of such mass and charge,
Led by a delicate and tender prince,
Whose spirit, with divine ambition puffed,
Makes mouths at the invisible event,   50
Exposing what is mortal and unsure
To all that fortune, death, and danger dare,
Even for an eggshell. Rightly to be great
Is not to stir without great argument,
But greatly to find quarrel in a straw
When honour's at the stake. How stand I then,
That have a father killed, a mother stained,
Excitements of my reason and my blood,
And let all sleep, while to my shame I see
The imminent death of twenty thousand men   60
That for a fantasy and trick of fame
Go to their graves like beds, fight for a plot
Whereon the numbers cannot try the cause,
Which is not tomb enough and continent

To hide the slain? O, from this time forth,
My thoughts be bloody, or be nothing worth!   *Exit*

IV.5   *Enter the Queen, Horatio, and a Gentleman*

QUEEN
I will not speak with her.

GENTLEMAN
She is importunate, indeed distract.
Her mood will needs be pitied.   What would she have?

QUEEN

GENTLEMAN
She speaks much of her father; says she hears
There's tricks i'th'world, and hems, and beats her heart,
Spurns enviously at straws, speaks things in doubt
That carry but half sense. Her speech is nothing.
Yet the unshapèd use of it doth move
The hearers to collection. They aim at it,
And botch the words up fit to their own thoughts,
Which, as her winks and nods and gestures yield them,
Indeed would make one think there might be thought,
Though nothing sure, yet much unhappily.

HORATIO
'Twere good she were spoken with, for she may strew
Dangerous conjectures in ill-breeding minds.

QUEEN
Let her come in.   *Exit the Gentleman*
(*Aside*) To my sick soul, as sin's true nature is,
Each toy seems prologue to some great amiss.
So full of artless jealousy is guilt
It spills itself in fearing to be spilt.
          Enter Ophelia

OPHELIA
Where is the beauteous majesty of Denmark?

QUEEN How now, Ophelia?

OPHELIA (*sings*)

> How should I your true-love know
>> From another one?
> By his cockle hat and staff
>> And his sandal shoon.

QUEEN
  Alas, sweet lady, what imports this song?

OPHELIA Say you? Nay, pray you, mark.
  (*Sings*) He is dead and gone, lady.
>> He is dead and gone.   30
>>> At his head a grass-green turf,
>>> At his heels a stone.
  O, ho!

QUEEN Nay, but, Ophelia –

OPHELIA Pray you, mark.
  (*Sings*)   White his shroud as the mountain snow –
    Enter the King

QUEEN Alas, look here, my lord.

OPHELIA (*sings*)

> Larded all with sweet flowers,
>> Which bewept to the ground did not go
>> With true-love showers.   40

KING How do you, pretty lady?

OPHELIA Well, God dild you! They say the owl was a
  baker's daughter. Lord, we know what we are, but know
  not what we may be. God be at your table!

KING Conceit upon her father –

OPHELIA Pray let's have no words of this, but when they
  ask you what it means, say you this:
  (*sings*) Tomorrow is Saint Valentine's day,
>> All in the morning betime,
>> And I a maid at your window   50
>>> To be your Valentine.

> Then up he rose and donned his clothes,
>> And dupped the chamber door;
> Let in the maid, that out a maid
>> Never departed more.

KING Pretty Ophelia!

OPHELIA Indeed, la, without an oath, I'll make an end on't.

> (*Sings*) By Gis and by Saint Charity,
>> Alack, and fie for shame!
> Young men will do't if they come to't.
>> By Cock, they are to blame.

> Quoth she, 'Before you tumbled me,
>> You promised me to wed.'

He answers:

> 'So would I ha' done, by yonder sun,
>> An thou hadst not come to my bed.'

KING How long hath she been thus?

OPHELIA I hope all will be well. We must be patient. But I cannot choose but weep to think they would lay him i'th'cold ground. My brother shall know of it. And so I thank you for your good counsel. Come, my coach! Good night, ladies, good night. Sweet ladies, good night, good night.   *Exit*

KING

Follow her close. Give her good watch, I pray you.
                                                        Exit Horatio

O, this is the poison of deep grief. It springs
All from her father's death – and now behold!
O Gertrude, Gertrude,
When sorrows come, they come not single spies,
But in battalions: first, her father slain;
Next, your son gone, and he most violent author
Of his own just remove; the people muddied,

Thick and unwholesome in their thoughts and whispers
For good Polonius' death, and we have done but greenly
In hugger-mugger to inter him; poor Ophelia
Divided from herself and her fair judgement,
Without the which we are pictures or mere beasts;
Last, and as much containing as all these,
Her brother is in secret come from France,
Feeds on his wonder, keeps himself in clouds,   90
And wants not buzzers to infect his ear
With pestilent speeches of his father's death,
Wherein necessity, of matter beggared,
Will nothing stick our person to arraign
In ear and ear. O my dear Gertrude, this,
Like to a murdering-piece, in many places
Gives me superfluous death.
        A noise within
QUEEN
Alack, what noise is this?
KING
Attend. Where is my Switzers? Let them guard the
        door.
        Enter a Messenger
What is the matter?
MESSENGER   Save yourself, my lord.   100
The ocean, overpeering of his list,
Eats not the flats with more impiteous haste
Than your Laertes, in a riotous head,
O'erbears your officers. The rabble call him lord,
And, as the world were now but to begin,
Antiquity forgot, custom not known,
The ratifiers and props of every word,
They cry 'Choose we! Laertes shall be king!'
Caps, hands, and tongues applaud it to the clouds:
'Laertes shall be king! Laertes king!'   110

A noise within

QUEEN
How cheerfully on the false trail they cry!
O, this is counter, you false Danish dogs!

KING
The doors are broke.
     Enter Laertes with his followers

LAERTES
Where is this King? — Sirs, stand you all without.

HIS FOLLOWERS
No, let's come in.

LAERTES   I pray you give me leave.

HIS FOLLOWERS
We will, we will.

LAERTES
I thank you. Keep the door.   *Exeunt his followers*
                                        O thou vile King,
Give me my father.

QUEEN   Calmly, good Laertes.

LAERTES
That drop of blood that's calm proclaims me bastard,
Cries cuckold to my father, brands the harlot
Even here between the chaste unsmirchèd brows
Of my true mother.

KING   What is the cause, Laertes,
That thy rebellion looks so giant-like?
Let him go, Gertrude. Do not fear our person.
There's such divinity doth hedge a king
That treason can but peep to what it would,
Acts little of his will. Tell me, Laertes,
Why thou art thus incensed. Let him go, Gertrude.
Speak, man.

LAERTES
Where is my father?

KING   Dead.
QUEEN   But not by him.
KING
  Let him demand his fill.
LAERTES
  How came he dead? I'll not be juggled with.
  To hell allegiance! Vows to the blackest devil!
  Conscience and grace to the profoundest pit!
  I dare damnation. To this point I stand,
  That both the worlds I give to negligence,
  Let come what comes, only I'll be revenged
  Most throughly for my father.
KING   Who shall stay you?
LAERTES
  My will, not all the world's.
  And for my means, I'll husband them so well   140
  They shall go far with little.
KING   Good Laertes,
  If you desire to know the certainty
  Of your dear father, is't writ in your revenge
  That, swoopstake, you will draw both friend and foe,
  Winner and loser?
LAERTES
  None but his enemies.
KING   Will you know them then?
LAERTES
  To his good friends thus wide I'll ope my arms
  And like the kind life-rendering pelican
  Repast them with my blood.
KING   Why, now you speak
  Like a good child and a true gentleman.   150
  That I am guiltless of your father's death,
  And am most sensibly in grief for it,
  It shall as level to your judgement 'pear

As day does to your eye.
    A noise within
VOICES (*within*)   Let her come in.
LAERTES
How now? What noise is that?
    Enter Ophelia
O heat, dry up my brains! Tears seven times salt
Burn out the sense and virtue of mine eye!
By heaven, thy madness shall be paid with weight
Till our scale turn the beam. O rose of May,
Dear maid, kind sister, sweet Ophelia!
O heavens, is't possible a young maid's wits
Should be as mortal as an old man's life?
Nature is fine in love, and where 'tis fine,
It sends some precious instance of itself
After the thing it loves.
OPHELIA (*sings*)
        They bore him barefaced on the bier,
          Hey non nony, nony, hey nony,
          And in his grave rained many a tear –
Fare you well, my dove!
LAERTES
Hadst thou thy wits, and didst persuade revenge,
It could not move thus.
OPHELIA You must sing 'A-down a-down, and you call
him a-down-a.' O, how the wheel becomes it! It is the
false steward, that stole his master's daughter.
LAERTES This nothing's more than matter.
OPHELIA There's rosemary, that's for remembrance.
Pray you, love, remember. And there is pansies, that's
for thoughts.
LAERTES A document in madness: thoughts and re-
membrance fitted.
OPHELIA There's fennel for you, and columbines. There's

rue for you, and here's some for me. We may call it
herb of grace o'Sundays. O, you must wear your rue
with a difference. There's a daisy. I would give you some
violets, but they withered all when my father died. They
say 'a made a good end.

(*Sings*)   For bonny sweet Robin is all my joy.

LAERTES

Thought and afflictions, passion, hell itself,
She turns to favour and to prettiness.

OPHELIA (*sings*)

           And will 'a not come again?   190
           And will 'a not come again?
              No, no, he is dead.
              Go to thy deathbed.
           He never will come again.

           His beard was as white as snow,
           All flaxen was his poll.
              He is gone, he is gone,
              And we cast away moan.
           God 'a' mercy on his soul!
And of all Christian souls, I pray God. God bye you.   200

                                                      Exit

LAERTES

Do you see this? O God!

KING

Laertes, I must commune with your grief,
Or you deny me right. Go but apart,
Make choice of whom your wisest friends you will,
And they shall hear and judge 'twixt you and me.
If by direct or by collateral hand
They find us touched, we will our kingdom give,
Our crown, our life, and all that we call ours,
To you in satisfaction. But if not,

210   Be you content to lend your patience to us,
And we shall jointly labour with your soul
To give it due content.

LAERTES   Let this be so.
His means of death, his obscure funeral –
No trophy, sword, nor hatchment o'er his bones,
No noble rite nor formal ostentation –
Cry to be heard, as 'twere from heaven to earth,
That I must call't in question.

KING   So you shall.
And where th'offence is, let the great axe fall.
I pray you go with me.   *Exeunt*

IV.6   *Enter Horatio and a Gentleman*

HORATIO
What are they that would speak with me?

GENTLEMAN Seafaring men, sir. They say they have
letters for you.

HORATIO
Let them come in.   *Exit the Gentleman*
I do not know from what part of the world
I should be greeted if not from Lord Hamlet.
   Enter Sailors

SAILOR God bless you, sir.

HORATIO Let him bless thee, too.

SAILOR 'A shall, sir, an't please him. There's a letter for
10   you, sir – it came from th'ambassador that was bound
for England – if your name be Horatio, as I am let to
know it is.

HORATIO (*reads the letter*) *Horatio, when thou shalt have*
overlooked this, give these fellows some means to the King.
They have letters for him. Ere we were two days old at sea,
a pirate of very warlike appointment gave us chase. Find-

ing ourselves too slow of sail, we put on a compelled valour,
and in the grapple I boarded them. On the instant they got
clear of our ship. So I alone became their prisoner. They
have dealt with me like thieves of mercy. But they knew   20
what they did. I am to do a good turn for them. Let the
King have the letters I have sent, and repair thou to me
with as much speed as thou wouldst fly death. I have words
to speak in thine ear will make thee dumb. Yet are they
much too light for the bore of the matter. These good fel-
lows will bring thee where I am. Rosencrantz and Guilden-
stern hold their course for England. Of them I have much
to tell thee. Farewell.

> *He that thou knowest thine,*

> > > *Hamlet*   30

Come, I will give you way for these your letters,
And do't the speedier that you may direct me
To him from whom you brought them.   *Exeunt*

Enter the King and Laertes   IV.7

KING

Now must your conscience my acquittance seal,
And you must put me in your heart for friend,
Sith you have heard, and with a knowing ear,
That he which hath your noble father slain
Pursued my life.

LAERTES   It well appears. But tell me
Why you proceeded not against these feats
So criminal and so capital in nature,
As by your safety, greatness, wisdom, all things else,
You mainly were stirred up.

KING   O, for two special reasons,
Which may to you perhaps seem much unsinewed,   10
But yet to me they're strong. The Queen his mother

Lives almost by his looks, and for myself —
My virtue or my plague, be it either which —
She is so conjunctive to my life and soul
That, as the star moves not but in his sphere,
I could not but by her. The other motive
Why to a public count I might not go
Is the great love the general gender bear him,
Who, dipping all his faults in their affection,
Work like the spring that turneth wood to stone,
Convert his gyves to graces; so that my arrows,
Too slightly timbered for so loud a wind,
Would have reverted to my bow again,
And not where I had aimed them.

LAERTES

And so have I a noble father lost,
A sister driven into desperate terms,
Whose worth, if praises may go back again,
Stood challenger, on mount, of all the age
For her perfections. But my revenge will come.

KING

Break not your sleeps for that. You must not think
That we are made of stuff so flat and dull
That we can let our beard be shook with danger,
And think it pastime. You shortly shall hear more.
I loved your father, and we love ourself,
And that, I hope, will teach you to imagine —
      Enter a Messenger with letters
How now? What news?

MESSENGER   Letters, my lord, from Hamlet.
These to your majesty. This to the Queen.

KING

From Hamlet? Who brought them?

MESSENGER

Sailors, my lord, they say. I saw them not.

They were given me by Claudio. He received them   40
Of him that brought them.

KING   Laertes, you shall hear them. —
Leave us.   *Exit the Messenger*
    (*He reads*)
High and mighty, you shall know I am set naked on your
kingdom. Tomorrow shall I beg leave to see your kingly
eyes; when I shall, first asking your pardon thereunto,
recount the occasion of my sudden and more strange return.
                                                        Hamlet
What should this mean? Are all the rest come back?
Or is it some abuse, and no such thing?

LAERTES
Know you the hand?

KING   'Tis Hamlet's character. 'Naked'!   50
And in a postscript here, he says 'alone'.
Can you devise me?

LAERTES
I am lost in it, my lord. But let him come.
It warms the very sickness in my heart
That I shall live and tell him to his teeth
'Thus didest thou.'

KING   If it be so, Laertes —
As how should it be so? How otherwise? —
Will you be ruled by me?

LAERTES   Ay, my lord,
So you will not o'errule me to a peace.

KING
To thine own peace. If he be now returned,   60
As checking at his voyage, and that he means
No more to undertake it, I will work him
To an exploit now ripe in my device,
Under the which he shall not choose but fall;
And for his death no wind of blame shall breathe,

But even his mother shall uncharge the practice
And call it accident.

LAERTES   My lord, I will be ruled;
    The rather if you could devise it so
    That I might be the organ.

KING   It falls right.
70 You have been talked of since your travel much,
    And that in Hamlet's hearing, for a quality
    Wherein they say you shine. Your sum of parts
    Did not together pluck such envy from him
    As did that one, and that, in my regard,
    Of the unworthiest siege.

LAERTES   What part is that, my lord?

KING
    A very riband in the cap of youth,
    Yet needful too, for youth no less becomes
    The light and careless livery that it wears
    Than settled age his sables and his weeds,
80 Importing health and graveness. Two months since,
    Here was a gentleman of Normandy.
    I have seen myself, and served against, the French,
    And they can well on horseback. But this gallant
    Had witchcraft in't. He grew unto his seat,
    And to such wondrous doing brought his horse
    As had he been incorpsed and demi-natured
    With the brave beast. So far he topped my thought
    That I, in forgery of shapes and tricks,
    Come short of what he did.

LAERTES   A Norman was't?

KING
90 A Norman.

LAERTES
    Upon my life, Lamord.

KING   The very same.

LAERTES
    I know him well. He is the brooch indeed
    And gem of all the nation.
KING
    He made confession of you,
    And gave you such a masterly report
    For art and exercise in your defence,
    And for your rapier most especial,
    That he cried out 'twould be a sight indeed
    If one could match you; the scrimers of their nation
    He swore had neither motion, guard, nor eye,   100
    If you opposed them. Sir, this report of his
    Did Hamlet so envenom with his envy
    That he could nothing do but wish and beg
    Your sudden coming o'er to play with you.
    Now, out of this –
LAERTES   What out of this, my lord?
KING
    Laertes, was your father dear to you?
    Or are you like the painting of a sorrow,
    A face without a heart?
LAERTES   Why ask you this?
KING
    Not that I think you did not love your father,
    But that I know love is begun by time,   110
    And that I see, in passages of proof,
    Time qualifies the spark and fire of it.
    There lives within the very flame of love
    A kind of wick or snuff that will abate it,
    And nothing is at a like goodness still;
    For goodness, growing to a pleurisy,
    Dies in his own too-much. That we would do
    We should do when we would. For this 'would' changes,
    And hath abatements and delays as many

120   As there are tongues, are hands, are accidents.
       And then this 'should' is like a spendthrift sigh,
       That hurts by easing. But to the quick o'th'ulcer –
       Hamlet comes back. What would you undertake
       To show yourself in deed your father's son
       More than in words?

LAERTES   To cut his throat i'th'church!

KING
       No place, indeed, should murder sanctuarize.
       Revenge should have no bounds. But, good Laertes,
       Will you do this: keep close within your chamber?
       Hamlet returned shall know you are come home.
130   We'll put on those shall praise your excellence
       And set a double varnish on the fame
       The Frenchman gave you; bring you in fine together,
       And wager on your heads. He, being remiss,
       Most generous, and free from all contriving,
       Will not peruse the foils, so that with ease,
       Or with a little shuffling, you may choose
       A sword unbated, and, in a pass of practice,
       Requite him for your father.

LAERTES   I will do't,
       And for that purpose I'll anoint my sword.
140   I bought an unction of a mountebank,
       So mortal that, but dip a knife in it,
       Where it draws blood no cataplasm so rare,
       Collected from all simples that have virtue
       Under the moon, can save the thing from death
       That is but scratched withal. I'll touch my point
       With this contagion, that, if I gall him slightly,
       It may be death.

KING   Let's further think of this,
       Weigh what convenience both of time and means
       May fit us to our shape. If this should fail,

And that our drift look through our bad performance,   150
'Twere better not assayed. Therefore this project
Should have a back or second, that might hold
If this did blast in proof. Soft, let me see.
We'll make a solemn wager on your cunnings –
I ha't!
When in your motion you are hot and dry –
As make your bouts more violent to that end –
And that he calls for drink, I'll have preferred him
A chalice for the nonce, whereon but sipping,
If he by chance escape your venomed stuck,   160
Our purpose may hold there. – But stay, what noise?
    Enter the Queen
How, sweet Queen!

QUEEN

One woe doth tread upon another's heel,
So fast they follow. Your sister's drowned, Laertes.

LAERTES

Drowned! O, where?

QUEEN

There is a willow grows askant the brook,
That shows his hoar leaves in the glassy stream.
Therewith fantastic garlands did she make
Of crowflowers, nettles, daisies, and long purples,
That liberal shepherds give a grosser name,   170
But our cold maids do dead-men's-fingers call them.
There on the pendent boughs her crownet weeds
Clambering to hang, an envious sliver broke,
When down her weedy trophies and herself
Fell in the weeping brook. Her clothes spread wide,
And mermaid-like awhile they bore her up;
Which time she chanted snatches of old tunes,
As one incapable of her own distress,
Or like a creature native and indued

180 Unto that element. But long it could not be
Till that her garments, heavy with their drink,
Pulled the poor wretch from her melodious lay
To muddy death.

LAERTES   Alas, then she is drowned?

QUEEN
Drowned, drowned.

LAERTES
Too much of water hast thou, poor Ophelia,
And therefore I forbid my tears. But yet
It is our trick. Nature her custom holds,
Let shame say what it will. When these are gone,
The woman will be out. Adieu, my lord.
190 I have a speech o'fire that fain would blaze,
But that this folly drowns it.   *Exit*

KING   Let's follow, Gertrude.
How much I had to do to calm his rage!
Now fear I this will give it start again.
Therefore let's follow.   *Exeunt*

*

V. I   *Enter two Clowns*

FIRST CLOWN Is she to be buried in Christian burial
when she wilfully seeks her own salvation?

SECOND CLOWN I tell thee she is. Therefore make her
grave straight. The crowner hath sat on her, and finds
it Christian burial.

FIRST CLOWN How can that be, unless she drowned
herself in her own defence?

SECOND CLOWN Why, 'tis found so.

FIRST CLOWN It must be *se offendendo*. It cannot be else.
10   For here lies the point: if I drown myself wittingly, it

argues an act, and an act hath three branches – it is to
act, to do, and to perform. Argal, she drowned herself
wittingly.

SECOND CLOWN Nay, but hear you, Goodman Delver.

FIRST CLOWN Give me leave. Here lies the water – good.
Here stands the man – good. If the man go to this water
and drown himself, it is, will he nill he, he goes, mark
you that. But if the water come to him and drown him,
he drowns not himself. Argal, he that is not guilty of
his own death shortens not his own life.   20

SECOND CLOWN But is this law?

FIRST CLOWN Ay, marry, is't – crowner's quest law.

SECOND CLOWN Will you ha' the truth on't? If this had
not been a gentlewoman, she should have been buried
out o' Christian burial.

FIRST CLOWN Why, there thou sayst. And the more pity
that great folk should have countenance in this world to
drown or hang themselves more than their even-
Christian. Come, my spade. There is no ancient gentlemen but gardeners, ditchers, and grave-makers. They   30
hold up Adam's profession.

SECOND CLOWN Was he a gentleman?

FIRST CLOWN 'A was the first that ever bore arms.

SECOND CLOWN Why, he had none.

FIRST CLOWN What, art a heathen? How dost thou
understand the Scripture? The Scripture says Adam
digged. Could he dig without arms? I'll put another
question to thee. If thou answerest me not to the purpose, confess thyself –

SECOND CLOWN Go to!   40

FIRST CLOWN What is he that builds stronger than
either the mason, the shipwright, or the carpenter?

SECOND CLOWN The gallows-maker, for that frame
outlives a thousand tenants.

FIRST CLOWN I like thy wit well, in good faith. The gallows does well. But how does it well? It does well to those that do ill. Now thou dost ill to say the gallows is built stronger than the church. Argal, the gallows may do well to thee. To't again, come.

50 SECOND CLOWN Who builds stronger than a mason, a shipwright, or a carpenter?

FIRST CLOWN Ay, tell me that, and unyoke.

SECOND CLOWN Marry, now I can tell.

FIRST CLOWN To't.

SECOND CLOWN Mass, I cannot tell.

FIRST CLOWN Cudgel thy brains no more about it, for your dull ass will not mend his pace with beating. And when you are asked this question next, say 'a grave-maker'. The houses he makes lasts till Doomsday. Go,
60 get thee in, and fetch me a stoup of liquor.

Exit Second Clown

(*Sings*) In youth when I did love, did love,
   Methought it was very sweet
  To contract – O – the time for – a – my behove,
   O, methought there – a – was nothing – a – meet.

Enter Hamlet and Horatio

HAMLET Has this fellow no feeling of his business? 'A sings in grave-making.

HORATIO Custom hath made it in him a property of easiness.

HAMLET 'Tis e'en so. The hand of little employment
70 hath the daintier sense.

FIRST CLOWN (*sings*)
   But age with his stealing steps
    Hath clawed me in his clutch,
   And hath shipped me into the land,
    As if I had never been such.

He throws up a skull

HAMLET That skull had a tongue in it, and could sing
  once. How the knave jowls it to the ground, as if 'twere
  Cain's jawbone, that did the first murder! This might be
  the pate of a politician, which this ass now o'erreaches;
  one that would circumvent God, might it not?

HORATIO It might, my lord.   80

HAMLET Or of a courtier, which could say 'Good morrow, sweet lord! How dost thou, sweet lord?' This
  might be my Lord Such-a-one; that praised my Lord
  Such-a-one's horse when 'a meant to beg it, might it
  not?

HORATIO Ay, my lord.

HAMLET Why, e'en so, and now my Lady Worm's, chopless, and knocked about the mazzard with a sexton's
  spade. Here's fine revolution, an we had the trick to
  see't. Did these bones cost no more the breeding but   90
  to play at loggats with them? Mine ache to think on't.

FIRST CLOWN (*sings*)
         A pickaxe and a spade, a spade,
           For and a shrouding sheet.
         O, a pit of clay for to be made
           For such a guest is meet.

  He throws up another skull

HAMLET There's another. Why may not that be the skull
  of a lawyer? Where be his quiddities now, his quillets,
  his cases, his tenures, and his tricks? Why does he
  suffer this mad knave now to knock him about the
  sconce with a dirty shovel, and will not tell him of his   100
  action of battery? Hum! This fellow might be in's
  time a great buyer of land, with his statutes, his recognizances, his fines, his double vouchers, his recoveries.
  Is this the fine of his fines, and the recovery of his
  recoveries, to have his fine pate full of fine dirt? Will
  his vouchers vouch him no more of his purchases, and

double ones too, than the length and breadth of a pair
of indentures? The very conveyances of his lands will
scarcely lie in this box, and must th'inheritor himself
110   have no more, ha?

HORATIO Not a jot more, my lord.

HAMLET Is not parchment made of sheep-skins?

HORATIO Ay, my lord, and of calves' skins too.

HAMLET They are sheep and calves which seek out assurance in that. I will speak to this fellow. — Whose
grave's this, sirrah?

FIRST CLOWN Mine, sir.

   (*Sings*)   O, a pit of clay for to be made
                For such a guest is meet.

120   HAMLET I think it be thine indeed, for thou liest in't.

FIRST CLOWN You lie out on't, sir, and therefore 'tis
not yours. For my part, I do not lie in't, yet it is mine.

HAMLET Thou dost lie in't, to be in't and say it is thine.
'Tis for the dead, not for the quick. Therefore thou
liest.

FIRST CLOWN 'Tis a quick lie, sir. 'Twill away again
from me to you.

HAMLET What man dost thou dig it for?

FIRST CLOWN For no man, sir.

130   HAMLET What woman then?

FIRST CLOWN For none neither.

HAMLET Who is to be buried in't?

FIRST CLOWN One that was a woman, sir. But, rest her
soul, she's dead.

HAMLET How absolute the knave is! We must speak by
the card, or equivocation will undo us. By the Lord,
Horatio, this three years I have took note of it, the age
is grown so picked that the toe of the peasant comes so
near the heel of the courtier he galls his kibe. — How
140   long hast thou been grave-maker?

FIRST CLOWN Of all the days i'th'year, I came to't that
     day that our last King Hamlet overcame Fortinbras.

HAMLET How long is that since?

FIRST CLOWN Cannot you tell that? Every fool can tell
     that. It was that very day that young Hamlet was born —
     he that is mad, and sent into England.

HAMLET Ay, marry, why was he sent into England?

FIRST CLOWN Why, because 'a was mad. 'A shall re-
     cover his wits there. Or, if 'a do not, 'tis no great matter
     there.   150

HAMLET Why?

FIRST CLOWN 'Twill not be seen in him there. There
     the men are as mad as he.

HAMLET How came he mad?

FIRST CLOWN Very strangely, they say.

HAMLET How strangely?

FIRST CLOWN Faith, e'en with losing his wits.

HAMLET Upon what ground?

FIRST CLOWN Why, here in Denmark. I have been
     sexton here, man and boy, thirty years.   160

HAMLET How long will a man lie i'th'earth ere he rot?

FIRST CLOWN Faith, if 'a be not rotten before 'a die, as
     we have many pocky corses nowadays that will scarce
     hold the laying in, 'a will last you some eight year or
     nine year. A tanner will last you nine year.

HAMLET Why he more than another?

FIRST CLOWN Why, sir, his hide is so tanned with his
     trade that 'a will keep out water a great while, and your
     water is a sore decayer of your whoreson dead body.
     Here's a skull now hath lien you i'th'earth three-and-   170
     twenty years.

HAMLET Whose was it?

FIRST CLOWN A whoreson mad fellow's it was. Whose
     do you think it was?

HAMLET Nay, I know not.

FIRST CLOWN A pestilence on him for a mad rogue! 'A
poured a flagon of Rhenish on my head once. This same
skull, sir, was, sir, Yorick's skull, the King's jester.

HAMLET This?

180 FIRST CLOWN E'en that.

HAMLET Let me see. Alas, poor Yorick! I knew him,
Horatio. A fellow of infinite jest, of most excellent fancy.
He hath bore me on his back a thousand times. And
now how abhorred in my imagination it is! My gorge
rises at it. Here hung those lips that I have kissed I
know not how oft. Where be your gibes now? Your
gambols, your songs, your flashes of merriment that
were wont to set the table on a roar? Not one now to
mock your own grinning? Quite chop-fallen? Now get
190 you to my lady's table and tell her, let her paint an inch
thick, to this favour she must come. Make her laugh at
that. Prithee, Horatio, tell me one thing.

HORATIO What's that, my lord?

HAMLET Dost thou think Alexander looked o'this fashion
i'th'earth?

HORATIO E'en so.

HAMLET And smelt so? Pah!

HORATIO E'en so, my lord.

HAMLET To what base uses we may return, Horatio! Why
200 may not imagination trace the noble dust of Alexander
till 'a find it stopping a bunghole?

HORATIO 'Twere to consider too curiously to consider so.

HAMLET No, faith, not a jot. But to follow him thither
with modesty enough, and likelihood to lead it; as thus:
Alexander died, Alexander was buried, Alexander
returneth to dust; the dust is earth; of earth we make
loam; and why of that loam whereto he was converted
might they not stop a beer barrel?

Imperious Caesar, dead and turned to clay,
Might stop a hole to keep the wind away.   210
O, that that earth which kept the world in awe
Should patch a wall t'expel the winter's flaw!
But soft, but soft awhile!
Enter the King and Queen, Laertes, and the corpse of
Ophelia, with Lords attendant and a Priest
                                    Here comes the King,
The Queen, the courtiers. Who is this they follow?
And with such maimèd rites? This doth betoken
The corse they follow did with desperate hand
Fordo it own life. 'Twas of some estate.
Couch we awhile, and mark.
    He withdraws with Horatio

LAERTES

What ceremony else?

HAMLET

That is Laertes, a very noble youth. Mark.   220

LAERTES

What ceremony else?

PRIEST

Her obsequies have been as far enlarged
As we have warranty. Her death was doubtful,
And, but that great command o'ersways the order,
She should in ground unsanctified have lodged
Till the last trumpet. For charitable prayers,
Shards, flints, and pebbles should be thrown on her.
Yet here she is allowed her virgin crants,
Her maiden strewments, and the bringing home
Of bell and burial.   230

LAERTES

Must there no more be done?

PRIEST   No more be done.
We should profane the service of the dead

To sing a requiem and such rest to her
As to peace-parted souls.

LAERTES   Lay her i'th'earth,
And from her fair and unpolluted flesh
May violets spring! I tell thee, churlish priest,
A ministering angel shall my sister be
When thou liest howling.

HAMLET   What, the fair Ophelia?

QUEEN
Sweets to the sweet! Farewell.
She scatters flowers
240 I hoped thou shouldst have been my Hamlet's wife.
I thought thy bride-bed to have decked, sweet maid,
And not have strewed thy grave.

LAERTES   O, treble woe
Fall ten times double on that cursèd head
Whose wicked deed thy most ingenious sense
Deprived thee of! Hold off the earth awhile,
Till I have caught her once more in mine arms.
He leaps in the grave
Now pile your dust upon the quick and dead
Till of this flat a mountain you have made
T'o'ertop old Pelion or the skyish head
250 Of blue Olympus.

HAMLET (*coming forward*)
                        What is he whose grief
Bears such an emphasis, whose phrase of sorrow
Conjures the wandering stars, and makes them stand
Like wonder-wounded hearers? This is I,
Hamlet the Dane.

LAERTES   The devil take thy soul!

HAMLET
Thou prayest not well.
I prithee take thy fingers from my throat.

For, though I am not splenitive and rash,
Yet have I in me something dangerous,
Which let thy wisdom fear. Hold off thy hand.

KING
Pluck them asunder.

QUEEN   Hamlet, Hamlet!   260

ALL
Gentlemen!

HORATIO   Good my lord, be quiet.

HAMLET
Why, I will fight with him upon this theme
Until my eyelids will no longer wag.

QUEEN
O my son, what theme?

HAMLET
I loved Ophelia. Forty thousand brothers
Could not with all their quantity of love
Make up my sum. What wilt thou do for her?

KING
O, he is mad, Laertes.

QUEEN
For love of God, forbear him.

HAMLET
'Swounds, show me what thou't do.   270
Woo't weep? Woo't fight? Woo't fast? Woo't tear
       thyself?
Woo't drink up eisel? Eat a crocodile?
I'll do't. Dost thou come here to whine?
To outface me with leaping in her grave?
Be buried quick with her, and so will I.
And if thou prate of mountains, let them throw
Millions of acres on us, till our ground,
Singeing his pate against the burning zone,
Make Ossa like a wart! Nay, an thou'lt mouth,

280   I'll rant as well as thou.

QUEEN   This is mere madness.
       And thus a while the fit will work on him.
       Anon, as patient as the female dove
       When that her golden couplets are disclosed,
       His silence will sit drooping.

HAMLET   Hear you, sir.
       What is the reason that you use me thus?
       I loved you ever. But it is no matter.
       Let Hercules himself do what he may,
       The cat will mew, and dog will have his day.

KING
       I pray thee, good Horatio, wait upon him.
                              Exeunt Hamlet and Horatio

       (*To Laertes*)
290   Strengthen your patience in our last night's speech.
       We'll put the matter to the present push.
       Good Gertrude, set some watch over your son.
       This grave shall have a living monument.
       An hour of quiet shortly shall we see.
       Till then in patience our proceeding be.   *Exeunt*

V.2   *Enter Hamlet and Horatio*

HAMLET
       So much for this, sir. Now shall you see the other.
       You do remember all the circumstance?

HORATIO
       Remember it, my lord!

HAMLET
       Sir, in my heart there was a kind of fighting
       That would not let me sleep. Methought I lay
       Worse than the mutines in the bilboes. Rashly,
       And praised be rashness for it – let us know

Our indiscretion sometime serves us well
When our deep plots do pall, and that should learn us
There's a divinity that shapes our ends,   10
Rough-hew them how we will —

HORATIO   That is most certain.

HAMLET
Up from my cabin,
My sea-gown scarfed about me, in the dark
Groped I to find out them, had my desire,
Fingered their packet, and in fine withdrew
To mine own room again, making so bold,
My fears forgetting manners, to unseal
Their grand commission; where I found, Horatio —
Ah, royal knavery! — an exact command,
Larded with many several sorts of reasons,   20
Importing Denmark's health, and England's too,
With, ho! such bugs and goblins in my life,
That on the supervise, no leisure bated,
No, not to stay the grinding of the axe,
My head should be struck off.

HORATIO   Is't possible?

HAMLET
Here's the commission. Read it at more leisure.
But wilt thou hear now how I did proceed?

HORATIO
I beseech you.

HAMLET
Being thus be-netted round with villainies,
Or I could make a prologue to my brains   30
They had begun the play. I sat me down,
Devised a new commission, wrote it fair.
I once did hold it, as our statists do,
A baseness to write fair, and laboured much
How to forget that learning. But, sir, now

It did me yeoman's service. Wilt thou know
Th'effect of what I wrote?

HORATIO   Ay, good my lord.

HAMLET

An earnest conjuration from the King,
As England was his faithful tributary,
As love between them like the palm might flourish,
As peace should still her wheaten garland wear
And stand a comma 'tween their amities,
And many such-like as's of great charge,
That on the view and knowing of these contents,
Without debatement further, more or less,
He should those bearers put to sudden death,
Not shriving time allowed.

HORATIO   How was this sealed?

HAMLET

Why, even in that was heaven ordinant.
I had my father's signet in my purse,
Which was the model of that Danish seal,
Folded the writ up in the form of th'other,
Subscribed it, gave't th'impression, placed it safely,
The changeling never known. Now, the next day
Was our sea-fight, and what to this was sequent
Thou knowest already.

HORATIO

So Guildenstern and Rosencrantz go to't.

HAMLET

Why, man, they did make love to this employment.
They are not near my conscience. Their defeat
Does by their own insinuation grow.
'Tis dangerous when the baser nature comes
Between the pass and fell incensèd points
Of mighty opposites.

HORATIO   Why, what a king is this!

HAMLET

    Does it not, think thee, stand me now upon —
    He that hath killed my King and whored my mother,
    Popped in between th'election and my hopes,
    Thrown out his angle for my proper life,
    And with such cozenage — is't not perfect conscience
    To quit him with this arm? And is't not to be damned
    To let this canker of our nature come
    In further evil?   70

HORATIO

    It must be shortly known to him from England
    What is the issue of the business there.

HAMLET

    It will be short. The interim is mine;
    And a man's life's no more than to say 'one'.
    But I am very sorry, good Horatio,
    That to Laertes I forgot myself.
    For by the image of my cause I see
    The portraiture of his. I'll court his favours.
    But sure the bravery of his grief did put me
    Into a towering passion.

HORATIO   Peace, who comes here?   80

    Enter Osrick

OSRICK Your lordship is right welcome back to Denmark.

HAMLET I humbly thank you, sir. (*Aside to Horatio*) Dost
    know this waterfly?

HORATIO (*aside to Hamlet*) No, my good lord.

HAMLET (*aside to Horatio*) Thy state is the more gracious,
    for 'tis a vice to know him. He hath much land, and
    fertile. Let a beast be lord of beasts, and his crib shall
    stand at the king's mess. 'Tis a chough, but, as I say,
    spacious in the possession of dirt.

OSRICK Sweet lord, if your lordship were at leisure, I   90
    should impart a thing to you from his majesty.

HAMLET I will receive it, sir, with all diligence of spirit.
Put your bonnet to his right use. 'Tis for the head.

OSRICK I thank your lordship, it is very hot.

HAMLET No, believe me, 'tis very cold. The wind is
northerly.

OSRICK It is indifferent cold, my lord, indeed.

HAMLET But yet methinks it is very sultry and hot for my
complexion.

100 OSRICK Exceedingly, my lord. It is very sultry, as 'twere
– I cannot tell how. But, my lord, his majesty bade me
signify to you that 'a has laid a great wager on your head.
Sir, this is the matter –

HAMLET I beseech you remember.

He invites Osrick to put on his hat

OSRICK Nay, good my lord. For my ease, in good faith.
Sir, here is newly come to court Laertes; believe me,
an absolute gentleman, full of most excellent differences,
of very soft society and great showing. Indeed, to speak
feelingly of him, he is the card or calendar of gentry.
110 For you shall find in him the continent of what part a
gentleman would see.

HAMLET Sir, his definement suffers no perdition in you,
though, I know, to divide him inventorially would dizzy
th'arithmetic of memory, and yet but yaw neither in
respect of his quick sail. But, in the verity of extolment,
I take him to be a soul of great article, and his infusion
of such dearth and rareness as, to make true diction of
him, his semblable is his mirror, and who else would
trace him, his umbrage, nothing more.

120 OSRICK Your lordship speaks most infallibly of him.

HAMLET The concernancy, sir? Why do we wrap the
gentleman in our more rawer breath?

OSRICK Sir?

HORATIO Is't not possible to understand in another
   tongue? You will to't, sir, really.

HAMLET What imports the nomination of this gentleman?

OSRICK Of Laertes?

HORATIO (*aside to Hamlet*) His purse is empty already.
   All's golden words are spent.   130

HAMLET Of him, sir.

OSRICK I know you are not ignorant —

HAMLET I would you did, sir. Yet, in faith, if you did, it
   would not much approve me. Well, sir?

OSRICK You are not ignorant of what excellence Laertes
   is —

HAMLET I dare not confess that, lest I should compare
   with him in excellence. But to know a man well were to
   know himself.

OSRICK I mean, sir, for his weapon. But in the impu-   140
   tation laid on him by them, in his meed he's unfellowed.

HAMLET What's his weapon?

OSRICK Rapier and dagger.

HAMLET That's two of his weapons. But well!

OSRICK The King, sir, hath wagered with him six Barbary
   horses, against the which he has impawned, as I take it,
   six French rapiers and poniards, with their assigns, as
   girdle, hangers, and so. Three of the carriages, in faith,
   are very dear to fancy, very responsive to the hilts, most
   delicate carriages, and of very liberal conceit.   150

HAMLET What call you the carriages?

HORATIO (*aside to Hamlet*) I knew you must be edified
   by the margent ere you had done.

OSRICK The carriages, sir, are the hangers.

HAMLET The phrase would be more germane to the
   matter if we could carry a cannon by our sides. I would
   it might be 'hangers' till then. But on! Six Barbary

horses against six French swords, their assigns, and
three liberal-conceited carriages. That's the French bet
against the Danish. Why is this all impawned, as you
call it?

OSRICK The King, sir, hath laid, sir, that in a dozen
passes between yourself and him he shall not exceed you
three hits. He hath laid on twelve for nine; and it would
come to immediate trial if your lordship would vouchsafe the answer.

HAMLET How if I answer no?

OSRICK I mean, my lord, the opposition of your person
in trial.

HAMLET Sir, I will walk here in the hall. If it please his
majesty, it is the breathing time of day with me. Let the
foils be brought, the gentleman willing, and the King
hold his purpose, I will win for him an I can. If not, I
will gain nothing but my shame and the odd hits.

OSRICK Shall I re-deliver you e'en so?

HAMLET To this effect, sir, after what flourish your
nature will.

OSRICK I commend my duty to your lordship.

HAMLET Yours, yours.   *Exit Osrick*
He does well to commend it himself. There are no
tongues else for's turn.

HORATIO This lapwing runs away with the shell on his
head.

HAMLET 'A did comply, sir, with his dug before 'a sucked
it. Thus has he, and many more of the same bevy that I
know the drossy age dotes on, only got the tune of the
time and, out of an habit of encounter, a kind of yeasty
collection, which carries them through and through the
most fanned and winnowed opinions; and do but blow
them to their trial, the bubbles are out.
        Enter a Lord

LORD My lord, his majesty commended him to you by
  young Osrick, who brings back to him that you attend
  him in the hall. He sends to know if your pleasure hold
  to play with Laertes, or that you will take longer time.

HAMLET I am constant to my purposes. They follow the
  King's pleasure. If his fitness speaks, mine is ready,
  now or whensoever, provided I be so able as now.

LORD The King and Queen and all are coming down.

HAMLET In happy time.

LORD The Queen desires you to use some gentle enter-   200
  tainment to Laertes before you fall to play.

HAMLET She well instructs me.   *Exit the Lord*

HORATIO You will lose this wager, my lord.

HAMLET I do not think so. Since he went into France I
  have been in continual practice. I shall win at the odds.
  But thou wouldst not think how ill all's here about my
  heart. But it is no matter.

HORATIO Nay, good my lord —

HAMLET It is but foolery. But it is such a kind of gaingiving as would perhaps trouble a woman.   210

HORATIO If your mind dislike anything, obey it. I will
  forestall their repair hither and say you are not fit.

HAMLET Not a whit. We defy augury. There is special
  providence in the fall of a sparrow. If it be now, 'tis not
  to come. If it be not to come, it will be now. If it be not
  now, yet it will come. The readiness is all. Since no man
  knows of aught he leaves, what is't to leave betimes?
  Let be.

  Trumpets and drums
  A table prepared, with flagons of wine on it
  Enter officers with cushions, and other attendants
  with foils, daggers, and gauntlets
  Enter the King and Queen, Osrick, Laertes, and all
  the state

KING

>Come, Hamlet, come, and take this hand from me.
>
>*He puts Laertes's hand into Hamlet's*

HAMLET

220
>Give me your pardon, sir. I have done you wrong.
>But pardon't, as you are a gentleman.
>This presence knows, and you must needs have heard,
>How I am punished with a sore distraction.
>What I have done
>That might your nature, honour, and exception
>Roughly awake, I here proclaim was madness.
>Was't Hamlet wronged Laertes? Never Hamlet.
>If Hamlet from himself be ta'en away,
>And when he's not himself does wrong Laertes,

230
>Then Hamlet does it not. Hamlet denies it.
>Who does it then? His madness. If 't be so,
>Hamlet is of the faction that is wronged.
>His madness is poor Hamlet's enemy.
>Sir, in this audience,
>Let my disclaiming from a purposed evil
>Free me so far in your most generous thoughts
>That I have shot my arrow o'er the house
>And hurt my brother.

LAERTES   I am satisfied in nature,
>Whose motive in this case should stir me most

240
>To my revenge. But in my terms of honour
>I stand aloof, and will no reconcilement
>Till by some elder masters of known honour
>I have a voice and precedent of peace
>To keep my name ungored. But till that time
>I do receive your offered love like love,
>And will not wrong it.

HAMLET   I embrace it freely,
>And will this brothers' wager frankly play.

Give us the foils. Come on.

LAERTES   Come, one for me.

HAMLET

I'll be your foil, Laertes. In mine ignorance
Your skill shall, like a star i'th'darkest night,   250
Stick fiery off indeed.

LAERTES   You mock me, sir.

HAMLET

No, by this hand.

KING

Give them the foils, young Osrick. Cousin Hamlet,
You know the wager?

HAMLET   Very well, my lord.
Your grace has laid the odds o'th'weaker side.

KING

I do not fear it. I have seen you both.
But since he is bettered, we have therefore odds.

LAERTES

This is too heavy. Let me see another.

HAMLET

This likes me well. These foils have all a length?

OSRICK

Ay, my good lord.   260

They prepare to play

KING

Set me the stoups of wine upon that table.
If Hamlet give the first or second hit,
Or quit in answer of the third exchange,
Let all the battlements their ordnance fire.
The King shall drink to Hamlet's better breath,
And in the cup an union shall he throw
Richer than that which four successive kings
In Denmark's crown have worn. Give me the cups,
And let the kettle to the trumpet speak,

270   The trumpet to the cannoneer without,
The cannons to the heavens, the heaven to earth,
'Now the King drinks to Hamlet.' Come, begin.
    (*Trumpets the while*)
And you, the judges, bear a wary eye.

HAMLET
Come on, sir.

LAERTES   Come, my lord.
    They play

HAMLET   One.

LAERTES   No.

HAMLET   Judgement?

OSRICK
A hit, a very palpable hit.
    Drum, trumpets, and shot. Flourish. A piece goes off

LAERTES   Well, again.

KING
Stay, give me drink. Hamlet, this pearl is thine.
Here's to thy health. Give him the cup.

HAMLET
I'll play this bout first; set it by awhile.
Come.
    They play
        Another hit. What say you?

LAERTES
280   A touch, a touch. I do confess't.

KING
Our son shall win.

QUEEN   He's fat and scant of breath.
Here, Hamlet, take my napkin. Rub thy brows.
The Queen carouses to thy fortune, Hamlet.

HAMLET
Good madam!

KING   Gertrude, do not drink.

QUEEN

I will, my lord. I pray you, pardon me.
She drinks

KING (*aside*)

It is the poisoned cup. It is too late.

HAMLET

I dare not drink yet, madam. By and by.

QUEEN

Come, let me wipe thy face.

LAERTES (*aside to the King*)

My lord, I'll hit him now.

KING (*aside to Laertes*)   I do not think't.

LAERTES (*aside*)

And yet it is almost against my conscience.   290

HAMLET

Come for the third, Laertes. You do but dally.
I pray you, pass with your best violence.
I am afeard you make a wanton of me.

LAERTES

Say you so? Come on.
They play

OSRICK

Nothing neither way.

LAERTES

Have at you now!
*In scuffling they change rapiers, and both are wounded
with the poisoned weapon*

KING   Part them. They are incensed.

HAMLET

Nay, come. Again!
The Queen falls

OSRICK   Look to the Queen there. Ho!

HORATIO

They bleed on both sides. How is it, my lord?

OSRICK

 How is't, Laertes?

LAERTES

300 Why, as a woodcock to mine own springe, Osrick.

 I am justly killed with mine own treachery.

HAMLET

 How does the Queen?

KING   She swounds to see them bleed.

QUEEN

 No, no, the drink, the drink! O my dear Hamlet!

 The drink, the drink! I am poisoned.

  She dies

HAMLET

 O, villainy! Ho! Let the door be locked.

 Treachery! Seek it out.

LAERTES

 It is here, Hamlet. Hamlet, thou art slain.

 No medicine in the world can do thee good.

 In thee there is not half an hour's life.

310 The treacherous instrument is in thy hand,

 Unbated and envenomed. The foul practice

 Hath turned itself on me. Lo, here I lie,

 Never to rise again. Thy mother's poisoned.

 I can no more. The King, the King's to blame.

HAMLET

 The point envenomed too?

 Then, venom, to thy work.

  He wounds the King

ALL

 Treason! Treason!

KING

 O, yet defend me, friends. I am but hurt.

HAMLET

 Here, thou incestuous, murderous, damnèd Dane,

Drink off this potion.
> *He forces the King to drink*

                         Is thy union here?   320
Follow my mother.
> *The King dies*

LAERTES   He is justly served.
  It is a poison tempered by himself.
  Exchange forgiveness with me, noble Hamlet.
  Mine and my father's death come not upon thee,
  Nor thine on me!
> *He dies*

HAMLET
  Heaven make thee free of it! I follow thee.
  I am dead, Horatio. Wretched Queen, adieu!
  You that look pale and tremble at this chance,
  That are but mutes or audience to this act,
  Had I but time – as this fell sergeant, Death,   330
  Is strict in his arrest – O, I could tell you –
  But let it be. Horatio, I am dead.
  Thou livest. Report me and my cause aright
  To the unsatisfied.

HORATIO   Never believe it.
  I am more an antique Roman than a Dane.
  Here's yet some liquor left.

HAMLET   As th' art a man,
  Give me the cup. Let go. By heaven, I'll ha't!
  O God, Horatio, what a wounded name,
  Things standing thus unknown, shall I leave behind me!
  If thou didst ever hold me in thy heart,   340
  Absent thee from felicity awhile,
  And in this harsh world draw thy breath in pain,
  To tell my story.
> *A march afar off, and shout within*

                    What warlike noise is this?

OSRICK

Young Fortinbras, with conquest come from Poland,
To the ambassadors of England gives
This warlike volley.

HAMLET   O, I die, Horatio!
The potent poison quite o'er-crows my spirit.
I cannot live to hear the news from England.
But I do prophesy th'election lights
350   On Fortinbras. He has my dying voice.
So tell him, with th'occurrents, more and less,
Which have solicited – the rest is silence.
      He dies

HORATIO

Now cracks a noble heart. Good night, sweet Prince,
And flights of angels sing thee to thy rest!
      (*March within*)
Why does the drum come hither?
      *Enter Fortinbras, with the Ambassadors and with his
      train of drum, colours, and attendants*

FORTINBRAS

Where is this sight?

HORATIO   What is it you would see?
If aught of woe or wonder, cease your search.

FORTINBRAS

This quarry cries on havoc. O proud Death,
What feast is toward in thine eternal cell
360   That thou so many princes at a shot
So bloodily hast struck?

AMBASSADOR   The sight is dismal,
And our affairs from England come too late.
The ears are senseless that should give us hearing,
To tell him his commandment is fulfilled,
That Rosencrantz and Guildenstern are dead.

   Where should we have our thanks?
HORATIO   Not from his mouth,
   Had it th'ability of life to thank you.
   He never gave commandment for their death.
   But since, so jump upon this bloody question,
   You from the Polack wars, and you from England,   370
   Are here arrived, give order that these bodies
   High on a stage be placèd to the view.
   And let me speak to th'yet unknowing world
   How these things came about. So shall you hear
   Of carnal, bloody, and unnatural acts,
   Of accidental judgements, casual slaughters,
   Of deaths put on by cunning and forced cause,
   And, in this upshot, purposes mistook
   Fallen on th'inventors' heads. All this can I
   Truly deliver.
FORTINBRAS   Let us haste to hear it,   380
   And call the noblest to the audience.
   For me, with sorrow I embrace my fortune.
   I have some rights of memory in this kingdom,
   Which now to claim my vantage doth invite me.
HORATIO
   Of that I shall have also cause to speak,
   And from his mouth whose voice will draw on more.
   But let this same be presently performed,
   Even while men's minds are wild, lest more mischance
   On plots and errors happen.
FORTINBRAS   Let four captains
   Bear Hamlet like a soldier to the stage.   390
   For he was likely, had he been put on,
   To have proved most royal. And for his passage
   The soldiers' music and the rites of war
   Speak loudly for him.

Take up the bodies. Such a sight as this
Becomes the field, but here shows much amiss.
Go, bid the soldiers shoot.

Exeunt marching; after the which a peal of
ordnance is shot off

NOTE: The 1980 edition was almost complete at the time
of Professor T. J. B. Spencer's death in March 1978. His
typescript was edited and seen through the press by Stanley
Wells with the help of Mrs Katharine Spencer.

An Account of the Text

In the Account of the Text and the Commentary the abbreviation Q1 is used for the first ('bad') Quarto (1603), Q2 for the second ('good') Quarto (1604) and F for the first Folio (1623).

Hamlet was entered in the Register of the Stationers' Company on 26 July 1602 to James Roberts as 'A booke called the Revenge of Hamlett Prince Denmarke as yt was latelie Acted by the Lo: Chamberleyn his servantes'. But it first appeared in print from the press of Valentine Simmes, in 1603. It was then described on the title page as *The Tragicall Historie of Hamlet Prince of Denmarke By William Shake-speare*, and was said to be 'As it hath beene diuerse times acted by his Highnesse seruants in the Cittie of London: as also in the two Vniuersities of Cambridge and Oxford, and elsewhere'. This edition, printed in quarto (that is, on sheets of paper folded twice), is an unauthorized text which appears to derive not from Shakespeare's manuscript, or even from a good copy of it, but from a manuscript reconstructed from memory by one or more of the actors of Shakespeare's company. The performer of Marcellus, whose role is exceptionally well reported, is particularly open to suspicion.

The text of the first or bad Quarto is seriously corrupt. It contains only about 2200 lines, whereas there are about 3800 in the good Quarto. The reporter's memory is often imperfect, as may be seen from his garbling of part of 'To be, or not to be' (III.1.56–88):

To be, or not to be, I there's the point,
To Die, to sleepe, is that all? I all:

No, to sleepe, to dreame, I mary there it goes,
For in that dreame of death, when wee awake,
And borne before an euerlasting Iudge,
From whence no passenger euer retur'nd,
The vndiscouered country, at whose sight
The happy smile, and the accursed damn'd.

At other times the reporter remembered little more than the dramatic situation, and seems to have composed his own verse, with occasional echoes of the original wording, as in Hamlet's 'pictures' speech (III.4.54–89):

           . . . behold this picture,
It is the portraiture, of your deceased husband,
See here a face, to outface *Mars* himselfe,
An eye, at which his foes did tremble at,
A front wherin all vertues are set downe
For to adorne a king, and guild his crowne,
Whose heart went hand in hand euen with that vow,
He made to you in marriage, and he is dead.
Murdred, damnably murdred, this was your husband,
Looke you now, here is your husband,
With a face like *Vulcan*.
A looke fit for a murder and a rape,
A dull dead hanging looke, and a hell-bred eie,
To affright children and amaze the world.

Other plays by Shakespeare, such as *Romeo and Juliet*, *Henry V* and *The Merry Wives of Windsor*, also exist in 'bad' Quartos; and Q1 of *Hamlet* shares some of their characteristics. But also, and more puzzlingly, it shows signs of deriving from a version of the play significantly different from that which we know today. Polonius is called Corambis; Reynaldo, Montano. Hamlet's madness is much more pronounced, and the Queen's innocence of her husband's murder much more explicitly stated. (In these respects the earlier play corresponds more closely with the original story.) The Queen is represented as concerting and actively cooperating with Hamlet against the King's life. And there are structural differences; the 'nunnery' scene (III.1.56–150) comes earlier than in the accepted text, and a scene in which Horatio tells the Queen of Hamlet's return to Denmark from England replaces those in which Horatio receives Hamlet's letter (IV.6) and the episode in which Hamlet and Horatio discuss the events of the voyage (V.2.1–74). The bad Quarto, then, arouses suspicions that the play may have been performed soon after it was written in a text that has otherwise not come down to us, possibly an earlier version, possibly a shortened form of what we now regard as the authentic text, made conceivably for a touring company.

For all its faults, Q1 is occasionally useful to the editor. Once or twice it is the only source of what seems an authentic reading (as at III.2.261; see the Commentary). It provides supporting evidence for other readings. Its stage directions, scanty though they are, are of exceptional interest, since they give us information about the early staging of the play which is not available elsewhere (the more interesting of them are given in the seventh collation list below). And it reports an expansion of Hamlet's comments to the First Player on 'those that play your clowns' which may well derive from Shakespeare's own theatre, and perhaps from his pen. The 1980 New Penguin Shakespeare edition was the first to include this passage in the text (III.2.43–55).

The entry of *Hamlet* to James Roberts in 1602, mentioned above, was probably what is known as a 'staying entry', designed, that is, to prevent unauthorized publication. The players may well have wished to keep the play out of print while it was one of their main assets. If so, they failed, but after Q1 was published they appear to have authorized the play's publication; it is pleasant to think that this may have been in an attempt to redeem Shakespeare's reputation. James Roberts was the printer (though not the publisher) of the second Quarto, which appeared late in 1604 (some copies are dated 1605), described on the title page as: 'The Tragicall Historie of Hamlet, Prince of Denmarke. By William Shakespeare. Newly imprinted and enlarged to almost as much againe as it was, according to the true and perfect Coppie.' This is the longest single version that we have. The enlargement is mainly in the contemplative and imaginative parts, little being added in the way of action and incident. The play appears to have been printed largely from Shakespeare's own manuscript, with some use of Q1. Unfortunately it is badly printed, with many obvious misprints and errors of omission, transposition and so on, probably because the manuscript was difficult to read. And the punctuation is chaotic. Moreover, Q2 does not include passages totalling about 95 lines which were later printed in the first Folio. The two main omissions are II.2.239–69 and 336–61, and slight awkwardnesses in the surrounding dialogue suggest that they were cuts in Q2, rather than later rewritings. Although Q2 is the best single surviving text, it does not tell us all that we need to know.

The good Quarto was reprinted several times, without authoritative alteration. The only other early text of the play of importance to an editor is the one included in the collected edition of Shakespeare's plays, known as the first Folio, which appeared in 1623. Here, as at the beginning of the text of Q2, it is called *The Tragedie of Hamlet, Prince of Denmarke*. Again the situation is not straightforward. The printers seem sometimes to have consulted a copy of Q2, but to have taken as their primary source either the prompt copy, or a transcript of it, which bore witness to changes made in the theatre, whether with or without Shakespeare's help and approval. Their text (which, on the whole, is well printed) omits about 230 lines that are found in Q2; most of these are in Hamlet's role, and they include one of his soliloquies ('How all occasions . . .', IV.4.32–66). A few of the omissions are clearly accidental, but most are deliberate cuts, made presumably to lighten the actor's task. The stage directions are rather more explicitly theatrical than those of Q2, especially in the final scene. And the text includes additions and repetitions of words and phrases unnecessary to the sense, along with indications for sounds 'within', that may be theatrical in origin. There are, then, good grounds for belief that the Folio comes closer than Q2 to representing the play as it was performed by Shakespeare's company. But in some respects it also offers a more carefully prepared, 'literary' version, correcting lacking concord between subject and verb (II.2.20; IV.5.99), regularizing the logic (II.2.216) and correcting words interpreted as being erroneous ('sulleyes' for 'sallies', II.1.39).

The modern editor, then, is faced with three different versions of the play. How can he best provide a single text which will not betray Shakespeare's intentions? When variants are indifferent, Q2 may claim superior authority as the text that is closest to Shakespeare's manuscript. Other variants have to be judged on their intrinsic merits (which usually means literary merits) in the light of all the information available. The Folio has its own kind of authority, both because it corrects many obvious errors in Q2, and because it represents the practice of the playhouse for which Shakespeare wrote. In this edition changes made in F are admitted into the text when they seem to represent a genuine amendment of a probable error in Q2. When the changes are merely a 'modernization' of grammar or of the form of a word the Q2 reading is usually retained. The longer passages contained in F but not printed in Q2 are included. So also are many of the repetitions in Hamlet's speech not found in Q2 (for example 'well, well, well' at III.1.92, where Q2 has only 'well'). Although these have sometimes been regarded by recent editors as 'actors' interpolations' and therefore denied a place in Shakespeare's 'authentic text', there is no need to take so derogatory a view of them. *Hamlet* was performed by the company to which Shakespeare belonged, and presumably he acted in it (there is a tradition that he played the Ghost). So changes in the Folio text may represent his own minor improvements to help the actors. We have reason to respect the modifications made in the acting versions of his plays; indeed a director of the play might find it convenient to use some of F's slightly more theatrical readings that an editor feels obliged to exclude, and he could do so with the confidence that there is a good chance that they indicate Shakespeare's second thoughts.

Few additions have been made to the stage directions; usually the stage business that can be deduced from the text or derived from theatre traditions is discussed in the Commentary. The number of elisions of vowels has been reduced. The practice of the printers in the early texts is inconsistent and unreliable, and any relation to the pronunciation of words on the stage is not known. It seems likely that the scansion of the verse line demands the weakening of syllables, and that the vowels were pronounced lightly, retaining the rhythm of the line, rather than suppressed entirely and so causing uncouth consonant clusters.

In both Q1 and Q2 the play is printed continuously, without

division into acts and scenes. In F only a perfunctory attempt at division occurs, extending no further than II.2. In this edition the traditional division is followed.

COLLATIONS

The collation lists are *selective*. They are arranged as follows: (1) readings of this text derived from F, not Q2; (2) readings derived from Q1, not Q2 or F; (3) readings not derived from Q1, Q2 or F; (4) alterations of Q2's stage directions; (5) readings of F and Q1 not accepted in this text; (6) passages found in Q2 but omitted in F; (7) stage directions in Q1.

Quotations from early editions are unmodernized, except that 'long s' (ʃ) is replaced by 's'.

1

The following readings in the present text of *Hamlet* derive from F, not from Q2. F's reading (as given in this edition) is followed by the Q2 form, unmodernized. The list includes passages found in F only, totalling about 95 lines. In general, F's adoption of more familiar variant spellings and its correction of obvious misprints are not noted here.

I.1

    16 soldier] souldiers
    21 MARCELLUS] *Hora.*
    44 harrows] horrowes
    63 sledded] sleaded
    73 why] with
       cast] cost
    91 returned] returne
    93 covenant] comart
  139 you] your
  176 conveniently] conuenient

I.2

    58 He hath] Hath
    67 Not so] Not so much

77 good] coold
83 denote] deuote
96 a] or
132 self] seale
133 weary] wary
137 to this] thus
143 would] should
149 even she] *not in* Q2
175 to drink deep] for to drinke
178 see] *not in* Q2
224 Indeed, indeed] Indeede
237 Very like, very like] Very like
257 Foul] fonde

I.3

3 convoy is] conuay, in
12 bulk] bulkes
18 For . . . birth] *not in* Q2
49 like] *not in* Q2
68 thine] thy
74 Are] Or
75 be] boy
76 loan] loue
83 invites you. Go.] inuests you goe,
125 tether] tider
131 beguile] beguide

I.4

2 a] *not in* Q2
71 beetles] bettles

I.5

20 fretful] fearefull
47 a] *not in* Q2
55 lust] but
56 sate] sort
68 posset] possesse
95 stiffly] swiftly
116 bird] and
122 my lord] *not in* Q2

II.1

28 no] *not in* Q2

        38 warrant] wit
        39 sullies] sallies
        40 i'th'] with
    52–3 at 'friend' . . . 'gentleman'] *not in* Q2
        63 takes] take
       105 passion] passions
       112 quoted] coted

II.2

        43 Assure you,] I assure
        57 o'erhasty] hastie
        73 three] threescore
        90 since] *not in* Q2
       126 above] about
       137 winking] working
       143 his] her
       148 watch] wath
       149 a] *not in* Q2
       151 'tis] *not in* Q2
       189 far gone, far gone] farre gone
       210 sanity] sanctity
   212–13 and suddenly . . . between him] *not in* Q2
       213 honourable] *not in* Q2
       214 most humbly] *not in* Q2
       215 sir] *not in* Q2
       224 excellent] extent
       228 over-happy] euer happy
       229 cap] lap
       236 that] *not in* Q2
   239–69 Let me . . . dreadfully attended] *not in* Q2
       272 even] euer
       278 Why] *not in* Q2
       303 What a piece] What peece
       305 moving how] moouing, how
           admirable, in] admirable in
       306 angel, in] Angell in
       309 woman] women
       320 of] on
   323–4 the clown . . . o'th'sere] *not in* Q2
       325 blank] black

336–61 How comes . . . load too] *not in* Q2
   363 mows] mouths
   372 lest my] let me
397–8 tragical-historical, tragical-comical-historical-
          pastoral] *not in* Q2
   424 By'r] by
   428 French falconers] friendly Fankners
   442 affectation] affection
   445 tale] talke
   472 Then senseless Ilium] *not in* Q2
   477 reverend] reuerent
   479 And] *not in* Q2
   502 'Mobled Queen' is good] *not in* Q2
   512 husband's] husband
   537 ha't] hate
   551 his] the
   558 the cue] that
   579 O, vengeance!] *not in* Q2
   597 devil . . . devil] deale . . . deale

III.1
     1 And] an
    28 too] two
    32 lawful espials] *not in* Q2
    46 loneliness] lowlines
    55 Let's] *not in* Q2
    83 of us all] *not in* Q2
    85 sicklied] sickled
    92 well, well, well] well
    99 the] these
   107 your honesty] you
   121 to] *not in* Q2
   129 all] *not in* Q2
   138 Go] *not in* Q2
   142 O] *not in* Q2
   143 too] *not in* Q2
   145 lisp] list
146–7 your ignorance] ignorance
   153 expectancy] expectation
   157 music] musickt

158 that] what
160 feature] stature
189 unwatched] vnmatcht

III.2

10 tatters] totters
22 own] *not in* Q2
25 make] makes
26 of the which] of which
29 praise] praysd
36 sir] *not in* Q2
99 detecting] detected
123–4 HAMLET I . . . lord] *not in* Q2
144 *very lovingly*] *not in* Q2
She kneels, and makes show of protestation unto him]
not in Q2
146 is miching] munching
151 counsel] *not in* Q2
165 orbèd] orb'd the
173 your] our
178 In neither] Eyther none, in neither
179 love] Lord
200 like] the
209 joys] ioy
233 If, once a widow, ever I be wife] If once I be a
widdow, euer I be a wife
262 Pox] *not in* Q2
265 Confederate] Considerat
275 HAMLET What, frighted with false fire?] *not in* Q2
285 two] *not in* Q2
287 sir] *not in* Q2
317 start] stare
326 of my] of
366 thumb] the vmber
375 the top of] *not in* Q2
379 can fret me] fret me not
393–4 POLONIUS I will say so. HAMLET 'By and by' is
easily said. *Exit Polonius* Leave me, friends.]
Leaue me friends. | I will, say so. By and by is
easily said,

396 breathes] breakes
398 bitter business as the day] busines as the bitter
       day
403 daggers] dagger

III.3

19 huge] hough
22 ruin] raine
23 with] *not in* Q2
50 pardoned] pardon
58 shove] showe
73 pat] but
79 hire and salary] base and silly
89 drunk] drunke,

III.4

5 with him] *not in* Q2
6 HAMLET . . . mother] *not in* Q2
7 warrant] wait
21 inmost] most
50 Yea] Ore
53 That . . . index] *spoken by Hamlet*
60 heaven-kissing] heaue, a kissing
89 panders] pardons
90 mine] my very
   very] *not in* Q2
91 grainèd] greeued
92 not leave] leaue there
96 mine] my
98 tithe] kyth
140 Ecstasy?] *not in* Q2
144 I] *not in* Q2
159 live] leaue
166 Refrain tonight] to refraine night
187 ravel] rouell
216 foolish] most foolish

IV.2

2 GENTLEMEN (*within*) Hamlet! Lord Hamlet!] *not
   in* Q2
6 Compounded] Compound
30–31 Hide fox, and all after] *not in* Q2

IV.3

42 With fiery quickness] *not in* Q2
54 and so] so
70 were . . . begun] will . . . begin

IV.5

9 aim] yawne
42 God] good
57 la] *not in* Q2
83 their] *not in* Q2
90 his] this
98 QUEEN Alack . . . this?] *not in* Q2
108 They] The
159 Till] Tell
162 an old] a poore
163–5 Nature . . . loves] *not in* Q2
167 Hey . . . nony] *not in* Q2
183 O, you must] you may
196 All] *not in* Q2
200 Christian] Christians
I pray God] *not in* Q2
201 see] *not in* Q2

IV.6

9 an't] (and't); and
21 *good*] *not in* Q2
25 *bore*] bord
29 *He*] So
31 give] *not in* Q2

IV.7

6 proceeded] proceede
14 conjunctive] concliue
22 loud a wind] loued Arm'd
24 And] But
had] haue
36 How . . . news] *not in* Q2
Letters . . . Hamlet] *not in* Q2
45 *your pardon*] you pardon
46 *and more strange*] *not in* Q2
47 *Hamlet*] *not in* Q2
55 shall] *not in* Q2

    56 didest] didst
    61 checking] the King
    87 my] me
  133 on] ore
  139 that] *not in* Q2
  155 ha't] hate
  162 How, sweet Queen] *not in* Q2
  167 hoar] horry
  171 cold] cull-cold
  177 tunes] laudes

V.1

    9 *se offendendo*] so offended
    12 and to perform. Argal,] to performe, or all;
  34–7 SECOND CLOWN Why . . . arms?] *not in* Q2
    43 frame] *not in* Q2
    60 stoup] soope
    84 meant] went
    88 mazzard] massene
 104–5 Is . . . recoveries] *not in* Q2
  106 his vouchers] vouchers
  107 double ones too] doubles
  118 O] or
  119 For . . . meet] *not in* Q2
  141 all] *not in* Q2
  163 nowadays] *not in* Q2
 170–71 three-and-twenty] 23
  181 Let me see] *not in* Q2
  204 as thus] *not in* Q2
  212 winter's] waters
 222, 231 PRIEST] *Doct.*
  225 have] been
  227 Shards] *not in* Q2
  257 and] *not in* Q2
  273 thou] *not in* Q2
  281 thus] this
  294 shortly] thereby

V.2

    6 bilboes] bilbo
    9 pall] fall

17 unseal] vnfold
43 as's] (Assis); as sir
52 Subscribed] Subscribe
57 Why . . . employment] *not in* Q2
68–80 To quit . . . here] *not in* Q2
93 Put] *not in* Q2
98 sultry] sully
for] or
101 But] *not in* Q2
148 hangers] hanger
154 carriages] carriage
160 impawned, as] (impon'd as); *not in* Q2
175 re-deliver] deliuer
e'en] *not in* Q2
179–80 Yours, yours. He] Yours
184 comply] so
185 bevy] breede
187 yeasty] histy
189 winnowed] trennowed
203 this wager] *not in* Q2
206 But] *not in* Q2
209–10 gaingiving] gamgiuing
214 now, 'tis] tis
234 Sir, in this audience] *not in* Q2
244 keep] *not in* Q2
till] all
248 Come on] *not in* Q2
257 bettered] better
266 union] Onixe
280 A touch, a touch] *not in* Q2
293 afeard] sure
307 Hamlet. Hamlet,] *Hamlet,*
310 thy] my
319 murderous] *not in* Q2
320 thy union] the Onixe
345 the] th'
358 proud] prou'd
373 th'] *not in* Q2
377 forced] for no

          386 on] no
          393 rites] right

                                    2

The following readings in the present text derive from Q1, and
not from Q2 or F. Q1's reading (as given in this edition) is followed
by the Q2 and F forms, unmodernized.

I.2
     209 Where, as] Whereas Q2, F
III.2
     43–55 And then you . . . Well] *not in* Q2, F
      261 must take] mistake Q2, F

                                    3

The following readings in the present text are emendations of the
words found in Q1 (for III.2.45), Q2 or F (which are printed,
unmodernized, after the reading of this edition, with where appropriate the forms found in other early texts). A few of these alterations were made in the later Quartos or Folios. Most of the other
emendations were made by the eighteenth-century editors.

The Characters in the Play] *not in* Q2, F
I.1
      94 designed] desseigne Q2; designe F
     121 feared] feare Q2
I.2
      82 shapes] chapes Q2; she wes F
     129 sullied] sallied Q2; solid F
I.3
     109 Running] Wrong Q2; Roaming F
     130 bawds] bonds Q2, F
I.4
      27 the] their Q2
      36 evil] eale Q2
      70 summit] somnet Q2; Sonnet F

I.5

      43 wit] wits Q2, F

II.2

    324 tickle] tickled F
    341 berattle] be-ratled F
    348 most like] like most F
    493 fellies] follies Q2; Fallies F
    517 whe'er] where Q2, F
    581 father] *not in* Q2, F

III.2

     45 quote] quotes
    229 An] And Q2

III.3

      6 near us] neer's Q2; dangerous F
     17 or 'tis] or it is Q2; It is F

III.4

    170 master] *not in* Q2

IV.1

     40 So haply slander] *not in* Q2, F

IV.2

  17–18 like an ape an apple] like an apple Q2; like an Ape F

IV.5

     16 QUEEN Let her come in] *spoken by Horatio in* Q2; *printed in italic as part of a stage direction in* F
    121 brows] browe Q2; brow F
    144 swoopstake] soopstake Q2; Soop-stake F
    154 VOICES (*within*) Let her come in] *spoken by Laertes in* Q2; F *substitutes the stage direction* 'A noise within. Let her come in'

IV.7

    121 spendthrift] spend thirfts Q2

V.1

    272 eisel] Esill Q2; *Esile* F

V.2

     19 Ah] A Q2; Oh F
     29 villainies] villaines Q2, F
     73 interim is] *interim's* F

   78 court] count F
  109 feelingly] sellingly Q2
  140 his] this Q2
  141 them, in his meed he's] them in his meed, hee's Q2
  189 fanned] prophane Q2; fond F
  217 knows of aught he leaves,] of ought he leaues,
      knowes Q2; ha's ought of what he leaues. F

                                    4

The directions in this edition are based on those of Q2, with some
additions from F. The original directions have been normalized
and clarified. Further directions have been added where necessary
to clarify the action. There are no directions for speeches to be
spoken aside or addressed to a particular character in Q2 or F,
except that Hamlet's interjections in the play scene (III.2.191 and
234) are printed to the right of the dialogue in Q2, as if to indicate their special nature. Below are listed some of the more important additions and alterations to Q2's directions. When these derive
in whole or part from F, this is noted. The list also includes the
more interesting F directions not accepted in this edition. Minor
alterations to Q2, such as the addition of a character's name to
'*Exit*', the change of '*Exit*' to '*Exeunt*' or '*Song*' to '*sings*', the
normalization of character names, and the provision of exits and
entrances where these are obviously required, are not listed here.

I.1

  127 *He spreads his arms*] *It spreads his armes* Q2; *not
       in* F
I.2

    0 *Flourish. Enter Claudius, King of Denmark, Gertrude the
      Queen, and the council, including Polonius with his son
      Laertes, Hamlet, Voltemand, Cornelius, and attendants*]
      *Florish. Enter Claudius, King of Denmarke, Gertrad the
      Queene, Counsaile: as Polonius, and his Sonne Laertes,
      Hamlet, Cum Alijs* Q2; *Enter Claudius King of
      Denmarke, Gertrude the Queene, Hamlet, Polonius,
      Laertes, and his Sister Ophelia, Lords Attendant* F (F
      directs Voltemand and Cornelius to enter after line 25)

II.1

    0 *Enter Polonius, with his man Reynaldo*] *Enter old Polonius, with his man or two* Q2; *Enter Polonius, and Reynoldo* F

II.2

   76 (*He gives a paper to the King*)] not in Q2, F

  167 *Enter Hamlet*] Q2; *Enter Hamlet reading on a Booke* F

  170 *Exeunt the King and Queen*] *Exit King and Queene* Q2 (*after line* 169); *Exit King & Queen* F (*after* Ile boord him presently)

III.1

   42 *Exit the Queen*] not in Q2, F

III.2

   0 *Enter Hamlet and the Players*] *Enter Hamlet, and three of the Players* Q2; *Enter Hamlet, and two or three of the Players* F

  101 *Danish march. Flourish. Trumpets and kettledrums. Enter the King and Queen, Polonius, Ophelia, Rosencrantz, Guildenstern, and other Lords attendant, with the guard carrying torches*] *Enter Trumpets and Kettle Drummes, King, Queene, Polonius, Ophelia* Q2; *Enter King, Queene, Polonius, Ophelia, Rosincrance, Guildensterne, and other Lords attendant, with his Guard carrying Torches. Danish March. Sound a Flourish* F

  144 *The trumpets sound*] Q2; *Hoboyes play* F

  269 *He pours the poison in the King's ears*] not in Q2; *Powres the poyson in his eares* F

  352 *Enter a Player with recorders*] *Enter the Players with Recorders* Q2; *Enter one with a Recorder* F

III.4

   8 *Polonius hides behind the arras*] not in Q2, F

   25 *He makes a thrust through the arras and kills Polonius*] not in Q2; *Killes Polonius* F

   31 *He sees Polonius*] not in Q2, F

  218 *Exeunt Hamlet, tugging in Polonius, and the Queen*] *Exit* Q2; *Exit Hamlet tugging in Polonius* F

IV.2

   4 *Guildenstern*] not in Q2

IV.3

    11 *Guildenstern*] not in Q2

IV.6

    0 *Enter Horatio and a Gentleman*] Enter Horatio and others
      Q2; Enter Horatio, with an Attendant F

    4 *Exit the Gentleman*] not in Q2, F

V.1

    64 *Enter Hamlet and Horatio*] Q2; Enter Hamlet and Horatio
      a farre off F (after line 55)

    74 *He throws up a skull*] not in Q2, F

    95 *He throws up another skull*] not in Q2, F

    213 *Enter the King and Queen, Laertes, and the corpse of
      Ophelia, with Lords attendant and a Priest*] Enter K. Q.
      Laertes and the corse Q2; Enter King, Queene, Laertes,
      and a Coffin, with Lords attendant F; Enter King and
      Queene, Leartes, and other lordes, with a Priest after the
      coffin Q1

    218 *He withdraws with Horatio*] not in Q2, F

    239 *She scatters flowers*] not in Q2, F

    246 *He leaps in the grave*] not in Q2; Leaps in the graue F

V.2

    80 *Enter Osrick*] Enter a Courtier Q2; Enter young Osricke
      F

    104 *He invites Osrick to put on his hat*] not in Q2, F

    218 *Trumpets and drums. A table prepared, with flagons of
      wine on it. Enter officers with cushions, and other atten-
      dants with foils, daggers, and gauntlets. Enter the King
      and Queen, Osrick, Laertes, and all the state*] A table
      prepard, Trumpets, Drums and officers with Cushions,
      King, Queene, and all the state, Foiles, daggers, and
      Laertes Q2; Enter King, Queene, Laertes and Lords, with
      other Attendants with Foyles, and Gauntlets, a Table and
      Flagons of Wine on it F

    219 *He puts Laertes's hand into Hamlet's*] not in Q2, F

    260 *They prepare to play*] not in Q2; Prepare to play F (after
      line 259)

    274 *They play*] F; not in Q2

    275 *Drum, trumpets, and shot. Flourish. A piece goes off*] Q2;
      Trumpets sound, and shot goes off F (after line 277)

279 *They play*] not in Q2, F
285 *She drinks*] Q1; *not in* Q2, F
294 *They play*] not in Q2; *Play* F
296 *In scuffling they change rapiers, and both are wounded with the poisoned weapon*] not in Q2; *In scuffling they change Rapiers* F
297 *The Queen falls*] not in Q2, F
304 *She dies*] not in Q2, F
316 *He wounds the King*] not in Q2; *Hurts the King* F
320 *He forces the King to drink*] not in Q2, F
321 *The King dies*] not in Q2; *King Dyes* F
325 *He dies*] not in Q2; *Dyes* F
343 *A march afar off, and shout within*] *A march a farre off* Q2; *March afarre off, and shout within* F
352 *He dies*] not in Q2; *Dyes* F
354 *March within*] not in Q2, F
355 *Enter Fortinbras, with the Ambassadors and with his train of drum, colours, and attendants*] *Enter Fortenbrasse, with the Embassadors* Q2; *Enter Fortinbras and English Ambassador, with Drumme, Colours, and Attendants* F
397 *Exeunt marching; after the which a peal of ordnance is shot off*] F; *Exeunt* Q2

5

The following are some of the variant readings and forms of words more commonly found in other editions (especially nineteenth-century ones). The reading of this edition, with its origin, is given first, followed by the rejected variant. (Emendations proposed by other editors but not adopted here are discussed in the Commentary to I.4.33, II.2.255, III.3.7, III.4.4, 122, 163, and 170, IV.4.25–6, IV.5.39, and V.2.42 and 281.)

I.I

33   have two nights] Q2; two Nights haue F
87   heraldy] Q2; Heraldrie F
88   these] Q2; those F
141 strike] Q2; strike at F
162 stir] Q2; walke F

I.2

11 an . . . a] Q2; one . . . one F
24 bands] Q2; Bonds F
50 My dread lord] Q2; Dread my Lord F
85 passes] Q2; passeth F
127 heaven] Q2; Heauens F
198 waste] Q2, F; vast Q1
213 watch] Q2; watcht F

I.3

26 particular act and place] Q2; peculiar Sect and
       force F
63 unto] Q2; to F
65 courage] Q2; Comrade F
77 dulleth] Q2; dulls the F
123 parle] Q2; parley F

I.4

49 interred] Q2; enurn'd F

I.5

33 roots] Q2; rots F
62 hebona] Q2; Hebenon F
112–13 *Enter Horatio and Marcellus* HORATIO My lord,
       my lord!] Q2; *Hor. & Mar. within.* My Lord, my
       Lord. | *Enter Horatio and Marcellus* F
132 I will] Q2; Looke you, Ile F

II.2

20 is] Q2; are F
97 he's] Q2; he is F
142 prescripts] Q2; Precepts F
203 yourself] Q2; you your selfe F
203–4 shall grow] Q2; should be F
216 will not] Q2; will F
278 anything but] Q2; any thing. But F
446 when] Q2; where F
454 heraldy] Q2; Heraldry F
522 abstract] Q2; Abstracts F
556 her] Q2; *Hecuba* F
585 stallion] Q2; Scullion F

III.1

1 conference] Q2; circumstance F

19 are here] Q2; are F
33 We'll] Q2; Will F
72 despised] Q2; dispriz'd F
145 and amble] Q2; you amble F
148 marriage] Q2; Marriages F
159 time] Q2; tune F

III.2

79 commeddled] Q2; co-mingled F
191 That's wormwood] Q2; Wormwood, Wormwood F
328 ROSENCRANTZ] Q2; *Guild.* F

III.3

15 cess] Q2; cease F
25 about] Q2; vpon F

III.4

23 Help] Q2; Helpe, helpe F
24 Help] Q2; helpe, helpe, helpe F
38 brassed] Q2 (brasd); braz'd F
51 heated] Q2; tristfull F
180 This] Q2; Thus F

IV.3

15 Ho! Bring in the] Q2; Hoa, *Guildensterne?* Bring in my
F
66 congruing] Q2; coniuring F

IV.5

39 ground] Q2; *graue* F
99 is] Q2; are F
158 paid with] Q2; payed by F
201 O God] Q2; you Gods F

IV.7

7 criminal] Q2; crimefull F
8 safety, greatness,] Q2; Safety, F
20 Work] Q2; Would F
52 devise] Q2; aduise F
91 Lamord] Q2; *Lamound* F
104 you] Q2; him F
124 in deed your father's son] Q2; your Fathers sonne
indeed F
158 preferred] Q2 (prefard); prepar'd F
166 askant] Q2; aslant F

168 Therewith . . . make] Q2; There with . . . come F
191 drowns] Q2; doubts F

V.1

60 in] Q2; to *Yaughan* F
65 'A] Q2; that he F
73 into] Q2; *intill* F
86–7 chopless] Q2; Chaplesse F
170 now hath lien you] Q2; now: this Scul, has laine F
183 bore] Q2; borne F
190 table] Q2; Chamber F
233 a] Q2; sage F
243 double] Q2; trebble F
259 wisdom] Q2; wisenesse F

V.2

63 think] Q2; thinkst F
105 my ease] Q2; mine ease F
187 out of an] Q2; outward F
339 I leave] Q2; liue F
352 silence.] Q2; silence. O, o, o, o. F

6

The following are the more important passages found in Q2 but omitted in F. They total about 230 lines. Odd words and insignificant phrases are not included here.

I.1

108–25 BARNARDO I think . . . countrymen

I.2

58–60 wrung . . . consent

I.4

17–38 This heavy-headed . . . scandal
75–8 The very . . . beneath

II.2

17 Whether . . . thus
443–4 as wholesome . . . fine
463 So, proceed you

III.2

176–7 women fear . . . And

181–2 Where love . . . there
228–9 To desperation . . . scope

III.4

72–7 Sense sure . . . difference
79–82 Eyes without . . . mope
162–6 That monster . . . put on
168–71 the next . . . potency
181 One word more, good lady
203–11 There's letters . . . meet

IV.1

4 Bestow . . . while
41–4 Whose whisper . . . air

IV.3

25–7 KING Alas . . . that worm

IV.4

8–66 *Enter Hamlet . . . worth*

IV.7

67–80 LAERTES My lord . . . graveness
99–101 the scrimers . . . opposed them
113–22 There lives . . . ulcer

V.2

106–41 Sir, here is . . . unfellowed (*replaced by* 'Sir, you are not ignorant of what excellence *Laertes* is at his weapon')
152–3 HORATIO . . . I knew . . . done
190–202 *Enter a Lord . . . Exit the Lord*
218 Let be

7

The following are the more interesting of the stage directions in Q1. Some of them probably indicate impressions drawn from a contemporary performance of the play. The line references are to this edition.

I.1

0 *Enter two Centinels*

I.2

0 *Enter King, Queene, Hamlet, Leartes, Corambis, and the two Ambassadors, with Attendants*

I.5

149 *The Gost under the stage*

II.1

0 *Enter Corambis, and Montano*

II.2

0 *Enter King and Queene, Rossencraft, and Gilderstone*

39 *Enter Corambis and Ofelia*

378 *The Trumpets sound, Enter Corambis*

III.2

144 *Enter in a Dumbe Shew, the King and Queene, he sits downe in an Arbor, she leaues him: Then enters Lucianus with poyson in a Viall, and powres it in his eares, and goes away: Then the Queene commeth and findes him dead: and goes away with the other*

163 *Enter the Duke and Dutchesse*

III.3

72 *hee kneeles. enters Hamlet*

III.4

103 *Enter the ghost in his night gowne*

218 *Exit Hamlet with the dead body*

IV.4

0 *Enter Fortenbrasse, Drumme and Souldiers*

IV.5

20 *Enter Ofelia playing on a Lute, and her haire downe singing*

155 *Enter Ofelia as before*

V.1

0 *enter Clowne and an other*

213 *Enter King and Queene, Leartes, and other lordes, with a Priest after the coffin*

246 *Leartes leapes into the graue*

253 *Hamlet leapes in after Leartes*

V.2

80 *Enter a Bragart Gentleman*

296 *They catch one anothers Rapiers, and both are wounded, Leartes falles downe, the Queene falles downe and dies*

355 *Enter Voltemar and the Ambassadors from England. enter Fortenbrasse with his traine*

Commentary

Biblical quotations are given, with modernized spelling and punctuation, from the Bishops' Bible (1568 etc.), the official English translation of Elizabeth's reign.

I.1

The action of the scene takes place on a *platform* (I.2.213) – a level place for mounting guns – of the Danish royal castle at Elsinore. Historically, the castle included a gun-platform where batteries commanded the narrow entrance to the Baltic Sea between Denmark and (modern) Sweden, exacting tolls from ships passing through. It was well known to British voyagers.

0 *Enter Francisco and Barnardo, two Sentinels*: Francisco is on duty, presumably pacing up and down. Barnardo enters to relieve him.

1 *Who's there*: Perhaps he fancies he sees the Ghost.

2 *Nay, answer me. Stand and unfold yourself*: The emphasis is on *me* and (perhaps) *yourself*. Francisco is the sentinel at his post, and it is his duty, not Barnardo's, to challenge anyone who approaches. By putting the challenge in the mouth of the new arrival, Shakespeare creates a feeling of tension.

unfold: Identify.

6 *carefully upon your hour*: Considerately on time.

7 *twelve*: When ghosts begin to walk; this prepares for I.4.3–6: cf. III.2.395–7.

8 *'Tis bitter cold*: Shakespeare carefully establishes the winter night, of which we are reminded at I.4.1–2.

9 *I am sick at heart*: This, from an unimportant soldier, contributes to the emotional atmosphere and prepares for the Prince's heart-sickness at I.2.129–59. It oddly contrasts with the disciplined military scene.

10 *Have you had quiet guard*: Francisco's *I am sick at heart* prompts Barnardo to think of the apparition and so to ask his vague question.

Not a mouse stirring: The ordinary image gives a sense of reality to the soldiers' language, preparing us to accept the supernatural happenings. It also implies the silence and acuteness of perception which anticipate the coming awareness of the Ghost.

13 *rivals*: Partners.

bid them make haste: Barnardo does not want to be left alone now that it is time for the feared appearance of the Ghost.

15 *this ground*: The land of Denmark.

liegemen: The soldiers in this scene seem to be nationals, not like the *Switzers* (IV.5.99), who are the King's personal bodyguard and imply a tyrant's reliance on foreign mercenaries.

the Dane: The King of Denmark.

16, 18 *Give you good night*: May God give you good night. The repetition suggests Francisco's effort to get away as soon as he can.

19 *What, is Horatio there*: This adds to the impression that we are witnessing a night scene.

21 *What . . . tonight*: Marcellus at once asks the question which is uppermost in their minds. The phrase *this thing* indicates his puzzled awe. The line is attributed to Horatio in the second Quarto (Q2), but to Marcellus in the first Quarto (Q1) (a good authority in this scene) and in the Folio (F). It seems to come more naturally from Marcellus in view of Barnardo's promptly understanding reply and of Horatio's disbelief.

29 *approve our eyes*: Corroborate the existence of what we have seen.

speak to it: See the note to 42.

30, 33 *Sit . . . sit*: Referring to Horatio and Marcellus, not

Barnardo, who is at his post.

31 *assail your ears*: Try to overcome your incredulity by
narrating to you. The military imagery is appropriate
in a soldier's speech.

34 *let us hear Barnardo*: He has already heard the story
from Marcellus.

36 *yond same star*: Barnardo presumably points to the sky
at one side of the stage, guiding the eyes of the audience away from where the Ghost will enter. A soldier
on night duty notices the stars and their changing positions as the hours pass; and Shakespeare throughout
the scene gives an impression of a clear, frosty, starlit
sky.

   the pole: The point where the Pole Star shines.

37 *Had made his course*: This, together with the strong
words *illume* and *burns*, seems to imply that the *star* is
a planet.

39 *Enter the Ghost*: It passes close to them (*Within his truncheon's length* (I.2.204), that is, only a few feet), and so
can be imagined as seen clearly in the dim light. It is
in full armour, carries a truncheon, and walks in military fashion, as is frequently iterated (47, 60 and 110;
I.2.200–204, 226–30 and 255; I.4.52). Further visual
details are given at I.2.231–4 and 242. On the
Elizabethan stage it would almost certainly have
emerged from a trapdoor and have descended by the
same means. This is appropriate, for it later *cries under
the stage* (I.5.148) and is called *this fellow in the cellarage*
(I.5.151).

41 *like the King that's dead*: The likeness, insisted on (43–4,
47–9 and 58–63), helps the watchers to believe that it
is really King Hamlet's spirit, not a demon.

42 *Thou art a scholar. Speak to it*: Horatio was a fellow
student of Hamlet, and would therefore know Latin,
in which language ghosts were conventionally
addressed (though theatrical convention permitted
English), and the correct form of words for exorcism.
Hamlet in fact uses a Latin phrase in addressing the
Ghost at I.5.156.

42, 45 *Speak to it. . . . It would be spoke to*: Ghosts could not initiate conversation. See 128–39 and III.4.105–10.

43 *'a*: The weakened, unstressed form of 'he'.

44 *harrows*: Distresses.

45 *would be*: Wants to be.

46 *usurpest*: Because this is not a time when human beings are expected to be out walking, and because you are bearing the form of one we know to be dead and buried.

48 *buried Denmark*: The dead King of Denmark.

49 *sometimes*: Formerly.

50 *It is offended*: Presumably by Horatio's *usurpest*.

54 *fantasy*: See 23.

57 *sensible*: Affecting my senses.
   avouch: Assurance.

61 *he the ambitious Norway combated*: The episode is described later (80–95). Horatio seems to speak from personal observation of the occasion, which we learn at V.1.141–60 was thirty years ago. But such details are not to be pressed as evidence for a time-scheme or as indications of Horatio's age.
   ambitious: The word was generally derogatory; Hamlet describes himself as *very proud, revengeful, ambitious* (III.1.124–5). At I.1.83 this King of Norway is described as *pricked on by a most emulate pride*.
   Norway: The King of Norway.

62 *So frowned he*: Presumably this connects with Marcellus's *It is offended*, and refers only to that moment; when Hamlet later asks *looked he frowningly?*, Horatio replies *A countenance more in sorrow than in anger* (I.2.231–2), apparently describing the Ghost's usual expression.
   parle: Parley (one syllable).

63 *sledded poleaxe*: Long military axe, weighted with lead (like a 'sledgehammer'): a favourite Scandinavian weapon. Q2 (and Q1) reads *sleaded pollax*, and F *sledded Pollax*. Later in the play an inhabitant of Poland is called a *Polack* (II.2.63 etc.), as well as *Pole* (IV.4.21). It has therefore often been supposed that the phrase should be 'sledded Polacks', that is, 'Poles on their

sleighs', referring to a different military episode from
the quarrel with the King of Norway. But the King is
said to have been frowning during heated verbal nego-
tiations (*angry parle*), and this does not seem an appropriate moment for his raining blows upon the enemy
Poles, mounted on their sledges, during a battle on a
frozen lake or river. In *Love's Labour's Lost*, V.2.571 the
word 'poleaxe' is spelt 'Polax' by Q1 (1598) and 'Pollax'
by F and by Q2 (1631).

65 *jump*: Exactly.

67 *thought to work*: Train of thinking to act upon.

68 *in the gross and scope of mine opinion*: So far as I can
make a general surmise without going into details.

69 *strange eruption to our state*: Startling disturbance in the
affairs of our country.

70 *Good now*: If you please.

71 *watch*: Literally, keeping awake; both the military night-
watch and the night labours of the citizens in manu-
facturing armaments and building ships.

72 *toils*: Causes to toil.
   subject: Subjects.

73 *cast*: Casting in a foundry.

74 *foreign mart for implements of war*: Seeking foreign
trade in armaments.

75 *impress*: Conscription, forced enrolment.

75–6, 78 *whose sore task | Does not divide the Sunday from the
week | . . . the night joint-labourer with the day*: They
are working on Sundays and night shifts.

77 *toward*: Impending.

79 *That can I*: Horatio provides the information needed
by the audience to understand the situation. But in the
next scene (I.2.164–9) he has recently arrived from
Wittenberg, ignorant of events, and at I.4.12 he has to
be informed about a local Danish custom. Later he
becomes Hamlet's confidant and often receives from
him the information the audience requires. He is clearly
a Dane at V.2.335. There is consistency in his character,
but not in his role in the play.

80 *whisper*: Rumour.

80–95 *Our last King . . . His fell to Hamlet*: The account of
the Danish successes against Norway emphasizes the
strength of Denmark under the late King Hamlet and,
potentially, under his successor. This impression is
increased by the success of the diplomatic pressure put
on the King of Norway at I.2.17–39 and II.2.60–80,
and the reference to Danish power in England at
IV.3.60–64.

81 *even but*: Only just.

83 *emulate*: Emulous, full of jealous rivalry (a strong
word).

84 *our valiant Hamlet*: This is the first mention of the family
name, identifying *the majesty of buried Denmark* (48)
and *Our last King* (80). Throughout, old Hamlet's virtue,
dignity, valour, physical prowess and personal beauty
are strongly emphasized. It is in the shadow of his worth
that Hamlet has to reveal himself to us, and to act.

85 *so*: That is, *valiant*.
this side of our known world: All Europe, or the western
hemisphere.

86–7 *Did slay . . . heraldy*: This personal combat between
King Hamlet and King Fortinbras, authorized by
heraldy and so on, seems to belong to a different and
older world from that of King Claudius, who is a
modern politician and works through his ambassadors.

86 *sealed compact*: Certified agreement.

87 *heraldy*: Chivalric formalities (an alternative form of
'heraldry').

89 *stood seised*: Was possessed (*stood* is an emphatic auxil-
iary). The pronunciation of *seised* is the same as
'seized'. What Fortinbras offered as a wager was his
personal possessions of land. The fate of the two king-
doms was, of course, not involved in this personal
wager.

90 *moiety competent*: Equivalent portion of land.

91 *gagèd*: Wagered.
returned: Passed (not necessarily 'passed back again').

92 *inheritance*: Subsequent possession (not necessarily with
the notion of heirship)

93 *covenant*: This is F's reading (spelt *Cou'nant*). It is intel-
   ligible, but metrically clumsy. Q2 has *comart*, which is
   a possible word ('co-mart', presumably meaning
   'mutual bargain'), but there is no adequate evidence of
   its existence.

94 *carriage of the article designed*: Fulfilment of the article
   or clause in the prearranged compact.

95 *sir*: Horatio seems to be addressing only Marcellus here,
   though it is Barnardo who next comments.
   young Fortinbras: The parallel between the fathers and
   sons, Fortinbras and Hamlet, is deliberate. It becomes
   clear from I.2.30 and II.2.62 and 70 that in Norway, as
   in Denmark, a brother has succeeded to the throne in
   preference to the late monarch's son. Just as a remarkable contrast between old and young Hamlet is given
   us (see the note to 84), so a difference of personality
   between old and young Fortinbras is implied. Old
   Fortinbras was a worthy opponent of old Hamlet. They
   met in personal combat. But young Fortinbras acts by
   a different code of conduct: he seeks by *terms compulsatory*, with *a list of lawless resolutes*, to wrest back what
   his father had honourably lost.

96 *unimprovèd mettle*: Vigour of mind and body uncultivated and unchastened by experience.

97 *skirts*: Outskirts or borders (less in the control of the
   King's government).

98 *Sharked up*: (Presumably) recruited indiscriminately,
   like a shark seizing its prey at haphazard.
   list: Collection (perhaps disparagingly), mere catalogue
   (but cf. I.2.32).
   lawless resolutes: Determined and desperate characters,
   with nothing to lose because they have rejected the
   obligations and protection of the law. But when
   Fortinbras and his army appear in IV.4, they do not
   correspond to this derogatory description. The reading
   lawless comes from Q2 and is supported by Q1. But
   F's *Landlesse* might be preferred on the grounds that
   Fortinbras was himself one who had lost his inheritance of lands.

99 *For*: (Acting) in return for.

    diet: Daily pay.

100 *stomach*: Exercise of stubborn courage (with a quibble on *food*). The *lawless resolutes* appreciate an enterprise with the excitement of danger.

101 *our state*: The government of Denmark.

102 *of*: From.

103 *compulsatory*: Involving compulsion (accented on the second syllable, and with a weakened fourth syllable).

106 *head*: Fountain-head.

107 *romage*: Commotion.

109–11 *Well may it . . . these wars*: There is no hint in this scene of suspicion that the late King has met his death by foul play. See the note to 129–40.

109 *sort*: Be appropriate.

111 *question*: Cause.

112 *A mote it is to trouble the mind's eye*: The apparition is, after all, a trifle. Yet a speck of dust can be troublesome in the eye, and so this apparition troubles our mental vision.

113–20 *In the most high . . . eclipse*: This passage on the portents which preceded Caesar's murder recalls I.3 and II.2 of *Julius Caesar*, probably written shortly before *Hamlet*. Both derive from Plutarch's *Life of Julius Caesar* in Sir Thomas North's translation (1579, etc.). Horatio, a *scholar* (42), discourses impressively to the two soldiers from his reading of Roman history. Perhaps he also shows an unexpectedly superstitious side.

113 *the most high and palmy state of Rome*: Julius Caesar was regarded as the first Roman emperor and his rule as the high point of Roman prosperity (ordained by Divine Providence to produce a world at peace in readiness for the birth of Christ). But Horatio means simply 'in ancient Rome, whose glories we all know about'.

    palmy: Flourishing.

    state: Government.

115 *sheeted*: Wearing their shrouds.

116 *gibber*: Pronounced with hard 'g' as in 'give'. The

shrill, weak, piping cries of the souls of the dead are
a detail from classical poetry.

117 *As stars with trains . . . blood*: The syntax here is much
broken; probably a line or two have been lost between
116 and 117, to the effect that 'there were prodigies
visible in the heavens as well as on earth, for example
. . .' An alternative explanation is that some lines have
been misplaced: to insert 121–5 between 116 and 117
makes good sense.

stars with trains of fire: Comets (rather than shooting
stars).

dews of blood: The phenomenon of 'red dews' is now
known to be caused by insects.

118 *Disasters*: (Astrological) unfavourable appearances:
here probably eclipses or sunspots.

the moist star: The moon (*moist* because of its relation
to the tides). The *influence* of its movements upon
marine tides was well known and accurately calculated
in Shakespeare's time; but the cause of the relation
between the moon and the oceans was not known.

119 *Neptune's empire*: The sea.

120 *sick almost to Doomsday*: On the Day of Judgement, it
was prophesied, the second coming of Christ would
be accompanied by eclipses of the sun and moon.
Scriptural language colours this whole passage; see
especially Matthew 24:29, Luke 21:25–6 and Revelation
6:12–13.

121 *precurse*: Forerunner.

feared: Q2 reads *feare*, which could easily be a
misreading of 'feard'.

122 *still*: Always.

123 *prologue*: This is the first instance of the theatrical
language which becomes prominent in the play.

omen: Ominous event, calamity.

125 *our*: The word is emphasized: such prodigies have
occurred not only in ancient Roman times but also in
the history of our own people. English history, as read
by the Elizabethans, contained a good many supernatural warnings, and in recent years several eclipses had

occurred, which superstitious persons (like Gloucester
in *King Lear*, I.2.103–4) regarded with anxiety.

climatures: Regions of the earth.

127 *cross it*: Stand in its path and so attempt to halt it. This
was a dangerous action.

He spreads his arms: Q2 has the direction *It spreads his
armes*. This would seem to refer to an action by the
Ghost. But the stage business required is that Horatio,
with arms outstretched, should *cross* the Ghost, and *It*
is usually regarded as an error for 'He'. Horatio thus
also resembles the Cross, which would repel the spirit
if it were of diabolical origin.

128 *illusion*: Presumably Horatio retains his scepticism
about the Ghost's true nature.

129–40 *If thou hast . . . Stay and speak*: Horatio interrogates
the Ghost and suggests, one by one, the usual explanations for its walking: (a) it needs something to be done
(for example, burial of its body) to give it rest; (b) it
is a warning spirit (a *harbinger* of *feared events*, such as
was discussed at 122–5); (c) it has buried treasure on
its conscience. Horatio does not reach, before the cock
crows, the fourth possible explanation – the true one:
(d) a demand of revenge for murder.

130, 133, 136 *Speak to me . . . O, speak*: The short lines no doubt
indicate pauses while Horatio awaits an answer.

135 *happily*: Haply (and perhaps also 'fortunately').

138 *Extorted*: Ill-gotten.

141 *partisan*: Pike with a broad head and (sometimes) a side
projection.

142 *stand*: Stop.

144 *being*: Since it is.

145–6 *offer it the show of violence, | For*: Offer it violence –
which is only a show of violence, because.

151 *trumpet*: Trumpeter.

152 *his*: Its.

shrill-sounding: High-pitched (not necessarily un-
pleasant).

153 *god of day*: Sun god, Phoebus Apollo.

his: The cock's.

155 *extravagant*: Vagrant outside its legitimate boundaries.
    erring: Wandering.
    hies: Hastens.

156 *confine*: Place of confinement.

157 *This present object made probation*: The Ghost that has
    just appeared affords a proof.

158–76 *It faded . . . conveniently*: From the spectral terrors of
    this night, the mood of the scene now changes to the
    contemplation of the health and grace of Christmas
    nights, and then to the dawn of the new day with a
    revival of courage and determination.

159–65 *Some say . . . that time*: This belief is not recorded else-
    where. Perhaps Shakespeare invented it for his theatrical
    purpose. Brilliantly written, it is also made plausible by
    Horatio's response (166).

159 *'gainst that season comes*: In expectation of that season.

162 *stir*: This is the Q2 reading; but *walk* in Q1 and F is
    the more appropriate word for a ghost.

163 *The nights are wholesome*: The night air was prover-
    bially bad for the health at ordinary times.
    strike: Exert their malign influence (presumably upon
    night travellers).

164 *takes*: Bewitches (not 'takes away').
    charm: Work magic.

165 *gracious*: Full of divine grace.

167–8 *the morn . . . hill*: The rising sun is personified as a
    countryman appearing on the horizon at the break of
    day.

167 *the morn*: The period of time between midnight (7) and
    dawn has been shortened for dramatic purposes.
    russet: The word can mean either 'grey' or 'reddish'.
    Either meaning would be suitable here; perhaps
    Shakespeare intended both. The light and colour replace
    the darkness and shadow of the early part of this
    episode.

171 *young Hamlet*: The first reference to the hero. The
    epithet, doubtless intended to differentiate him from the
    late King Hamlet, is the first indication of his youth-
    fulness, emphasized in the early part of the play.

Towards the end, he is felt to be older than the university student he was at the beginning. This does not mean that the time-scheme need include the passage of an equivalent amount of time. Shakespeare gives clear indications that Hamlet has matured, knowing that we shall not notice or protest that time has been inadequate.

I.2

It is not stated when exactly the marriage of Claudius and Gertrude, and their coronation, took place. This scene seems to be the first formal gathering after these events. We are perhaps given the impression that the Ghost began to walk three nights before, at the same time as the festivities commenced.

0 *Flourish*: This royal trumpet call would have been very prominent in production.

1 *our*: The King uses the 'royal plural', but sometimes in this speech *we*, *us* and *our* refer to the Danish nation.

2 *that*: A substitute for *Though* in the previous line.

4 *contracted*: Drawn together (like the *brow* in a frown). *in one brow of woe*: With unanimous sorrow.

5 *so far hath discretion fought with nature*: To such an extent has our prudence struggled against our natural affection. This is also the theme of the King's speech to Hamlet at 87–106.

7 *Together with remembrance of ourselves*: This goes closely with *think on him* and explains *wisest*.

8 *our sometime sister, now our Queen*: The reprehensible nature of the relation between the King and his Queen (his former sister-in-law) is at once emphasized. Such a marriage was explicitly forbidden by the 'Table of Kindred and Affinity, wherein whosoever are related are forbidden in scripture and our laws to marry together', first printed in 1563 and incorporated into the Book of Common Prayer.
sometime: Former.

9 *jointress*: Joint heretrix. No explanation is given of how Claudius's claim to the throne could be strengthened by his marriage to the late King's widow. It is not mentioned again.

    this warlike state: This reminds us of the condition of vigorous military preparedness initiated by King Claudius, already described at I.1.71–8.

10 *defeated*: Overcome (by its enemy, sorrow).

11 *With an auspicious and a dropping eye*: The comic or repulsive image (one eye smiling, the other weeping) is stronger in the F reading: *With one Auspicious, and one Dropping eye*.

13 *In equal scale weighing*: Weighing out an equal quantity of.
    dole: Grief.

14 *barred*: Kept out (of the discussion and the decision).

15–16 *Your better wisdoms . . . this affair along*: Claudius is shown as prudently consulting his Council of State and not as acting tyrannically; cf. IV.1.38–40.

17 *Now follows that you know*: The next matter for us to consider is something you know about already.

18 *weak supposal*: Low estimate.

20 *Our state to be disjoint and out of frame*: A curious anticipation (and refutation) of Hamlet's later *The time is out of joint*, I.5.188.
    frame: Order.

21 *Colleaguèd with*: Having as an (imaginary) ally and supporter. But perhaps this is the main verb (*Young Fortinbras* being the subject), with a full stop after *advantage*.
    dream of his advantage: Fanciful estimate of his superiority.

23 *Importing*: Concerning.

25 *our most valiant brother*: Claudius tactfully praises the late King, in the same way as he had shown his affection for *our dear brother* (1 and 19). Cf. Horatio's *our valiant Hamlet* (I.1.84).
    F gives the entry of Voltemand and Cornelius at this point. It probably means that they come forward, to kneel and to receive the King's letter and their commission (38) from his hands.

28 *Norway*: The King of Norway.

29 *impotent*: Helpless.

31 *gait*: Proceedings.

31 *in that*: Because.
32 *lists*: Enlistments.
    full proportions: Supporting forces and supplies.
33 *his subject*: Those subject to him.
35 *greeting*: Perhaps to be spoken ironically.
36–8 *no further . . . allow*: They are not plenipotentiaries but
    are to negotiate only in accordance with the limits laid
    down in Claudius's instructions.
38 *delated*: Set out in detail.
    allow: The plural form is used after *scope* because influ-
    enced by *articles*.
39 *let your haste commend your duty*: Show by your haste
    your high sense of duty.
42 *Laertes*: Accented on the second syllable: lay-ér-tees.
43 *suit*: Formal request.
44 *Speak of reason*: Make any reasonable request.
    Dane: King of Denmark.
45 *lose your voice*: Ask to no purpose.
    thou: The King shifts to the singular form and further
    softens to *my* (not 'our') *offer* at 46.
46 *That shall not be my offer, not thy asking*: 'whenever
    they call, I will answer them; while they are yet but
    thinking how to speak, I will hear them' (Isaiah 65:24).
47 *native*: By its very nature closely related.
48 *instrumental*: Serviceable.
49 *the throne of Denmark*: The King tactfully generalizes
    Polonius's personal services to him into a devotion to
    the whole royal family.
50 *dread*: Revered.
51 *leave and favour*: Kind permission.
    return to France: To Paris: II.1.7. Shakespeare carefully
    builds up Laertes as a *foil* (V.2.249) to Hamlet, by
    sending one to Paris, the other to Wittenberg.
53 *To show my duty in your coronation*: Laertes, as a loyal
    subject and the son of the principal minister, returned
    to swear fealty to the new King. Horatio says (176)
    that he has returned to see King Hamlet's funeral.
56 *bow*: As in entreaty.
    pardon: Permission to depart.

57 *Polonius*: Pronounced with the first 'o' short and the second 'o' (accented) long. This is Latin for 'of Poland': a surprising choice for the name of the principal minister of Denmark in a play which involves the conquest of part of the adjacent kingdom of Poland. In real life there is no reason why someone who happened to be named Mr Britain should not be President of the United States, or a M. Langlais Minister of Defence in France. But in fiction we expect things to be more carefully arranged.

58–61 *He hath . . . go*: Polonius's first speech is characterful: he takes thirty-three words to say 'yes'.

58 *slow*: Reluctantly given.

60 *will*: Perhaps punning on the sense 'testament', which needs to have a *seal* impressed upon it.
hard: Obtained with difficulty.

62 *Take thy fair hour*: Enjoy your time of youth.
Time be thine: (Presumably) stay away as long as you please. The King grants Laertes's request and dismisses him. But it would presumably be a violation of court etiquette to insert an exit for Laertes: he withdraws to the side, and can watch Hamlet, in preparation for his talk to Ophelia in the next scene.

64 *my cousin Hamlet, and my son*: Perhaps Claudius keeps his stepson (*son*) waiting while he dispatches other business; thus Hamlet is kept in his place. Certainly Claudius's refusal to permit Hamlet's return to Wittenberg contrasts with his treatment of Laertes.

65 *A little more than kin, and less than kind*: This must be spoken aside, as it interrupts Claudius's sentence. Hamlet's first words are, characteristically, a sardonic and cryptic pun. As Claudius's nephew he is more than a *cousin*, but he resents being called *son*, for any natural relationship (*kind*), such as a father and son feel, is impossible between them. Perhaps *kind* also means 'kindly' but we see no action of the King towards Hamlet which is not, at least on the surface, affectionate.

66 *the clouds still hang on you*: Hamlet's disaffection and melancholy, evident in his costume, are stressed after

we have seen the King deal efficiently with state business.

67 *too much in the sun*: Another cryptic pun: presumably Hamlet refers to Claudius's *my son* (64) as well as to his being in the sunshine of court favour. He insinuates his resentment at having been deprived of the succession and at his new position of Claudius's stepson.

68 *nighted colour*: His black mourning garments and his melancholy.

69 *Denmark*: The King of Denmark.

70 *vailèd lids*: Downcast eyelids.

75 *particular*: Personal.

78 *customary*: Either 'following the conventions of society in wearing mourning for several months' or 'having now become usual with me'.

79 *windy suspiration of forced breath*: An elaborate phrase for 'uncontrollable sighs'.

80 *fruitful*: Flowing copiously.

82 *moods*: Modes, appearances.
   shapes: In theatrical language, 'assumed roles'.

83 *denote*: Portray.

84 *play*: Like an actor.

85 *passes*: Surpasses, goes beyond.

86 *These*: Both his clothes and his general behaviour.

87 *commendable*: Accented on the first syllable.

90 *That father*: Your grandfather.
   bound: Was bound.

92 *obsequious*: Dutifully mourning in a way appropriate to his obsequies.
   persever: Accented on the second syllable.

93 *condolement*: Sorrowing.

95 *incorrect to heaven*: Behaving contrary to piety.

96 *unfortified*: Against the inevitable misfortunes of life.
   impatient: Lacking in the important Christian virtue of patience.

99 *any the most vulgar thing to sense*: (Death is as common as) the most familiar experience we could have through our senses.

100 *peevish*: Obstinate, foolish.

103–4 *whose . . . who*: Reason.

104 *still*: Always.

105 *the first corse*: Actually the first *corse* ('corpse') in the
    world's history was a son and brother (Abel) not a
    father (Genesis 4:8). Further allusions to the biblical
    fratricide are at III.3.37–8 and V.1.77.

107 *unprevailing*: Unavailing.

109 *the most immediate*: Closest in succession. Hamlet's
    position as heir under a quasi-elective system is strong.
    Ophelia testifies to his courtly qualities (III.1.151–5)
    and Claudius to his being loved by the people (IV.3.4
    and IV.7.18). Claudius seeks to placate Hamlet with
    the expectation that his succession to the throne has
    been merely postponed. But with this public declara-
    tion he loses some of his power: by taking a secret
    revenge, Hamlet could now easily achieve the throne.
    It is only when Hamlet's disaffection shows him to be
    apparently irresponsible and dangerous and (eventu-
    ally) to know about the fratricide that Claudius changes
    his intention about the succession. Shakespeare shows
    Claudius not as a usurper, but as duly elected. Later,
    facing death, Hamlet himself supports the election of
    Fortinbras, and Horatio thinks that this recommenda-
    tion will win Fortinbras more votes (V.2.349–50 and
    382–6).

112 *I*: Claudius adopts the singular pronoun when he
    addresses Hamlet as a *father* to a *son*.
    impart toward: Bestow (my affection) upon. The syntax
    seems awkward; *with* at 110 expects a different verb.
    For: as for.

113 *school*: University. Wittenberg was famous as Luther's
    university (founded in 1502), where in 1517 he nailed
    up his ninety-five theses. Elizabethan audiences also
    knew it as Dr Faustus's university, from Marlowe's
    play.

114 *retrograde*: Contrary.

115 *bend you*: Incline yourself (imperative).

117 *cousin*: Probably a vocative.

120 *I shall . . . obey you, madam*: Hamlet pointedly accedes
     to his mother's appeal to his affection, not to the King's
     ingratiating plea. But the King, with skilful tact, appro-
     priates Hamlet's compliance as *a loving and a fair reply*.
     in all my best: In so far as I can.

127 *rouse*: Bumper of wine.
     bruit: Echo.

129–59 *O that this too too sullied . . . hold my tongue*: The impor-
        tance of this soliloquy lies in its establishing Hamlet's
        personality and revealing his mental condition. The
        syntax is abrupt; the sentences progress by increments
        and interruptions; exclamations are followed by clari-
        fications, questions, and imperatives.

129 *sullied*: Q2 reads *sallied* (which could be a spelling of
     sullied). F reads *solid*, which contrasts well with *melt*, |
     Thaw, and resolve itself . . . and until the twentieth
     century was generally preferred by editors. But it may
     have an unpleasantly comic effect, especially if Richard
     Burbage, the actor who first played Hamlet, were
     putting on weight (cf. *He's fat and scant of breath*,
     V.2.281). *sullied* fits well into the feeling of contami-
     nation expressed by Hamlet; and for *sullies* (F *sulleyes*)
     at II.1.39 Q2 has the spelling *sallies*.

130 *resolve*: Dissolve.

132 *His canon 'gainst self-slaughter*: The sixth command-
     ment, 'Thou shalt not kill' (Exodus 20:13), was gener-
     ally regarded as a sufficient condemnation of suicide.
     canon: Religious law.

134 *all the uses*: The whole routine of affairs.

136 *rank*: Coarsely luxuriant.

137 *merely*: Completely.

139, 140 *to this . . . to a satyr*: Compared to this . . . compared
          to a satyr.

140 *Hyperion to a satyr*: Hamlet's insistence (here and at
     III.4.65–103) on Claudius's unworthiness for the king-
     ship is not corroborated by what Claudius does before
     the eyes of the audience, at any rate in the first half of
     the play. We are doubtless expected to feel that Hamlet
     is exaggerating Claudius's incompetence, while we

share his moral indignation at the homicide and incest.
Hyperion: The sun god. See also III.4.57. From his
scansion here and in other plays it is clear that
Shakespeare thought the accent was on the second
syllable. Owing to the influence of these two famous
passages in *Hamlet* and to false analogy with such names
as Tiberius and Valerius, the customary pronunciation
has become 'high-peer-i-on', and more 'correct'
pronunciations – 'hipper-eye-on' or 'highper-eye-on'
– would be intolerable.

satyr: Pronounced 'satter'. In classical mythology a
satyr had a goat's legs, tail, ears and budding horns,
the rest of his form being human.

141 *beteem*: Permit.

146 *Frailty, thy name is woman*: Shakespeare early establishes Hamlet's generalizing frame of mind.

147 *or e'er*: Before. Cf. 183 below. Probably Shakespeare
and his contemporaries supposed the second word to
be 'ever'. In fact both *or* and *e'er* (or *ere*) are forms of
the same word, meaning 'before'.

149 *Niobe*: The type of the grieving mother – her seven
sons and seven daughters were slain by Apollo and
Diana. She shed so many tears that she was turned into
stone.

150 *wants discourse of reason*: Lacks the (human) faculty of
reason.

153 *Hercules*: The amount of classical allusion (*Hyperion*,
satyr, *Niobe*, *Hercules*) by the university-educated
Hamlet is doubtless intended to be a character-
indication.

154 *unrighteous*: Impiously insincere.

155 *Had left the flushing in her gallèd eyes*: Had had time to
cause redness in her eyes, that her salt tears had made
sore; or, perhaps, 'had left off causing redness . . .'
Here *flushing* means 'reddening', not 'filling with
water'.

156 *post*: Hasten.

157 *dexterity*: Facility.

159 *break, my heart*: A powerful phrase which derived its

currency from its use in the Bible: 'He healeth those
that are broken in heart' (Psalm 147:3; also 51:17
(Geneva Bible, 1587) and 69:20; Isaiah 61:1 (Geneva
Bible); Luke 4:16–18). Cf. *Now cracks a noble heart*
(V.2.353). The modern use of the phrase as referring
sentimentally to amorous disappointment came much
later.

160 *I am glad to see you well*: At first, Hamlet merely gives
a polite reply; then he recognizes Horatio.

163 *I'll change that name with you*: I will be your *servant*,
instead of your being mine.

164 *make you from*: Are you doing away from.

165 *Marcellus*: Presumably Hamlet recognizes Marcellus.
He greets Barnardo formally as if not previously known
to him, though Barnardo seems to be of the same military rank as Marcellus. Horatio refers to them as
gentlemen (194 and 196).

169 *A truant disposition*: A disposition to play truant (from
his university studies).

175 *teach you to drink deep*: Probably ironical, perhaps
prompted by a piece of stage business such as the
passing of a drink-laden servant or a burst of drunken
hilarity offstage.

180 *Thrift, thrift*: The repetition of words is soon felt to be
characteristic of Hamlet. Cf. 224 and 237 below. But
these are more common in F than in Q2; so they may
be due to an actor's affectation of a trick of speech.

180–81 *The funeral baked meats | Did coldly furnish forth the
marriage tables*: Hamlet's bitter jest seems to derive
from the King's remark about *mirth in funeral* and *dirge
in marriage* (12). There was of course *A little month*
(147) between the ceremonies.

180 *baked meats*: Pies.

181 *coldly*: As cold dishes.

182 *dearest*: Closest, and therefore deadliest.

185 *Where, my lord*: Horatio, who has come to give the
news of the Ghost, is momentarily startled by the
thought that Hamlet is himself seeing an apparition.

186 *once*: This seems inconsistent with I.1.59–63 (which

implies that Horatio was thoroughly familiar with
King Hamlet's appearance) and with 211–12 and 241
below.

187 *'A was a man*: Hamlet has a view of moral worth largely
based on stoical ideals. This is elaborated in his description of Horatio in III.2.75–81.

192 *Season your admiration*: Control your amazement.

193 *attent*: Attentive.
deliver: Report.

198 *dead waste*: Desolate time (of night), as still as death.
Q1 reads *dead vast*, which many editors have found
attractive.

200 *at point*: (As if) in readiness.
cap-a-pe: From head to foot.

203 *oppressed*: Distressed, troubled.

204 *truncheon*: Military baton.
distilled: Melted.

205 *act*: Effect.

207 *dreadful*: Full of dread.

212 *These hands are not more like*: These hands are not more
like each other than the Ghost was like your father. An
expressive gesture for the actor.

216 *it*: Its.

216–17 *address . . . would*: Begin to move as if it were about
to.

222 *writ down*: Prescribed.

229 *Then saw you not his face*: Hamlet is testing his inform-
ants. This may be a question, or a statement of in-
ference which throws doubt upon their story of
recognizing the late King Hamlet.

230 *beaver*: Visor of a helmet (the movable upper part which
could be drawn down over the face for protection but
was normally kept in the lifted position except when
fighting).

235 *constantly*: Unchangingly, fixedly.

236 *amazed*: (A strong word) confounded.

238 *tell*: Count.

240 *grizzled*: Grey.

242 *A sable silvered*: Black streaked with white.

242 *watch*: Keep the watch (with you). But the everyday meaning of *watch* was 'stay awake'.

243 *warrant*: Guarantee.

248 *tenable in your silence*: Kept secret.

249 *whatsomever*: Whatsoever.

251 *requite your loves*: Reward your affectionate behaviour.

254 *loves*: Not merely *duty*.

256 *doubt*: Suspect. Hamlet is already suspicious of the cause of his father's death, and the Ghost's revelations confirm his *prophetic soul* (I.5.40).

257–8 *Foul deeds . . . men's eyes*: Cf. II.2.591–2.

I.3

This scene informs the audience of the strong family feeling in Polonius's family. Laertes's love for his sister Ophelia, whom we see for the first time, and their regard for their father, in spite of his foibles, prepare for the violence of Laertes's impulses to revenge later. There is nothing to show that Laertes and Ophelia are contemptuous of Polonius's long-windedness.

1 *necessaries*: Personal baggage for the journey.

2–3 *as the winds give benefit | And convoy is assistant*: Whenever the wind is favourable for the sailing of a ship to France and whenever any other means of sending a letter is available.

5 *For Hamlet, and the trifling of his favour*: This remark introduces the love affair between Hamlet and Ophelia. Both Polonius and Laertes suppose that Hamlet has only a passing interest in the girl and that, since they see no hope of a royal marriage for their family, she will be either jilted or seduced. Yet she is the second lady in the land and might seem eligible.

6 *fashion*: Modish way of behaving.
   a toy in blood: Mere whim of amorous passion.

7 *violet*: It was proverbial for transient existence, as well as being associated with love.
   the youth of primy nature: Its spring-like prime.

8 *Forward*: Blossoming precociously early.

9 *suppliance*: Pastime.

11 *crescent*: Increasing by the passage of time.

alone: Only.

12   *thews*: Muscles, bodily strength.

     this temple: The human body that each of us possesses
     (a biblical phrase: 'ye are the temple of God' (1
     Corinthians 3:16, etc.)).

13   *inward service*: Faculties which are not visible in our
     physical exterior.

14   *withal*: Also. Laertes is suggesting that Hamlet will
     soon grow out of his shallow love for Ophelia. These
     lines suggest Hamlet's youth.

15   *soil*: Blemish.

     cautel: Deceitfulness.

16   *will*: Sexual impulse, as well as 'intentions'; and Laertes
     continues the complex meanings of *will* by using it at
     17 as 'faculty of making decisions'.

     fear: Be anxious about the fact that.

17   *His greatness weighed*: If you take into account his high
     rank.

18   *he himself is subject to his birth*: He may be a member
     of the royal family and we his subjects, but he too is
     subject to the princely rank into which he was born.
     This line was omitted from Q2, presumably by acci-
     dent.

19   *unvalued persons*: Those whose social and political posi-
     tion is of no importance.

20   *Carve for himself*: Make his own choice of a royal consort
     (like one who chooses to take his own slice of meat at
     the dinner table).

     choice: Of a wife.

23   *voice*: Declared opinion (or approval).

     yielding: Compliance.

     body: Nation (the 'body politic').

26   *he in his particular act and place*: One who is in his
     personal position (as a prince). But the text may be
     wrong, for F reads the even more difficult phrase *he in
     his peculiar Sect and force*.

27   *give his saying deed*: Fulfil by his actions what his words
     promise.

28   *main voice*: Majority opinion.

28 *withal*: Along with.

30 *credent*: Trustful.

   list: Listen to.

   songs: Seductive avowals of love.

32 *unmastered*: Uncontrolled.

34 *keep you in the rear of your affection*: Do not go as far as your feelings would lead you.

35 *shot*: Feelings of love were often imagined as provoked by Cupid's arrows. But here perhaps the image is from gunshot.

36 *chariest*: Most cautious.

   prodigal enough: Quite sufficiently prodigal (if she does no more than *unmask her beauty* merely *to the* chaste *moon*, whose pale light will show little of it).

39 *canker*: Canker-worm or caterpillar.

   galls: Injures.

   infants of the spring: Young spring-time plants.

40 *buttons*: Flower-buds.

   disclosed: Opened out.

41–2 *in the morn . . . most imminent*: It is in the moist air of the morning that infectious diseases are most likely to strike. Similarly, it is young people who are especially vulnerable.

42 *blastments*: Blights.

43 *Best safety lies in fear*: To be afraid of doing something dangerous is the best way of keeping safe.

44 *Youth to itself rebels, though none else near*: Young people are both frightened and adventurous. Their fearfulness is in conflict with their adventurousness, and may keep them safe when no other help is available. Or perhaps: the passions of youth lead to instinctive rebellion against self-restraint, even though no temptation is near.

47 *ungracious*: Without grace.

   pastors: The word is carefully chosen. The 'good shepherd', unlike the *ungracious pastors*, will 'put forth his own sheep; he goeth before them, and the sheep follow him' (John 10:4).

48 *the steep and thorny way to heaven*: This, and *the prim-rose path of dalliance* (50), seem to derive from Matthew

7:13–14: 'Wide is the gate, and broad is the way, that leadeth to destruction . . . Strait is the gate, and narrow is the way, which leadeth unto life.'

49 *puffed*: Swollen with pride (or excess).

50 *primrose path of dalliance*: Similar phrases are used in *All's Well That Ends Well*, IV.5.51–3: 'the flowery way that leads to the broad gate and the great fire', and by the Porter in *Macbeth*, II.3.18: 'the primrose way to the everlasting bonfire'.

51 *recks not his own rede*: Disregards his own advice.
   fear me not: Don't worry about me.

53 *A double blessing*: Laertes has already once said goodbye to his father and received his blessing.

54 *Occasion smiles upon a second leave*: It is a lucky chance when there is a second leave-taking.

56 *sits in the shoulder of your sail*: An elaborate way of saying 'is favourable'.

57 *There*: Polonius places his hand on the head of the kneeling Laertes.

59 *Look*: Be sure that.
   character: Inscribe (accented on the second syllable).

60 *unproportioned*: Inappropriate to the circumstances (or perhaps 'badly calculated' and so 'reckless').
   his: Its.

61 *Be thou familiar, but by no means vulgar*: Be affable in dealing with others, but don't make yourself cheap among the common people.

62 *and their adoption tried*: Once their association in friendship with you has been tested.

64 *do not dull thy palm*: So that your handshake becomes meaningless, or so that you lose your power of discrimination among true friends.

65 *courage*: Young man of bravado. F reads *Comrade*.

67 *Bear't*: Sustain it, carry it through.

68 *voice*: Spoken opinion, support.

69 *Take each man's censure*: Take notice of the opinions expressed by other people (on any matter).

71 *expressed in fancy*: Designed in some peculiar and fanciful way.

74 *Are of a most select and generous*: (Perhaps) show their refined and well-bred taste. But the line is difficult to interpret, and its twelve syllables suggest an error in the text.

    chief in that: Especially in that respect (of good taste in clothes).

77 *husbandry*: Thrift.

81 *season this in thee*: In due season bring my good advice to fruition in you (or 'make it palatable').

83 *invites you*: Requests your presence.

    tend: Attend you.

90 *Marry*: A mild oath: 'by the Virgin Mary'.

    well bethought: Well remembered ('I am glad you reminded me'; or perhaps 'That was a good idea of his').

93 *audience*: Attention (to what Hamlet has said).

94 *put on me*: Impressed upon me.

101 *green*: Inexperienced.

102 *Unsifted*: Untried.

107 *Tender*: Polonius puns on *tenders* meaning 'offers' (103, 106 and 99) and to *Tender* (107) meaning 'look after' or 'have a proper esteem for'.

108 *crack the wind*: The image is from the excessive galloping of a horse or over-exertion of a hound, which will get the stitch.

109 *tender me a fool*: As the father of a girl who is intriguing with the heir to the throne, or who has been seduced; or perhaps 'exhibit yourself to me as a fool, a girl who has been seduced'. Ophelia's reply shows that she understands her father to think she might be seduced.

111 *fashion*: Ophelia uses the word simply as 'manner', but Polonius interprets it like Laertes at 6 above.

112 *Go to*: An interjection of impatience.

113 *countenance*: Support, favourable appearance.

115 *springes to catch woodcocks*: Proverbially the woodcock was a foolish bird which easily fell into snares (*springes*, pronounced to rhyme with 'hinges'). Cf. *as a woodcock to mine own springe* (V.2.300).

116 *prodigal*: Prodigally.

118 *extinct in both*: Both the light and heat of which are extinguished.

121 *something*: Somewhat.

122 *your entreatments*: His solicitations of your favour.

123 *a command to parle*: An invitation to carry on a love conversation with him. Polonius sees the relationship between Hamlet and Ophelia as a siege of her chastity.

125 *with a larger tether*: With a longer tethering-rope (and so with less control).

126 *In few*: In brief.

127 *brokers*: Go-betweens.

128 *investments*: Garments (especially of a religious or otherwise imposing kind).

129 *implorators*: Solicitors.

130 *Breathing*: Speaking persuasively.
    bawds: This is an emendation of *bonds* (Q2 and F), which has been defended as meaning 'marriage bonds'.

131 *beguile*: Cheat.
    This is for all: To sum up.

133 *slander*: Misuse.
    moment: Moment's.

135 *Come your ways*: Come away.

I.4

0 *Enter Hamlet, Horatio, and Marcellus*: Barnardo is not now included in the group, though from I.2.225 and 253 we are led to expect him. As a sentinel he could not abandon his post; and it would be awkward to leave him on stage when Horatio and Marcellus rush off after Hamlet.

1 *shrewdly*: 'Wickedly', sharply.

2 *eager*: Biting.

3 *lacks of*: Is a little before.

5 *season*: Time of day.

6 *pieces of ordnance*: The gun salutes honour Hamlet's *gentle and unforced accord* (I.2.123), so celebrate a kind of triumph of the King over Hamlet.

8 *The King doth wake tonight . . .*: Cf. I.2.124–8.
    doth wake: Stays awake, holds a late-night revel.
    rouse: Bumper of wine.

9 *Keeps wassail*: Gives a drinking-party.

swaggering upspring reels: Probably the rare noun *upspring* indicates some kind of Teutonic dance which Shakespeare introduces as local colour.

10 *Rhenish*: Rhineland wine (imported in large quantities into England in Shakespeare's time).

12 *The triumph of his pledge*: His glorious achievement as a drinker of toasts (usually that of drinking a vessel of wine down at one draught).

15 *to the manner born*: Habituated to it from my birth.

16 *More honoured in the breach than the observance*: Which it is more honourable to disregard than to keep.

17–38 *This heavy-headed . . . scandal*: This passage about the drunkenness of the Danes is not in F. Probably it seemed tactless after the accession of James VI of Scotland to the English throne, with his Danish consort, Anne.

17 *heavy-headed*: Presumably the *revel* causes heavy heads, rather than being characterized by them.

east and west: (Presumably) throughout the length and breadth of Denmark (but perhaps the phrase goes with *Makes us traduced* and means 'throughout Europe').

18 *Makes us traduced and taxed of*: Causes us to be calumniated and to have faults imputed to us by.

19 *clepe us*: Describe us as.

with swinish phrase: In comparing us to pigs.

20 *Soil*: Blemish.

addition: Honorary title (and so 'good name').

it: The Danish custom of drunkenness.

21 *though performed at height*: Though they are the summit of our endeavour.

22 *our attribute*: The reputation attributed to us by others.

23 *particular men*: Individuals.

24 *vicious mole of nature*: Natural blemish.

25 *As*: For instance.

26 *his*: Its.

27 *o'ergrowth of some complexion*: Overdevelopment of some natural trait.

28 *pales*: Fences.

29 *habit*: Acquired habit.

too much o'er-leavens: Has too strong an effect upon (like something damaged by excessive fermentation).

30 *form of plausive*: Behaviour resulting from pleasing.

32 *Being nature's livery or fortune's star*: Which is due either to their subservience to nature or to the influence of ill fortune (the *defect* is either natural or accidental).

33 *His*: So Q2, and probably the shift from plural to singular is Shakespeare's; but some editors emend to 'Their'.

virtues else: Other qualities.

34 *may undergo*: Can support.

35 *general censure*: Overall opinion of him.

35–6 *take corruption | From*: Be falsely esteemed because of. Hamlet means that a man may have many virtues and one fault, but this one fault will so damage his reputation that his virtues will be misjudged.

36–8 *The dram of evil . . . scandal*: These words do not make grammatical sense. It seems best to take the rather complicated sentence as broken off in the middle by the Ghost's appearance.

36 *dram*: Tiny quantity.

evil: Q2 prints *eale* (Q1 and F omit this passage), perhaps a misreading of 'evil'.

37 *of a doubt*: Plausible emendations are 'oft adulter' ('often adulterate or corrupt') and 'often dout' ('often efface').

38 *his*: That man's.

scandal: Shame.

39 *ministers of grace*: Messengers from God.

40–41 *Be thou . . . from hell*: Hamlet has initial doubts about the Ghost, but these are soon displaced by his (and the audience's) conviction that it is a veritable vision of his father. On two later occasions Hamlet suspects that *The spirit that I have seen | May be a devil*, which *Abuses me to damn me* (II.2.596–601 and III.2.92).

40 *Be thou*: Whether you are.

spirit of health: Benevolent spirit (or possibly 'saved soul').

40 *goblin damned*: Evil spirit that has suffered damnation.

41 *Bring*: Whether you bring.

42 *Be thy intents*: Whether your intentions are.

43 *questionable*: Inviting interrogation by me (since you appear like my father).

44 *call thee*: Invoke you by the name of.

47 *thy canonized bones, hearsèd in death*: Hamlet's father had been properly buried with all due religious rites (see the note to I.1.129–40).
   canonized: Consecrated by Christian burial (accented on the second syllable).
   hearsèd: Coffined.

48 *cerements*: Waxed shroud (two syllables, pronounced 'seer–').

49 *interred*: F's reading, *enurn'd*, is attractive, although the Roman-style obsequies of placing ashes in an urn would be inconsistent with the Christian burial of the shrouded body (the *canonized bones* in their *cerements*). Possibly *enurn'd* merely means 'put into a coffin'.

52 *complete steel*: Full armour.
   complete: Accented on the first syllable.

53 *the glimpses of the moon*: The earth illuminated by the uncertain light of the moon.

54 *fools of nature*: Weak creatures limited by nature (but now having to face experience of the supernatural).

55 *horridly*: Probably with the notion of 'making our hair stand on end'.
   disposition: Composure of feelings.

56 *reaches*: Capacity.

59 *impartment*: Communication.

65 *a pin's fee*: The value of a trifle.

69 *flood*: Sea.

71 *beetles*: Projects.

73 *your sovereignty of reason*: Your reason of its control over you.

75 *toys of desperation*: Fanciful impulses leading to despair (and suicide).

82 *petty*: (Relatively) weak.
   artere: Channel through which flowed the 'vital spirits'

(not the blood; two syllables: an alternative form of 'artery').

83 *Nemean lion*: The killing of the terrible lion of Nemea was one of the twelve labours of Hercules.
Nemean: Accented on the first syllable, which is short: 'nemm-ee-an'.

85 *lets*: Hinders.

87 *waxes*: Becomes increasingly.

89 *Have after*: I will follow.

91 *Nay*: A mild contradiction to *Heaven will direct it*, implying that they themselves can do something.

1.5

3 *sulphurous and tormenting flames*: This sounds more like hell than the purgatory referred to in 9–13 below.

6 *bound*: Ready (but the Ghost takes it to mean 'obliged').

11 *fast*: Do penance.

12 *foul crimes*: The Ghost does not necessarily imply that he has been particularly wicked, but refers to the common situation of a sinner in this mortal life.
my days of nature: This mortal life.

17 *spheres*: In which the heavenly bodies normally moved: see the note to IV.7.15.

19 *an*: On.

20 *fretful porpentine*: Porcupine when it has become angry. Q2 has *fearefull* ('timid') for F's *fretfull*.

21 *eternal blazon*: Revelation about what has been appointed for all eternity.

25, 28 *unnatural*: Because contrary to family feeling.

27 *in the best*: Even at best.

30 *meditation*: Thought.

32 *shouldst thou be*: You would have to be.

32–3 *the fat weed | That roots itself in ease on Lethe wharf*: Lethe is a river of Hades: according to the classical poets, it caused oblivion in those who drank it. The word *wharf* is used because the spirits were supposed to embark on Charon's boat in order to cross the river. As *the fat weed* Shakespeare may have had in mind asphodel, which grew in the fields of Hades.

33 *roots*: F reads *rots*, which perhaps gives a more

expressive meaning and is supported by *Antony and Cleopatra*, I.4.45–7.

35 *orchard*: Garden (as at III.2.270).

36–8 *the whole ear of Denmark . . . abused*: Old Hamlet's anticipation of his account of his own poisoned ear (63–4; see also III.2.144, stage direction) is almost like one of his son's characteristic puns. The many allusions in the play to ears (especially damaged ones) – e.g. I.1.31, I.2.171, II.2.475 and 560, III.2.10, III.4.65 and 96, and IV.5.91 – produce a half-conscious reminder of the circumstances of the murder.

37 *forgèd process*: Fabricated official report.

38 *abused*: Deceived.

40 *prophetic soul*: See I.2.255–8.

42 *adulterate*: This word, and the whole passage 42–57, seem to imply that Claudius had seduced Gertrude before her husband's death. But nothing in the rest of the play supports this, except perhaps Hamlet's *whored my mother* (V.2.64) and, conceivably, Horatio's words *carnal . . . acts* (V.2.375). In the play of *The Murder of Gonzago* the wooing definitely takes place after the poisoning (III.2.144, stage direction, and 270–73).

47 *falling off*: Both 'decline in moral standards' and 'desertion'.

50–51 *decline | Upon*: Sink to the level of.

52 *To*: In comparison with.

53 *virtue as it*: As virtue.

54 *lewdness*: Lust.
   a shape of heaven: A physical appearance of angelic attractiveness.

56 *sate itself in a celestial bed*: Grow weary of sexual union with a lawful and virtuous partner. The F and Q1 reading *sate* seems to be required, against Q2's *sort* ('separate'), which gives only a strained meaning.

57 *garbage*: (Originally) the offal and entrails of animals.

61 *secure*: Thoughtlessly unguarded (accented on the first syllable).

62 *juice of cursèd hebona*: It is doubtful what precisely Shakespeare and his contemporaries meant by this

poison. F uses the form *Hebenon*. The word is related
to 'ebony', but here it seems to be combined with some
of the qualities of henbane.

63 *porches of my ears*: Poisoning through the ears was a
legendary Italian method; but according to medical
authority it could not be effective.

64 *leperous distilment*: Distillation causing a disease like
leprosy (still fairly common in Shakespeare's England).

67 *gates and alleys*: The body is represented under the
image of a city.

68 *sudden*: Rapid in action.

vigour: Power, efficacy.

posset: Curdle (so that the blood is clotted). A posset
was a drink made from milk curdled with wine or ale.

69 *eager*: Sharp, sour (and so curdling the milk).

70 *thin*: Not curdled into clots.

71 *tetter*: Scurf.

barked about: Coated with a *crust*.

72 *lazar-like*: Like leprosy (the disease usually attributed
to the beggar Lazarus in Luke 16:20).

75 *dispatched*: Deprived.

76–9 *Cut off . . . With all my imperfections on my head*: Hamlet
remembers this at III.3.80–81.

76 *in the blossoms of my sin*: When my sins were at their
height.

77 *Unhouseled*: Without having received the sacrament.

disappointed: Unprepared (for death, as having had no
opportunity for repentance, confession, and absolution).

unaneled: (Rhyming with 'healed') without having been
given extreme unction.

78 *reckoning*: Assessing and settling of my debts (his sins)
to God.

my account: At God's judgement seat.

80 *O . . . Most horrible*: On the stage, from Garrick's time,
this line has often been transferred to Prince Hamlet.
The interruption serves to break up the Ghost's long
speech.

81 *nature*: Natural feelings of a son for a father.

83 *luxury*: Lechery.

86 *Leave her to heaven*: Entrust her to God's judgement. According to usual religious teaching, revenge upon Claudius should also be left *to heaven*.

89 *matin*: Morning.

90 *uneffectual*: Becoming feeble as day dawns. The glow-worm's *fire* contrasts imaginatively with the purgatorial fires to which the Ghost is about to return (11–13).

92 *host of heaven*: Angels.

93 *couple hell*: Include hell in my invocation.

   O, fie: Presumably a rejection of the powers of hell.

   Hold: Hold together, remain unbroken.

94 *instant*: Immediately.

95 *stiffly*: Strongly. This is F's reading; Q2 has *swiftly*, which, though awkward, perhaps has some support from 29–30.

97 *this distracted globe*: Probably his head, which he holds, rather than the world itself or 'the little world of man'.

98 *the table of my memory*: My memory, which is now like a memorandum tablet on which experience writes. The *table* was generally made of thin leaves of ivory or slate, from which one could *wipe away* previous *records* or notes. The customary contents of such notebooks are listed in 99–101.

99 *fond*: Foolish.

   records: Accented on the second syllable.

100 *saws*: (Usually somewhat derogatory) wise sayings, platitudes.

    forms: General ideas.

    pressures past: Impressions previously received.

110 *there you are*: I have set down my comment on you, accordingly, in my notebook.

    word: Watchword, motto (or perhaps 'promise given').

113 *secure him*: Keep him safe.

114 *So be it*: Either a continuation of his own thought, *I have sworn't*, or a response to Horatio's *Heavens secure him!*

115 *Illo, ho, ho*: Originally the falconer's cry in calling a hawk down.

116 *Come, bird, come*: In his excited mood, Hamlet mocks his friends' cries as if they were birdcalls.

121 *once think it*: Ever believe what the Ghost has told me.

124 *But he's an arrant knave*: Probably Hamlet intends to say 'who is worse than King Claudius', or something similar, but checks himself, deciding not to tell anyone what the Ghost has revealed to him.

127 *without more circumstance*: Cutting the matter short.

136 *Saint Patrick*: Hamlet swears by him because Saint Patrick was a keeper of purgatory (whence the Ghost comes), having found an entrance to it in Donegal; or perhaps because he banished serpents from Ireland (see *Richard II*, II.1.157–8), and Hamlet's task is to get rid of a *serpent* (39).

137 *much offence*: Hamlet deliberately mistakes Horatio's word *offence* and takes it as concerning the revelation of the Ghost, which has told him of the terrible *offence* of Claudius.

138 *honest ghost*: Hamlet assures them that the Ghost is a *spirit of health*, not a *goblin damned* (I.4.40).

141 *scholars, and soldiers*: Probably generic, including Horatio in the one category and Marcellus in the other.

142 *Give*: Grant.

146 *not I*: I will never make known what I have seen. (Horatio is not refusing to take the oath.)

147 *Upon my sword*: The handle of a sword forms a cross upon which an oath can be administered. Hamlet is not content with oaths *in faith*.

149 *Swear*: The Ghost's insistence on, or approval of, the oath upon the hilt of the sword as a Cross and its response to the appeals to God's mercy at 169 and 180 are further evidence that it is not a diabolical tempter. Presumably Hamlet's mockery of the Ghost is intended to conceal from Horatio and Marcellus how seriously he takes it and its revelations.

150 *truepenny*: Honest fellow.

151 *You hear this fellow*: It is not certain that they do hear the Ghost any more than the Queen does in III.4.103–40.

151 *cellarage*: Not a particularly appropriate word for a *platform* (I.2.252). But the space under the stage in the Elizabethan theatre was known as the cellarage.

153 *Never to speak of this that you have seen*: The first oath concerns what they have *seen*, the second, what they have *heard* (from each other, not the Ghost), the third, Hamlet's subsequent behaviour (170–79). So it seems that they swear three times, though no words are given to them. But the scene is usually played as if their words were interrupted by the Ghost at 155 and 161, and only at 181 do they silently complete their oaths (see the note).

156 *Hic et ubique*: (Latin) here and everywhere?
     Then we'll shift our ground: Hamlet seems to move his companions around inexplicably. But Horatio and Marcellus perhaps flee in terror from the spot whence the Ghost's voice comes, and Hamlet follows them to different parts of the stage.

163 *pioneer*: Miner.

165 *stranger*: Punningly, alluding to the proverb that a guest (*stranger*) should be received hospitably, with no questions asked.

167 *your philosophy*: The exact meaning of *your* is difficult to decide. It may refer to Horatio's rationalist philosophy (he was established as a sceptic at I.1.23–32); or *your philosophy* may express a general disdain for rationalizing explanations, not Horatio's modes of thought particularly.

169 *help you mercy*: May God's mercy save you at his judgement seat

170 *How strange or odd some'er I bear myself*: Hamlet's assumption of madness in order to lull suspicion seems to have been an essential element in the Hamlet story, and would be expected by an audience familiar with the earlier play on the stage.

172 *antic*: Fantastically disguised.

174 *encumbered*: Folded.

176 *an if*: If.

177 *list*: Wished.

There be, an if they might: There *are* persons – meaning
themselves – who could explain things if only they
were at liberty to do so.

178 *giving out*: Intimation.

to note: To draw attention to the fact.

179 *know aught*: Have confidential knowledge.

181 *Swear*: But Horatio and Marcellus are not given any
words of an oath as they place their hands on the sword.

185 *friending*: Friendliness.

186 *lack*: Be lacking.

187 *still*: Always.

188–9 *cursèd spite, | That ever I was born to set it right*: Hamlet
seems to be following Job (3:1–3) in cursing the day
of his nativity. He laments, not merely his task, but
that he was ever born.

188 *spite*: Of Fortune.

190 *together*: Without an order of precedence. Hamlet's friendliness and avoidance of formality seem to be emphasized.

II.I

Some time has elapsed: Laertes has arrived in Paris and
is settling down there; Ophelia has repelled Hamlet's
letters and *denied | His access* (109–10); the King already
knows of *Hamlet's transformation* (II.2.5) and has
summoned Rosencrantz and Guildenstern. This scene
reveals that the King's chief minister is skilful at organ-
izing spying – in this case, upon his own son. So
Hamlet's danger, and the justification of his putting on
an *antic disposition*, are understandable.

1 *Reynaldo*: A suitable name for a 'foxy' character.

3 *marvellous*: Very.

7 *me*: The indefinite indirect object (the 'ethic dative'),
used so as to give an air of ingratiating ease.

Danskers: Danes (his fellow-countrymen). The unusu-
ally correct form of the word seems to imply
Shakespeare's interest in giving local colour.

8 *what means*: What their financial position is.

keep: Maintain an establishment.

10 *encompassment and drift of question*: Roundabout and
gradual inquiry.

11 *more nearer*: The 'double comparative' is common in Shakespeare's grammar.

12 *particular demands will touch it*: Detailed questions would achieve.

   it: The scheme for finding out how Laertes is behaving.

13 *Take you*: Assume.

19 *put on*: Attribute to.

20 *forgeries*: Fictions (invented accounts of wrong-doing).

   rank: Gross.

26 *Drabbing*: Pursuing loose women.

28 *season it in the charge*: Modify (or soften) the accusation.

30 *incontinency*: Habitual sexual indulgence.

31 *breathe . . . quaintly*: Allude to, hint at . . . subtly.

32 *taints of liberty*: Faults resulting from freedom.

34–5 *A savageness . . . | Of general assault*: A wildness . . . that attacks all indiscriminately.

34 *unreclaimèd*: Unreformed (like an untamed hawk).

38 *fetch of warrant*: Justifiable device. For F's *warrant*, Q2 reads *wit*.

39 *sullies*: See the note to I.2.129.

40 *a little soiled i'th'working*: Somewhat blemished as a result of contact with the world.

42 *converse*: Conversation.

43 *Having*: If he has.

   prenominate: Before-mentioned.

45 *closes with you in this consequence*: Will end by becoming confidential with you and speak as follows.

47 *addition*: Polite form of address.

49 *does 'a*: He does.

50 *By the mass*: An oath.

58 *o'ertook in's rouse*: Overcome by drunkenness when carousing.

61 *Videlicet*: That is to say.

64 *we of wisdom and of reach*: Those of us characterized by (or 'we who by means of') wisdom and penetration.

65 *windlasses and . . . assays of bias*: Roundabout methods and indirect attacks. A *windlass* in this sense was a circuit made by a portion of a hunting party to intercept and

head back the game. In the game of bowls the *bias* is the curved course of a bowl which reaches its aim (the jack) by not going in a straight line.

66 *indirections*: Indirect approaches.
   directions: Ways of proceeding.

68 *have*: Understand.

69 *God bye ye*: God be with you.

71 *in yourself*: For yourself (as well as by report).

73 *let him ply his music*: Perhaps with a literal meaning, or perhaps 'let him go his own way'.

77 *closet*: Small private room.

78–80 *his doublet . . . ankle*: Hamlet's disordered clothing, presumably deliberately assumed, and the rest of his behaviour here, resemble the usual symptoms of love-sickness as described in *As You Like It*, III.2.363–6.

78 *doublet*: Close-fitting jacket with short skirt.
   unbraced: Not laced up or fastened.

79 *No hat upon his head*: Elizabethans normally wore hats indoors, even in church and at meals. Cf. V.2.93.

80 *down-gyvèd to his ankle*: Fallen down like fetters ('gyves') around the ankles.

82 *purport*: Expression.

89 *his other hand thus o'er his brow*: Ophelia places her open hand palm downwards shading her eyes.

91 *As*: As if.

95 *bulk*: Body from neck to waist.

102 *ecstasy*: Madness.

103 *violent property*: Quality of being violent.
    fordoes: Damages.

105 *passion*: Violent state of feeling.

112 *quoted*: Made my observation of.

113 *wrack*: Dishonour (by seducing).
    beshrew my jealousy: A curse upon my suspiciousness.

114 *proper to*: Characteristic of.
    our age: That is, old age.

115 *cast beyond ourselves*: Overestimate in our calculations.

117 *go we to the King*: But Q2 and F give no indication of Ophelia's being present in the next scene, and there are strong reasons for not introducing her there.

118 *This must be known*: We must make this known to the
King (probably, rather than 'whatever we may do to
conceal it, the story of this will soon become common
knowledge').

close: Secret.

118–19 *move | More grief to hide than hate to utter love*: Cause
more ill-feeling if I conceal this love (by leading to
further derangement of Hamlet's mind) than will be
the indignation provoked in the King if I reveal (*utter*)
it. Polonius feels that his daughter is no match for
Hamlet; but later the Queen approves, discreetly at
III.1.38–42 and (after Ophelia's death) plainly at
V.1.240–41.

II.2

0 *attendants*: An interpretation of F's *Cum alijs* ('with
others'); not in Q2. *Go, some of you* (36) implies that
attendants are onstage, or easily summoned.

1 *Rosencrantz and Guildenstern*: They seem to be young
noblemen, chosen as the childhood companions of the
Prince.

2 *Moreover that*: In addition to the fact that.

5 *transformation*: Metamorphosis, involving both the *exterior* (his appearance) and *the inward man* (his mental
qualities).

6 *Sith nor*: Since neither.

11 *of so young days*: From such an early age.

12 *sith*: Since that time (probably, rather than 'because' as
at 6).

13 *vouchsafe*: Be pleased to agree to.

rest: Residence.

14 *your companies*: The company of each of you.

16 *occasion*: Opportunity.

18 *opened*: When it is revealed (perhaps a medical image:
'lanced').

20 *is*: F amends Q2's *is* to *are*, but such lack of concord,
often in emphatic speech, is not uncommon in
Shakespeare.

21 *adheres*: Feels united.

22 *gentry*: Courtesy.

24 *For the supply and profit of our hope*: In order to feed
   our hopes and cause them to progress successfully.

26 *fits a king's remembrance*: Would be fitting to be paid
   by a king who takes note of the services rendered him.

27 *of us*: Over us.

28 *dread pleasures*: Revered wishes.

30 *in the full bent*: Completely (like a bow in archery).

38 *practices*: Conduct of this affair (but perhaps implying
   'sharp practices').

40–41 *The ambassadors . . . returned*: This indicates the passage
      of time since I.2, where Cornelius and Voltemand were
      dispatched on their embassy.

42 *still*: Always.

47 *Hunts . . . the trail*: Like a dog following the scent.
   policy: Investigation.

52 *fruit*: At the end of the *feast*.

53 *do grace to them*: Conduct them into the royal presence
   (as if he were saying grace before a *feast*). This gives
   Claudius an opportunity for a private word with
   Gertrude.

55 *distemper*: Malady.

57 *His father's death and our o'erhasty marriage*: Gertrude
   shrewdly enough interprets Hamlet's original state of
   mind, but she is ignorant of the murder, knowledge of
   which has transformed Hamlet.

58 *sift him*: Question Polonius carefully.

59 *brother*: Monarchs of different countries were 'brothers'.

60 *desires*: Good wishes.

61 *Upon our first*: Immediately upon our making our representations.

62 *His nephew's levies*: Described at I.1.95–104.

63 *the Polack*: The inhabitants of Poland.

66 *impotence*: Helplessness.

67 *falsely borne in hand*: Deluded.
   arrests: Summons to desist.

69 *fine*: Conclusion.

71 *give th'assay of arms*: Make trial of a military engagement.

73 *three thousand*: Q2 reads *threescore thousand*, but this is

unmetrical, and 60,000 crowns is rather a large *annual* sum for a comparatively small expedition; moreover, F's reading, adopted here, is supported by Q1.

76, 80   *herein . . . therein*: In the document which they have brought. The change from *herein* to *therein* seems to justify the addition of the stage direction.

77   *quiet pass*: Peaceful passage.

79   *regards of safety*: Conditions concerning safety (or 'conditions that may be safely granted').
      allowance: The permission granted.

80   *likes*: Pleases.

81   *considered*: Fit for considering.

86   *expostulate*: Expound.

90   *wit*: Intelligence, wisdom.

93–4   *to define . . . mad*: Polonius probably means 'it would be madness to try to define madness, for everyone knows what it is', rather than 'the definition of madness is to be mad'. It may be an intentional bathos: Polonius embarks on a definition and breaks down.

95   *art*: Rhetorical art.

97   *'Tis true, 'tis pity*: Of course it is a pity.

98   *figure*: Of speech.

102   *defect*: Weakness of Hamlet's mind.

103   *this effect defective*: The effect we have been aware of, which is a mental deficiency.

104   *Thus it remains, and the remainder thus*: This is the situation; and now here is the solution (in so far as one can paraphrase Polonius's verbal tangles).

105   *Perpend*: Consider carefully (probably a comic pomposity).

106   *while she is mine*: Until she is married.

109, 110   *beautified*: Probably an affected word for 'beautiful' (Robert Greene in 1592 described Shakespeare as an 'upstart crow, beautified with our feathers'). Presumably Polonius objects to the word as being a past participle of the verb 'to beautify' and therefore an incorrect usage for 'beautiful'.

112   *these*: This letter (a common phrase).
      et cetera: Sometimes interpreted as if Polonius were

omitting indecorous allusions suggested by *bosom*; but
probably he is merely indicating that he is glancing at,
and omitting, some superfluous comments.

114 *faithful*: To the contents of the letter.

115–18 *Doubt thou . . . I love*: This little poem is a clever
epitome of some of the poetical tendencies of the 1590s:
cosmological imagery, the Copernican revolution,
moral paradoxes, all illustrating amorous responses.

117 *Doubt truth*: In this line *Doubt* means 'suspect' (as at
I.2.256).

119 *ill at*: Unskilful in making.
numbers: Verses.

123 *this machine*: His body.
to him: His.

126–8 *more above hath . . . given*: She has in addition given.

126 *solicitings*: Not necessarily deceitful or immoral impor-
tunings.

127 *fell out*: Took place.
by: According to.

131 *would fain*: Should very much wish to.

136 *played the desk or table-book*: Served as a mute and
useful means of communication (between the lovers;
or possibly 'noted the matter privately for myself ').
table-book: Notebook (like *table*, I.5.98).

137 *given my heart a winking*: Shut my eyes (to what was
going on). For F's *winking*, Q2 reads *working*, a word
Shakespeare often uses of the heart and of mental activities (cf. 551 and I.1.67); but it seems to have the contrary
meaning to what is required here.

138 *idle sight*: Careless observation.

139 *round*: Roundly, straightforwardly.

140 *bespeak*: Summon to address her.

141 *star*: Sphere.

142 *prescripts*: Orders. F's reading, *Precepts*, seems a simpli-
fication.

143 *resort*: Visits.

148 *watch*: Sleeplessness.

149 *lightness*: Lightheadedness.
declension: Downward course.

151 *all*: (Into) everything that.

152 *like*: Likely.

156 *Take this from this*: Generally interpreted as 'Cut my head off'; but Polonius might more decorously point to his staff or chain of office – 'Remove me from my office as your chief minister'; cf. 166–7.

159 *centre*: Of the earth, which, according to medieval cosmology, was the centre of the universe.
    try: Judge.

162 *loose*: Release (like an animal in a stud).

163 *arras*: A tapestry hanging, such as covered the full height of the walls of rooms in great Elizabethan houses.

165 *thereon*: On account of this (disappointed love).

166 *assistant for a state*: Government minister.

167 *Enter Hamlet*: It has been suggested that Hamlet should enter a little earlier and overhear something of the plot at 159–67. This would provide a justification for his bitterness to Polonius at 171–219 and his treatment of Ophelia at III.1.89–150.

168 *sadly*: Seriously (not 'sorrowfully').
    reading: The symbol of his detachment from revenge is striking.

170 *board him presently*: Accost him immediately (drawing alongside like a sea-vessel).
    give me leave: Excuse me (as he hurries the King and Queen offstage).
        In Q1 the soliloquy *To be, or not to be* is placed here; see the note to III.1.56–88.

172 *God-a-mercy*: Thank you.

174 *fishmonger*: Probably the primary allusion is to the smell of corruption that seems to emanate from Polonius, though the word is sometimes thought to imply 'bawd'. This is the first occasion on which the audience sees Hamlet assume his *antic disposition* (I.5.170–72). He deceives Polonius, who has been boasting of his own shrewdness.

181–2 *For if ... carrion*: Possibly spoken from the book Hamlet is carrying.

182 *a good kissing carrion*: The phrase is difficult: the carrion

is good for kissing, as the sun shines on a dead dog and breeds maggots in it. Hamlet is deliberately indulging in mad-talk; but there is generally *method in't* (206), and it is not easy to see the point here. Eighteenth-century editors emended *good* to 'god' (the sun god Apollo), with great probability. Perhaps Hamlet is obscurely saying: 'Honesty is rare in this world, which is so corrupt that even the sun produces nothing but maggots in shining upon carrion.'

184 *walk i'th'sun*: Spenser in *The Faerie Queene* (III.vi) had told how Amoret and Belphoebe were begotten by the impregnating rays of the sun.

187 *harping on*: Like a harper playing on one string.

194 *matter*: Subject-matter.

199 *purging*: Exuding.

199–200 *plum-tree gum*: Sap from the bark of a plum tree.

201 *hams*: Thighs and buttocks.

203 *honesty*: Decent.

  set down: In print.

204 *backward*: Actually, of course, crabs move sideways.

206 *method*: Logical organization of thought. Polonius does not mean that Hamlet is using his apparent madness as a device for certain ends.

  out of the air: (Probably) out of the fresh air into a confined room (since the open air was regarded as dangerous to the sick).

209 *pregnant*: Full of meaning. The image is continued in *be delivered of* (211).

209–10 *A happiness that often madness hits on*: This was the doctrine of 'poetic fury' (*furor poeticus*), to which Theseus also refers in linking 'The lunatic, the lover, and the poet' (*A Midsummer Night's Dream*, V.1.7).

209 *happiness*: Felicity of expression.

212 *suddenly*: Immediately.

216 *not more*: F makes the sentence more rational by omitting *not*. But Q2 is probably correct, as confusing Polonius's wits still further by the double negatives – which the audience will take as emphatic.

  withal: With.

227 *indifferent*: Average.
    children of the earth: Ordinary fellows.

229 *button*: Summit.

230 *soles of her shoe*: So as to be trodden underfoot by Fortune.

232 *favours*: Hamlet alludes bawdily to her sexual *favours*; Guildenstern follows this by *her privates* ('intimates', and so 'sexual organs'), and Hamlet again by her *secret parts*. The progress then is to the commonplace notion of *Fortune* as a *strumpet* who bestows her favours in a fickle and indiscriminate manner (see 491).

245 *confines*: Places of confinement.

254 *count*: (Nevertheless) account.

255 *bad*: As nothing develops from *bad* in the subsequent dialogue, emendation to 'had' is attractive.

257–8 *the very substance . . . a dream*: What an ambitious man actually achieves is only a pale shadow of what he had set out to achieve.

262–3 *Then are our beggars bodies, and our monarchs and outstretched heroes the beggars' shadows*: If this is so, the beggars have substance, because they have no ambition, whereas great people are unreal (*shadows*) because they are filled with ambition. Therefore, as it is *bodies* that cast *shadows*, the great people may be regarded as the *shadows* of *beggars*. Or perhaps Hamlet means that *beggars* too have ambitions and long to be *monarchs* and *heroes*; since ambitions are *shadows*, *monarchs* and *heroes* are therefore *beggars' shadows*. Presumably this cryptic utterance baffles Rosencrantz and Guildenstern, for Hamlet promptly breaks off.

263 *outstretched heroes*: Great men whose ambitions stretch them. But *outstretched* also suggests their strutting gait and the length of their shadows.

264 *fay*: Faith.
    reason: Carry on an intellectual conversation at this level.

265–6 *wait upon you*: Accompany you (but Hamlet takes it to mean 'act as your servants').

267 *sort you with*: Put you in the category of.

269 *dreadfully attended*: Incompetently waited upon.

269–70 *in the beaten way of friendship*: As the course of our
friendship has been well-tried and reliable.

274 *too dear a halfpenny*: Cost a little too much. Presumably
Hamlet is being cryptically insulting: his friends' visit
is not worth his thanks because it is not a voluntary
kindness on their part. Or, if *a halfpenny* means 'at a
halfpenny' rather than 'by a halfpenny', he may mean:
'The thanks of a beggar such as I am are worthless.'

275 *free*: Voluntary.

278 *but to th'purpose*: Except a straightforward answer.

280 *modesties*: Sense of shame.
colour: Disguise.

283 *conjure*: Solemnly ask.

284 *consonancy*: Harmony.

286–7 *what more dear a better proposer can charge you withal*:
Whatever motive a more skilful speaker than I am might
propose in order to appeal to you (that you should be
frank with me).

287 *even*: Straightforward.

290 *of*: On.

291 *hold not off*: Do not remain aloof.

293–4 *my anticipation prevent your discovery*: My own statement about the matter be made before you have any
opportunity of revealing the truth to me.

294 *discovery*: Disclosure.

295 *moult no feather*: Be quite unimpaired.

296 *forgone*: Done without.

296–7 *custom of exercises*: Practice of manly sports.

298 *frame*: Ordered arrangement.

299 *sterile promontory*: Presumably this striking image is
that of a barren headland jutting out into the sea,
contrasted with the fertile cultivated countryside inland.

299, 301 *canopy . . . roof*: The roof overhanging the stage in an
Elizabethan public playhouse was known as the
'heavens' and seems to have been painted with stars.
This may have given special point to Hamlet's imagery
here.

300 *brave*: Fine.

301 *fretted with golden fire*: Adorned with the heavenly bodies, as a chamber roof is decorated (*fretted*) with bosses.

302–3 *pestilent congregation of vapours*: It was widely believed that diseases were borne upon the air and spread by winds.

congregation: Mass.

303 *piece of work*: Masterpiece.

305 *express*: (Probably) direct. This seems to go with *moving* rather than with *form*.

306 *apprehension*: Powers of comprehension.

307 *paragon*: Pattern of supreme excellence.

308 *quintessence of dust*: The reference is to Genesis 3:19: 'For dust thou art, and into dust shalt thou be turned again.'

309 *woman*: Q2 reads *women*, which may well be right.

316 *lenten entertainment*: The kind of meagre reception one would expect in Lent, not in a season of festivity when theatrical activities would be welcomed.

317 *coted*: Caught up with and passed.

320 *tribute*: The Prince will pay money to *the king*.

321 *foil and target*: Sword (blunted for fencing or for stage use) and light shield.

322 *gratis*: Without payment.

humorous man: Not the comic but the eccentric, capricious, or carping character, whose state of mind, according to Elizabethan physiology, was due to some excess of one of the humours.

324 *tickle o'th'sere*: Easily provoked. The image is of a gun whose trigger-catch (*sere*) was sensitive or unstable (*tickle*) and easily went off.

325 *freely*: Perhaps 'with a certain amount of ad-libbing' because the boy actor might not know his part very well; or perhaps 'with complete freedom of speech' (without feeling a need to omit indecent words or allusions). There is not much evidence for either explanation.

halt: Limp (scan badly).

328 *tragedians*: Actors (not necessarily performing only tragedies).

the city: In spite of the dramatic situation, London is in Shakespeare's mind, as the following dialogue makes clear.

329 *travel*: Are on tour.

residence: Normal place of performance.

331 *inhibition*: The word was used of the official indictment of stage plays by the authorities, but here seems to refer metaphorically to the players' inability to continue acting in the city.

332 *late*: Recent.

innovation: Fashion: The popularity of the boy actors in 1600–1601.

336–61 *How comes it? . . . his load too*: This passage, giving the reason for the decline in *estimation* of *the tragedians of the city*, is not in Q2. The discussion of the success of the child actors is somewhat intrusive into the play and the tone is more personal and acerb than we like to associate with Shakespeare. Its inclusion in F is surprising, because the episode must have become more obscure with the passage of years.

337 *keeps*: Continues.

338 *eyrie*: Nestful.

eyases: Hawk nestlings.

339 *on the top of question*: This probably means that their voices are heard above all others in the argument.

339–40 *tyrannically*: Outrageously.

341 *berattle*: Clamour abusively against.

common stages: That is, public theatres, as distinct from the 'private' playhouses, occupied by the boys' companies.

342 *rapiers*: The sign of a gentleman and man of quality.

are afraid of goosequills: Fear the satire and ridicule they would hear in the plays written for the boys' companies.

goosequills: The usual writing implement in Shakespeare's time.

345 *escoted*: Paid for.

345–6 *pursue the quality no longer than they can sing*: Follow their profession as actors only until their voices break.

348 *their means are not better*: They have no other resources for earning their livelihood.

349–50 *exclaim against their own succession*: Speak disdainfully about the profession to which they will themselves belong (as actors in adult companies).

351 *to-do*: Bustle, turmoil (an Elizabethan usage as well as a modern colloquialism).

352 *nation*: People in general (that is, the audiences).
    tarre: Incite (pronounced like 'tar').

353–4 *money bid for argument*: Payment offered (to an author) for the plot of a play (or perhaps 'money paid (by the audience) unless this particular controversy formed part of the entertainment').

354 *went to cuffs*: (Metaphorically) came to blows.

355 *in the question*: About the controversy.

357–8 *much throwing about of brains*: A great battle of wits.

359 *carry it away*: Win the day.

360–61 *Hercules and his load too*: The sign of the Globe Theatre was Hercules bearing up the globe (relieving Atlas). This passage implies, perhaps ironically, that the success of the boys' companies had had its effect on Shakespeare's company too.

363 *make mows*: Put on a mocking expression of face.

365 *ducats*: The ducat was a gold coin, worth about nine shillings, so Hamlet is speaking of considerable sums.
    picture in little: Miniature painting.
    'Sblood: By God's blood (in the eucharist).

366 *philosophy*: 'Natural philosophy' or (as we now call it) science.

370 *appurtenance*: Proper or usual accompaniment.

371 *fashion and ceremony*: Conventional ceremonious behaviour.

371–2 *comply with you in this garb*: Show you polite conduct in this manner (shaking your hands).

372 *my extent to*: The politeness that I intend to extend towards.

373 *show fairly outwards*: Give every evidence of cordiality.

373–4 *entertainment*: A good reception.

375 *deceived*: Mistaken (in thinking him to be mad).

377 *I am but mad north-north-west*: In the very assertion of
    his sanity Hamlet makes such a cryptic remark that
    they must regard him as having lost his senses: 'I am
    only a very little off compass – one point (22½°) out
    of sixteen (360°).'

378 *handsaw*: This is usually interpreted as a variant of
    'hernshaw', heron. Hamlet seems to be warning his
    companions that, though he may seem a bit mad, he
    usually has his wits about him and can distinguish
    between true and false friends.

383 *Happily*: Perhaps.

384 *twice*: For the second time.

386–7 *You say . . . indeed*: As Polonius comes onstage Hamlet
    pretends to be engaged in conversation.

386 *'A*: On.

389 *Roscius*: The most famous actor in ancient Rome.

392 *Buzz*: A contemptuous exclamation on hearing stale
    news.

396–9 *tragedy, comedy . . . unlimited*: This is a jest at the expense
    of the Renaissance theories of the specific 'kinds' of
    drama, with their special rules or principles.

397–8 *tragical-comical-historical-pastoral*: This mixture may
    seem absurd until one remembers that Shakespeare later
    wrote *Cymbeline*.

398 *scene individable*: Plays in which the scene is not
    changed, so that the so-called 'unity of place' is
    preserved.

398–9 *poem unlimited*: More imaginative plays in which the
    classicizing unities of place and time are not preserved
    – like nearly all of Shakespeare's.

399 *Seneca*: The ten tragedies attributed to him were well
    known in Shakespeare's time and represented the clas-
    sical type of tragedy more than did those of Aeschylus,
    Sophocles and Euripides. They were performed in
    academic circles in Latin and in English translation.
    Plautus: The two Latin comic playwrights Plautus and
    Terence had a considerable influence on Elizabethan
    drama. Shakespeare's *The Comedy of Errors* is based
    on Plautus' *Menaechmi* and *Amphitruo*.

400   *the law of writ and the liberty*: Plays (like those of Ben Jonson) in which the classical principles are followed, and plays (like those of Shakespeare) with greater freedom of structure.

402   *Jephthah, judge of Israel*: Jephthah made a vow to Jehovah that, if he were successful over the Ammonites, he would sacrifice the first living thing that came to meet him (Judges 11:9–40). This was his daughter.

406–7   *One fair daughter . . . well*: In 1567–8 the printing of 'A ballad entitled the song of Jephthah's daughter at her death' was authorized. No copy of this is known, but it is probably the same as a ballad authorized in 1624 with the title 'Jephthah Judge of Israel', which begins:

> I read that many year ago
> When Jephthah, Judge of Israel,
> Had one fair daughter and no more,
>   Whom he loved passing well,
> And as by lot, God wot,
> It came to pass most like it was
> Great wars there should be,
>   And who should be the chief but he.

407   *passing well*: Very well indeed.

412   *that follows not*: What you have just said is not the next line of the ballad I was quoting.

415   *lot*: Chance.

417   *as most like it was*: As was very probable.

418   *row*: Stanza.
      pious: Because it has a biblical subject.
      chanson: Song.

419   *abridgement*: (1) Interruption; (2) entertainment.

422   *valanced*: Fringed (with a beard). A valance is a draped edging of cloth.

423   *beard*: Defy (punningly).

423–4   *my young lady and mistress*: Hamlet is addressing the boy (probably in his early teens) who takes the female roles in the plays.

424–5   *is nearer to heaven*: Has grown taller.

426 *chopine*: The high bases on the fashionable Venetian-styled women's shoes ('chopines') raised them several inches. Hamlet continues to jest with the boy by allusions to women's roles.

426–7 *a piece of uncurrent gold*: A gold coin was regarded as no longer legally current at its full value if it had been 'clipped' or *cracked* within the ring surrounding the monarch's head.

428–9 *like French falconers: fly at anything we see*: This was the British opinion of French sportsmen, who allegedly did not select the prey for their falcons with sufficient care. Hamlet asks for a speech at once, without worrying much what it is to be. (In fact, however, he chooses one carefully.)

429 *straight*: Straightaway.

430 *taste of your quality*: Specimen of what your profession (acting) can provide.

435 *caviary*: Caviare, introduced into England in Shakespeare's time, was an expensive delicacy, unpalatable to those without an acquired taste for it.

436 *general*: Ordinary people.
received: Considered.

437 *cried in the top of*: Were spoken more loudly and with more authority than.

438 *digested*: Arranged.

439 *modesty*: Moderation in writing.
cunning: Skill.

440 *sallets*: Tasty bits (probably he means 'bawdy').

441 *indict*: Convict.

442 *affectation*: Q2 reads *affection*, perhaps a variant form.

443–4 *more handsome than fine*: Not showy in decoration, but genuinely beautiful in proportions.

444 *One speech in't I chiefly loved*: It concerns a revenge taken by a son and a vigorous homicide. At certain points – *blood of fathers* (456), *Did nothing* (480) – Hamlet probably responds with personal feeling.

445 *Aeneas' tale to Dido*: This is given in Books 2 and 3 of Virgil's *Aeneid*. The murder of King Priam by Pyrrhus, son of Achilles, during the night of the fall of Troy is

in 2.526–88. In writing the speech, Shakespeare derived many hints from Virgil.

448–516 *The rugged Pyrrhus . . . in the gods*: The old-fashioned style of this speech marks it off from the rest of the play as 'theatrical'. It is a serious performance and the First Player is a distinguished actor.

448 *Hyrcanian beast*: The tigers of Hyrcania (a province in Asia Minor near the Caspian Sea) were a commonplace image of ferocity. In the *Aeneid* (4.367) Dido says of Aeneas that Hyrcanian tigresses must have suckled him.

450 *rugged*: Hairy.
      sable: Black.

452 *ominous*: Fateful.
      horse: The wooden horse used by the Greeks to intrude men secretly inside the walls of Troy.

454 *dismal*: Disastrous (a strong word).

455 *total*: Entirely.
      gules: Red (a heraldic term; pronounced with a hard 'g').
      tricked: Spotted (a heraldic term).

457 *Baked and impasted with the parching streets*: The hot air (from the burning city of Troy) has congealed the blood smeared upon Pyrrhus as he went through the streets killing Trojans.
      impasted: Made into a paste.

458 *tyrannous*: Cruel.
      damnèd: Because resembling the flames of hell.

459 *their lord's murder*: Pyrrhus will soon be the murderer of Priam, the rightful *lord* of Troy and its *streets*.

460 *o'er-sizèd*: Covered with something like size, painted over.

461 *carbuncles*: Red and fiery precious stones.

466 *Anon*: Soon afterwards.

467 *too short*: With blows which fall short.

468 *Rebellious to*: Not obeying.

469 *Repugnant to command*: Offering resistance to its orders. The old man misses his blow and his arm is so jarred by this that he is unable to raise the sword again.

471 *fell*: Cruel.

472   *unnervèd*: Without energy.

      senseless: Although lacking the senses of a human being.

      Ilium: Troy (pronounced '*eye*-li-um').

475   *Takes prisoner*: Captures (so that he cannot act).

476   *Declining*: Falling.

      milky: White-haired.

478   *as a painted tyrant*: Like a tyrant represented in a painting (in which his sword is shown as held up in the act of descending but never descends).

479   *a neutral to his will and matter*: One who is inactive despite both his will and his duty. For a moment Pyrrhus becomes like Hamlet.

481   *against*: Just before.

482   *rack*: Cloud-formation.

485   *region*: Sky.

487   *the Cyclops' hammers*: The Cyclops assisted Vulcan in forging armour for the gods.

488   *Mars's armour*: In the *Iliad* it is Achilles' armour, in the *Aeneid* Aeneas', that is forged by Vulcan and the Cyclops. Neither hero is suitable for mention in this context. So Mars is reasonably supposed as having a suit of Cyclopean armour too.

      for proof eterne: To remain strong and impenetrable for ever.

489   *remorse*: Pity.

491   *strumpet Fortune*: See the note to 232.

492   *synod*: Assembly.

493   *fellies*: Curved wooden pieces which, when joined together, make the rim of a wheel.

      wheel: Fortune was generally imagined as standing on a wheel which revolved (cf. III.3.17–22).

494   *nave*: Hub of the wheel.

497   *shall to*: Will have to go to.

498   *jig*: In some theatres, but probably not at Shakespeare's Globe, performances concluded with a farcical playlet, called a *jig*, including singing and lively dancing.

499   *Hecuba*: Hamlet is interested in the effect of her husband's murder upon the wife.

500   *who . . . had*: Anyone who had.

500 *mobled*: Muffled up, veiled (a rare and homely word, rhyming with 'cobbled').

503–4 *threatening the flames | With bisson rheum*: Her profuse tears seem likely to put out the fires which are burning Troy.

504 *bisson*: Blinding.

clout: Piece of cloth.

505 *late*: Recently.

506 *all o'er-teemèd loins*: According to Homer and Virgil, Priam's wives and concubines bore him fifty sons. Perhaps this gave an impression that his chief wife, Hecuba, was worn out with bearing children.

508 *tongue in venom steeped*: Extremely bitter words.

515 *milch*: Moist (literally 'milky').

burning eyes of heaven: Heavenly bodies.

516 *passion*: (Would have made) sympathetic sorrow.

521 *bestowed*: Accommodated.

522 *abstract*: Summary. F has *Abstracts*, an easier reading.

523 *you were better*: It would be better for you to.

527 *God's bodkin*: One of the nails of Christ on the Cross; or *bodkin* may be a form of 'bodykin', a diminutive of 'body' referring originally to the unconsecrated wafer in the mass.

528 *after*: According to.

537–8 *for a need*: If necessary.

538 *study*: Learn by heart.

541 *mock*: Make fun by mimicking (not merely 'deride').

547 *rogue and peasant slave*: On the one hand a cheat, and on the other a spiritless coward.

peasant: Base (usually derogatory in Shakespeare).

549 *But*: Merely.

550 *force his soul so to his own conceit*: Make his imagination so control the workings of his mind and body.

551 *from her working*: As a result of this activity of his soul (commonly thought of as feminine).

wanned: Grew pale.

553–4 *his whole function suiting | With forms to his conceit*: All his bodily powers responding with physical expressiveness appropriate to these fictitious imaginings.

560 *the general ear*: The ears of people generally.
    horrid: Horrifying.
561 *appal*: Turn pale (and so 'dismay').
    the free: The innocent.
562 *ignorant*: Of the crime that has been committed.
    amaze: Bewilder, stun.
564 *muddy-mettled*: Sluggish.
    peak: Mope.
565 *John-a-dreams*: Apparently a byword for 'a dreamer'.
    unpregnant of my cause: Not stirred to action by my
    just cause.
568 *defeat*: Destruction.
570 *beard*: Presumably Hamlet must be imagined as bearded
    in the fashion of a young man of the early seventeenth
    century.
571 *Gives me the lie i'th'throat*: Calls me a downright liar.
572 *to the lungs*: Making him swallow the insult.
573 *'swounds*: By God's wounds.
    take it: Accept the insult.
574 *pigeon-livered and lack gall*: Pigeons were believed not
    to secrete gall (the reputed cause of anger).
575 *To make oppression bitter*: Which would make me resent
    the oppression.
576 *region kites*: Kites in the sky.
578 *kindless*: Inhuman.
580 *brave*: Fine (ironically).
582 *heaven and hell*: That is, a sense of natural justice and
    the fury of his anger.
585 *stallion*: A prostitute (like *drab*). F reads *Scullion*, an
    acceptable reading sometimes preferred by editors. But
    whore and *drab* perhaps lead naturally to *stallion*.
586 *About*: To work.
588 *by the very cunning of the scene*: Simply by the skill in
    presentation of the play.
589 *presently*: At once.
591-2 *murder . . . organ*: Cf. I.2.257-8.
595 *tent him to the quick*: Probe him until he feels the pain.
    blench: Flinch (not 'turn pale').
596-601 *The spirit . . . damn me*: Hamlet now explains or excuses

his inactivity by distrusting the Ghost's statements. Though he and his friends had already envisaged the possibility that the Ghost might be an evil spirit (*a spirit of health or goblin damned*, I.4.40–42, and Horatio's warning at I.4.69–74), Hamlet had concluded *It is an honest ghost* (I.5.138).

599–600 *my melancholy,* | *As he is very potent with such spirits*: According to Elizabethan physiology, persons suffering from an excess of black bile (*melancholy*) were prone to exercising strong imaginations, and were therefore subject to mental instability and hallucinations. So they were an easy prey to the devil.

601 *Abuses*: Deceives.

602 *relative*: Closely related to fact.
     this: The narrative and promptings of the Ghost.

III.1

0 *Enter the King and Queen*: Unlike I.2 and II.2, here the royal entry is not marked with a *Flourish* in Q2 or F. This may indicate a more private interview than the formal, though genial, reception of Rosencrantz and Guildenstern in II.2.

1 *drift of conference*: Directing of your conversations with him.

2 *puts on*: This indicates suspicion that Hamlet's *antic disposition* is a pose.
   confusion: Mental distraction.

3 *Grating*: Harassing,

7 *forward*: Readily disposed.
   sounded: Questioned.

8 *crafty*: Cunning.

12 *forcing of his disposition*: Constraint, forcing himself to be in an accommodating mood.

14 *assay him*: Try to win him.

17 *o'er-raught*: Overtook.

26 *give him a further edge*: Stimulate him to a keener desire.

29 *closely*: Privately.

31 *Affront*: Come face to face with.

32 *lawful espials*: Spies made excusable by the circumstances.

38–42 *for your part . . . honours*: This probably shows that
      Ophelia hears the plotting against Hamlet, so that she
      must take responsibility for deceiving him. But it cannot
      be regarded as certain, for the Elizabethan stage was
      large, and she could have been so placed that (by
      convention) she did not hear 32–7. Nothing in what
      she says at 90–162 implies that she knows she is being
      spied upon.

   40 *wildness*: This is a mild word for Hamlet's *confusion*,
      lunacy, *affliction*. To Ophelia the Queen tactfully avoids
      the word 'madness'.

   42 *To both your honours*: To the credit of you both.

   43 *Gracious*: To the King.

   44 *bestow*: Conceal.
      book: Clearly a prayer book: 45, 47–8, 89–90.

   45 *exercise*: Religious exercise.
      colour: Provide plausible explanation of.

   46 *loneliness*: Being alone (without a chaperon).

   47 *proved*: Found by experience.
      devotion's visage: An outward appearance of religious
      devotion.

   48 *pious action*: Performance of religious acts.

   49 *O, 'tis too true*: Probably this is spoken aloud, for the
      King is a self-controlled character. The '(*Aside*)' direc-
      tion at 50 is added by editors.

50–54 *How smart . . . burden*: This is the first sign that the
      King has a bad conscience. From now on, the audience
      has no reason to doubt the Ghost's veracity. It is just
      at this point that Hamlet has begun to have doubts
      (II.2.596–601).

   52 *to the thing*: In comparison with the cosmetic. But the
      meaning is strained. Possibly *the thing that helps it* is
      the harlot's servant who arranges her toilet and so
      knows how ugly she really is.

   53 *painted*: Hypocritically disguised.

   55 *Enter Hamlet*: It is possible that Hamlet enters reading
      a book and speaks his soliloquy while ruminating upon
      it. For Q1 has the introductory line spoken by the King:
      see where hee comes poring vpon a booke, which probably

indicates what the actor who reported the text had seen upon the stage. If, as seems probable, the soliloquy was originally spoken at II.2.170 (where Q1 places it), the Queen's *But look where sadly . . .* is a vestige of this stage business.

56–88 *To be, or not to be . . . action*: Q1 prints this soliloquy, and the meeting with Ophelia, after II.2.170, which may well indicate stage practice in early productions. Some modern directors have found that placing the soliloquy there, at a low point in Hamlet's despair, is more effective than it is here, just after his vigorous decision to test Claudius. The placing of the soliloquy here may indicate an afterthought – not altogether successful – influenced by the fact that including it in II.2 gives the actor a very long period onstage.

56 *To be, or not to be*: Whether or not to continue this mortal existence (the choice is between continuing to live and committing suicide). An alternative explanation is: 'is there an afterlife, or not?' This, though congruous with the line of thought later in the soliloquy, is more difficult to communicate on the stage.

57–60 *Whether 'tis nobler . . . end them*: It does not matter (in discussing *the question* of the advantages and disadvantages of suicide) whether we think a stoical attitude to misfortune or an active fighting back against the blows of fate is the more honourable course for a man to take. An alternative explanation is that 57–8 expand *To be* and 59–60 expand *not to be*: Hamlet can either endure his misfortunes (and so continue to live) or follow an active plan of attacking the King (and so expose himself to an inevitable avenger's death or suicide). At II.2.547 Hamlet had supposed that such an endurance of wrongs was fit only for a *rogue and peasant slave*.

57 *in the mind*: Probably goes with *to suffer* rather than with *nobler*.

58 *outrageous*: Hamlet seems to be emphasizing the unbearable irrationality of Fortune.

60 *by opposing*: As distinct from using other methods of

ending one's troubles, such as stoical endurance or suicide.

61 *No more*: Than to sleep.

63 *consummation*: Final completion (of life).

65 *rub*: Obstacle (in the game of bowls).

67 *shuffled off this mortal coil*: Like a snake shedding its slough, or perhaps a butterfly – a symbol of the soul – emerging from its chrysalis.

this mortal coil: The turmoil of this mortal life.

68 *give us pause*: Cause us to hesitate.

respect: Consideration.

69 *makes calamity of so long life*: Makes those afflicted by calamity willing to endure it for so long.

70 *time*: The world in which one lives, the times.

72 *despised*: Not necessarily by the lady. F has *dispriz'd* ('unvalued'), which also makes good sense.

the law's delay: A typically Elizabethan misfortune.

73 *office*: Those who hold official positions.

74 *patient merit of th'unworthy takes*: The deserving have to endure patiently from the unworthy.

75 *quietus*: Release from a debt ('*quietus est*', 'it is discharged') and so from the troubles of life.

76 *a bare*: Merely a.

bodkin: Dagger (but *bodkin* had come also to mean 'a large pin', and possibly that is the vivid image here).

fardels: Burdens.

79–80 *from whose bourn | No traveller returns*: The inconsistency between this statement and Hamlet's experience of his father's ghost is obvious. It might be intended to indicate his waning faith in the authenticity of the Ghost (see II.2.596–601). But it is more likely to be an imaginative intensification of his thoughts on death, not to be related too literally to the action in other parts of the play. Moreover, the image is that of a *traveller* returning to his home from a sojourn elsewhere – which is quite unlike the transitory visitation of a ghost.

79 *bourn*: Region, boundary.

80 *puzzles*: Bewilders (a strong word).

83 *conscience*: Introspection, reflection on the contents of the consciousness.

84 *native hue*: Complexion characteristic of a state of natural health.

85 *cast*: Tinge.

   thought: Anxiety.

86 *pitch*: High aspiration (the height of a soaring falcon's flight).

   moment: Importance.

87 *With this regard*: Owing to this consideration (because this is thought about).

88 *Soft you now*: An interjection expressing moderate surprise.

89–150 *The fair Ophelia! . . . To a nunnery, go*: The interview between Hamlet and Ophelia is difficult to interpret. We do not know whether Hamlet is talking with the knowledge that there are eavesdroppers; whether he thinks Ophelia is in the plot and is acting as a decoy; whether he becomes suspicious of her halfway through and thereupon turns nasty. The scene is usually played as if Hamlet were merely suspicious up to 130, when he asks *Where's your father?* From that point, realizing that the King and Polonius are listening, he puts on a vicious act intended for their ears.

The first part of the interview can be spoken by Hamlet in his typical cryptic ironic manner. At 130, it seems, he wonders what Ophelia is doing alone and unchaperoned after having been kept immured from him so long, and learns that her father is not with her. It is an easy step to suppose that she was brought here by the Queen and that, if anyone, it is the Queen who is listening to their conversation. Hamlet therefore begins an attack on womanhood intended for her ears. The irony is that it is not his mother but the King, with Polonius, who overhears his bitter words, and so he unknowingly betrays himself (*all but one – shall live*, 149) and prepares the King for the trick in the play scene (III.2).

There is no exit for the Queen at 42 in either Q2 or

F. If the audience can be made aware of the Queen's curiosity in observing what goes on between Hamlet and Ophelia, then the revelation at 162 that Hamlet has been mistaken, and the eavesdropper is not the Queen but — more importantly and more dangerously — the King, can be an exciting moment.

89 *orisons*: Prayers (because Ophelia carries a book of devotions, and is perhaps visibly at prayer).

93 *remembrances*: Gifts as souvenirs of affection.

99 *perfume*: Given by the *words of so sweet breath composed*.

103, 107 *honest*: Chaste (of a woman).

108 *admit no discourse to*: Permit no parleying with.

109–13 *Could beauty . . . likeness*: Ophelia supposes Hamlet to have said that *beauty* and chastity should not go together, and he accepts the misinterpretation as interesting and develops it.

109 *commerce*: Intercourse.

111–13 *the power of beauty . . . likeness*: This is very like the typical paradox on which academic wits exercised themselves in Shakespeare's time. In the second element Hamlet is presumably referring obscurely to the failure of his *honest* father to keep his beautiful mother in the path of virtue.

113 *translate*: Transform (probably with some implication of 'elevate').

    his likeness: The likeness of *honesty*.

114 *sometime*: Formerly (before his mother's disillusioning behaviour).

    the time: The times (but, in particular, his experience of his mother's behaviour).

118 *inoculate our old stock*: Be grafted (by the insertion of a bud) into the human inheritance of original sin (occasioned by an apple tree; and no doubt Hamlet is thinking of his family inheritance from his mother).

118–19 *relish of it*: Have a flavour of the original *stock*, with its inheritance of original sin.

121 *Get thee to a nunnery*: So avoiding sexual temptation, marriage, and the begetting of children. *Hamlet* is a play of long ago, set in a foreign country but in

Christian times, and it is given a vaguely Catholic
setting. The withdrawal of a noble young lady to a
convent to avoid the wickedness of the world is a not
unreasonable suggestion. After Shakespeare's time
'nunnery' was used facetiously to mean 'brothel', but
in this context (*Why wouldst thou be a breeder of sinners?*)
that meaning seems impossible.

122 *indifferent honest*: Of average honourableness.

124–5 *I am very proud, revengeful, ambitious*: This, although
it bitterly misrepresents Hamlet himself, is not unlike
the character of a hero-villain in a revenge story, such
as that derived from Belleforest in *The History of
Hamblet*.

131 *At home*: Ophelia's lie (if it is a lie and she knows
Polonius is listening) is the beginning of the calamity
that falls upon her, though she thinks she is only
humouring a madman.

133 *play the fool*: 'I have sinned . . . behold, I have played
the fool, and have erred exceedingly' (1 Samuel 26:21).

139 *monsters*: (Probably) cuckolds (who traditionally wear
horns and so look like monstrous animals. The actor
can make the gesture of horns with his fingers on his
head).
     you: Women in general, not Ophelia in particular.

143 *paintings*: Use of cosmetics.

145 *jig*: Dance, move jerkily.
     amble: Walk affectedly.
     lisp: Talk affectedly.

145–6 *nickname God's creatures*: Use foolish (or indecent)
invented names for creatures which were given their
proper names by Adam at God's direction (Genesis
2:19).

146–7 *make your wantonness your ignorance*: Affect ignorance
and use this as an excuse for your foolishness or wanton
speech.

148 *marriage*: So Q2; in F (as often happens) the meaning
is simplified by reading *Marriages*, the concrete for the
abstract word.

149 *all but one*: This clearly refers to the King. It is an

uncharacteristically and dangerously open warning if
Hamlet suspects that the King is listening. Perhaps it
is his first mistake, putting the King on his guard (as
is expressed at 163–76). But if he supposes that his
mother is listening (see the note to 89–150), then it is
a warning to *her* about what is going to happen. Or the
phrase may be spoken aside, rather than shouted as a
threat.

152 *The courtier's, soldier's, scholar's, eye, tongue, sword*:
The *eye*, *tongue* and *sword* do not seem to apply independently to the three types of a man, though *tongue*
and *sword* would go with the *scholar* and *soldier*. Rather,
Ophelia seems to be insisting on the unity of qualities
in Hamlet in his various capacities.

153 *expectancy*: Hope for the future.
rose: 'The very flower'.
fair: Perhaps 'made fair by Hamlet's presence and
participation', rather than vaguely approving of the
state of Denmark.

154 *glass*: Mirror.
mould of form: Pattern of behaviour (as distinct from
garments and physical appearance).

155 *of*: By.

157 *music*: This is the F reading. Q2 has *musickt*.

159 *out of time*: F has *tune* for Q2's *time*. The image of the
harmony of the human faculties under the government
of reason is common in Shakespeare.

160 *feature*: General physical appearance (not only the face).
blown youth: Youth in its bloom.

161 *Blasted*: Withered.
ecstasy: Madness.

162 *have seen what I have seen, see what I see*: See now such
a great change from what I have seen.

163 *affections*: Emotions.

164–5 *Nor . . . Was not*: The emphatic negative, not uncommon
in Shakespeare.

166 *sits on brood*: Like a bird on its eggs, leading to *hatch*
at 167.

167 *doubt*: Feel anxious that.

167 *disclose*: This also means 'hatching', as at V.1.283.

170 *he shall with speed to England*: Similarly in *The History of Hamblet* the Prince is sent to England. The King has now changed his mind from I.2.112–17, where he was intent on keeping Hamlet at home. At this point the King still claims to hope that Hamlet may be cured of his melancholy. But after he and Hamlet have confronted each other in the play scene he resolves to use the expedition to England as a means of sending Hamlet to his death (IV.3.60–70).

171 *tribute*: Shakespeare has a sense of the historical background of the play; this is the famous Danegelt.

173 *variable objects*: Variety of surroundings for him to observe.

174 *something-settled matter*: Somewhat-settled matter ('*idée fixe*').

175 *still beating*: For ever hammering in his head.

176 *From fashion of himself*: Out of his ordinary way of conducting himself.

178 *grief*: Grievance.

180–81 *You need not . . . all*: This could be taken to mean that Ophelia had not known that their conversation was being overheard. See the note to 38–42.

184 *be round with*: Speak bluntly to.

185 *in the ear*: Within earshot.

186 *find him not*: Fails to discover what is the matter with him.

187 *confine him*: Lock him up (as a madman rather than as a political danger).

189 *great ones*: Highly placed persons.

III.2

1–53 *Speak the speech . . . of it*: Hamlet begins by referring only to the elocution of *my lines*, the inserted *speech of some dozen lines or sixteen lines* (II.2.538) which he had himself written. But he soon moves to a consideration of the principles of acting generally.

5 *use all*: Treat everything.

9 *robustious*: Boisterous.

periwig-pated: With his head covered with a wig.

passion: Passionate speech.

10 *groundlings*: The part of the audience who stood on the ground in the open yard of the theatre, paying only a penny for entrance.

11 *capable of*: Capable of understanding.

13 *o'erdoing*: Outdoing.

Termagant: This imaginary deity believed to be worshipped by Mohammedans appears in the medieval religious plays as violent and overbearing.

13–14 *out-Herods Herod*: Gives a performance which is even more violent than that of Herod (represented in medieval religious plays as a wild tyrant).

19 *modesty*: Moderation.

20 *from*: Contrary to.

22 *the mirror up to nature*: This image of art as a mirror of reality had had a long history before Shakespeare used it.

22–3 *show virtue her own feature, scorn her own image*: The virtues and vices, by being represented in a lifelike way, are to be immediately recognizable for what they are, without confusing the spectator.

23 *scorn*: Folly (the object of scorn).

23–4 *very age and body of the time*: That is, present state of things.

24 *his*: Its (grammatically, their).

pressure: Impression (as in wax).

24–5 *come tardy off*: Imperfectly achieved.

25 *unskilful*: Uneducated part of the audience (contrasted with *the judicious*).

26–7 *censure of the which one*: Judgement of one of *the judicious*.

27 *must in your allowance*: You should allow to.

29–30 *not to speak it profanely*: By suggesting impiously that they were made not by God but by *some of Nature's journeymen*.

33 *journeymen*: That is, indifferent workmen.

34 *abominably*: This word was generally (but incorrectly) supposed to derive from the Latin '*ab homine*', interpreted as 'inhuman'; and both Q2 and F here spell it *abhominably*. So Hamlet is punning on *humanity*.

35–6 *indifferently*: To some extent. The First Player seems
      to give only a half-hearted assurance of reformation.

39   *there be of them that*: There are some of those (clowns)
      who.

43–55 *And then you . . . Well*: This passage is found only in
      Q1. This is generally unreliable, but there are good
      reasons for regarding this expansion of Hamlet's speech
      as a fairly accurate report of a passage later cut. It gives
      examples of the silly 'character' jests of the comic
      actors. This part of the scene is quite well remembered
      by the actor who betrayed the play to a piratical printer
      – he was obviously interested in this discussion of acting
      and appreciated the satirical comments on bad actors.
      Moreover, it is just the kind of passage which would
      soon become out of date and would therefore be
      cut in later performances. Since, however, we are
      dependent upon the actor's memory, we cannot trust
      the exact wording.

45   *quote*: Note.

46   *tables*: Notebooks.

49   *cullison*: A corruption of 'cognizance', a badge.

49–50 *blabbering*: Babbling.

50   *keeping in*: Perhaps 'accompanying', that is, the *gen-
      tlemen* speak the catchphrases along with the clown.
      cinquepace: A lively dance.

51   *warm*: Presumably as the result of his strenuous efforts
      to amuse.

56–7 *piece of work*: Masterpiece (ironically). Cf. II.2.303.

58   *presently*: Immediately.

64   *e'en*: Indeed.
      just: Honourable.

65   *conversation coped withal*: Dealings with people brought
      me into contact with.

70–71 *let the candied tongue . . . hinges of the knee*: Hamlet is
      describing an allegorical scene in which a figure of
      Flattery first licks another figure (Pomp), and then
      kneels down before him, expecting to be flattered.
      Hamlet is thinking of Rosencrantz and Guildenstern,
      whom he has just now dismissed.

70 *absurd*: Ridiculously unreasonable.

71 *crook the pregnant hinges of the knee*: Curtsy or kneel (as a gesture of respect).

pregnant: Productive of profit.

72 *thrift may follow fawning*: Personal profit may derive from sycophantic behaviour.

74 *of men distinguish her election*: Make discriminating choice among men.

75 *sealed*: Marked as a possession (like a legal document).

76 *one, in suffering all, that suffers nothing*: One who, however great his sufferings may be, shows none of the effects of suffering.

79 *blood and judgement*: Passion and reason.

commeddled: Mixed. F has *co-mingled*, a more usual word.

81 *stop*: Finger-hole (and the note produced by 'stopping' it).

83 *core . . . heart*: Probably a pun, on the supposition that *core* is related to Latin '*cor*', 'heart'.

89 *the very comment of thy soul*: Your closest observation.

90 *occulted*: Hidden.

91 *unkennel*: Reveal (like a dog emerging from its lair).

in one speech: At one speech. It is natural to suppose that this is the speech that Hamlet proposed to insert. This is not certain. He has chosen the play, *The Murder of Gonzago*, because of the resemblance of its plot to the actual situation in Denmark, and it may already contain a speech which will strike Claudius *to the soul* and make him *blench* (II.2.589, 595). Hamlet may from the first have intended his speech to be directed at his mother. See the note to 196–225.

94 *Vulcan's stithy*: The anvil of Vulcan, the blacksmith god, whose forge was supposed to be under Mount Etna, and so came to be connected with the idea of hell (therefore *foul*). Cf. *the Cyclops' hammers* (II.2.487).

96 *after*: Afterwards.

96–7 *we will both our judgements join | In censure of his seeming*: It is noteworthy that Hamlet has no plan for action if Claudius reveals his guilt, and he ignores the consequences of his revealing to Claudius that he is aware of the crime.

97 *censure of his seeming*: Assessment of the way he behaves outwardly.

98 *steal*: Hide by stealth (any emotion).

100 *be idle*: Seem to have nothing on my mind.

101 *Danish march. Flourish. Trumpets and kettledrums . . . guard carrying torches*: The *Trumpets and kettledrums* are in the Q2 direction, the *Flourish*, the *guard carrying torches*, and the *Danish march* in F. They indicate stage business for a formal entry with royal and national music. Probably early productions were content with trumpets and drums. The F direction suggests later elaboration. The phrase *Danish march* is interesting. The fact that King James I's consort was Anne of Denmark and that Christian IV of Denmark visited him in 1606 and 1614 may have meant that a *Danish march* had come to be recognizable to some of Shakespeare's audiences and was appropriately inserted into the play.

Trumpets . . . kettledrums: Probably to be heard offstage.

torches: Perhaps some of these are extinguished when the play begins (144), to give point to the King's and Polonius's demands for *light* (278–9).

102 *cousin*: Used of any close relative.

103 *chameleon's dish*: The chameleon was alleged to live on air alone. Hamlet takes up Claudius's *fares* as if it were an inquiry about his food.

104 *air*: Doubtless punning on 'heir'.

promise-crammed: This alludes to Claudius's promise of the succession to the throne (I.2.108–9 and 348–52 below).

105 *have nothing with*: Understand nothing of.

105–6 *These words are not mine*: What you have said is irrelevant to my remark.

107 *nor mine now*: Because he has spoken them and they have left him.

113 *Capitol*: In fact Caesar was not killed in the Capitol at

Rome, but the error (found also in *Julius Caesar* and *Antony and Cleopatra*) was common.

Brutus killed me: Hamlet encourages references to the murder of a tyrant.

114 *brute . . . capital*: Hamlet's jeering puns have an extra irony in that he will soon kill Polonius (III.4.24–34). *calf*: Fool.

116–17 *stay upon your patience*: Await your permission to begin.

119 *metal more attractive*: More magnetic metal (of Ophelia). By his behaviour Hamlet encourages Polonius's belief that distracted love is the cause of his trouble. But his other reason for sitting near Ophelia is that it is a position from which he can watch the King closely.

121 *shall I lie in your lap*: Hamlet's sexual innuendos in this scene are quite unlike any other lover's speech to his beloved in Shakespeare, but it must be admitted that several of Shakespeare's pure heroines listen to and tolerate ribald raillery from a man (e.g. Helena from Parolles, *All's Well That Ends Well*, I.1.109–61 and Desdemona from Iago, *Othello*, II.1.100–161).

122 *No, my lord*: Ophelia keeps Hamlet at a distance by addressing him in almost every speech as *my lord*, emphasizing her inferior position.

124 *Ay*: Probably she is accepting his interpretation of what he had said, rather than consenting to his suggestion.

125 *meant country matters*: Was referring to sexual intercourse.

130 *Nothing*: The figure nought. Presumably the actor makes the point about *country matters* by some such gesture as putting his thumb and first finger together to make a circle, representing the vagina, the *fair thought . . . between maids' legs*. Ophelia understands the obscenity: *You are merry, my lord*.

134 *your only jig-maker*: The very representative of mindless jesting. Cf. II.2.498.

136 *within's*: Within these.

137 *twice two months*: As the Ghost appeared when he was *But two months dead, nay, not so much, not two* (I.2.138), the information is thus given us that it is now more

than two months since the apparition, during which time Hamlet has done nothing.

138–9 *let the devil wear black, for I'll have a suit of sables*: That is, to hell with mourning! I'll wear a rich garment. 'Sables' could mean both 'black mourning garments' and 'expensive furs'.

139–40 *Die two months ago*: Hamlet seems to ignore the *twice two months* of Ophelia and to revert to *But two months dead*.

142 *build churches*: That is, endow chapels where prayers may be said for his soul.

142–3 *else shall 'a suffer not thinking on*: Otherwise he will have to endure being forgotten.

143 *with*: Like.

the hobby-horse: In morris dancing a man with a figure of a horse strapped around his waist. The word could also mean 'unchaste woman', and some association of thought may be intended here.

144 *For O . . . forgot*: This *epitaph* is apparently from some ballad not extant.

The trumpets sound: This is the direction in Q2. F has *Hoboyes play*, which may represent later theatrical practice. Perhaps the oboe was felt to be more suitable than the trumpet to accompany the following love scenes.

Dumb show: A mime, common in Elizabethan drama, usually foreshadowing part or all of a play, or summarizing part of the action. Claudius can sit through this dumb show with an outward appearance of calm because he is a practised hypocrite. It is only on the second telling of the story, where it is made a more intense experience, that he breaks down.

makes show of protestation: Gives a performance of one affirming strongly her love. There is no question of insincerity; the boy player is performing a role.

declines: Leans.

146 *miching mallecho*: An obscure phrase; *mallecho* may be related to the Spanish '*malhecho*', 'mischief'. It is usually pronounced to rhyme with 'calico' or 'pal echo'.

148 *Belike*: Probably.

show: Dumb show.

imports: Represents.

argument: Story.

149 *Prologue*: That is, speaker of the Prologue, a chorus-figure.

151 *keep counsel*: Keep a secret.

153–4 *Be not you*: Provided that you are not.

156 *naught*: Improper.

161 *the posy of a ring*: A motto inscribed in a ring (therefore short, and often in rhyme).

163 *As woman's love*: The injustice of this statement to Ophelia would be shocking were it not obvious that Hamlet is observing his mother and thinking of her. It also anticipates the situation in the playlet, where the Queen succumbs to the seductions of the poisoner.

164 *Phoebus' cart*: The chariot of Apollo, the sun god.

165 *Neptune's salt wash and Tellus' orbèd ground*: The sea and the earth.

Tellus: Goddess of the earth.

orbèd: Rounded (the earth being a sphere).

166 *borrowed sheen*: Because the light of the moon is only the reflection of the sun's.

168 *Hymen*: The pagan god of marriage.

169 *commutual*: Mutually.

173 *cheer*: Cheerfulness.

174 *distrust you*: Am anxious about you.

175 *Discomfort*: Trouble.

176 *even as they love*: As there is no rhyme, a line may have been accidentally omitted.

love: Love too much.

177 *hold quantity*: Are of equivalent amount.

178 *In neither aught, or in extremity*: Either there is nothing of either of them (*fear and love*) or both are present to the utmost limit.

179 *proof*: Your experience.

180 *as my love is sized*: According to the amount of my love for you.

182 *Where little fears grow great, great love grows there*: Where great anxiety develops from only small causes,

that is evidence of great love. The meaning is close to
that of 176.

184 *operant powers*: Vital faculties.

leave to do: Cease to perform.

185 *behind*: After I have gone.

190 *None wed the second but who*: Let no woman marry a
second husband except the one who.

191 *wormwood*: A plant of bitter taste, and so 'something
bitter to a person's feelings'.

192 *instances that . . . move*: Motives that lead to.

193 *base respects of thrift*: A dishonourable concern for
personal advantage.

194 *A second time I killed my husband dead*: I give offence
to the memory of my first husband and trouble his
spirit.

196–225 *I do believe . . . dead*: This is sometimes believed to be
the speech which Hamlet said (II.2.538–9) he would
insert into *The Murder of Gonzago*. It would be an ingenious device of Shakespeare to have Hamlet write a
speech about his own vacillations and his mother's
misconduct when he was expected to be writing one
about his uncle's guilt. But probably the promised lines
do not appear at all: it is enough for Hamlet to declare
that the playlet will contain something that will frighten
the King and then to keep us in suspense. Be that as it
may, this is an important speech, echoed by Hamlet and
the Ghost at III.4.107–12, by Hamlet at IV.4.32–66,
by Claudius at IV.7.110–22, and by Hamlet to Horatio
at V.2.10–11.

196 *you think*: Your real opinion is.

198 *Purpose is but the slave to memory*: Our decisions about
what we are going to do depend entirely upon our
being able to remember them afterwards.

199 *Of violent birth, but poor validity*: Our initial declara-
tions of our intentions may be emphatic, but they have
little stamina.

200 *Which*: Purpose (198).

202 *Most necessary 'tis*: It is inevitable.

203 *pay ourselves what to ourselves is debt*: Fulfil the

promises we have made about actions which we
ourselves have to perform.

204 *passion*: The heat of the moment.

207 *Their own enactures with themselves destroy*: Destroys
them even by putting them into action.

209 *joys . . . grieves*: Turns to joy . . . turns to grief.
on slender accident: For trivial causes.

210 *is not for aye*: Will not last for ever.
nor: And so.

212 *prove*: Decide by experience.

213 *lead*: Determine the direction of.

214 *down*: Being displaced.

215 *The poor advanced makes friends of enemies*: When a
humble man is promoted to a position of importance,
his enemies become his friends.

216 *hitherto*: To this extent.

217 *who not needs*: The rich and important, who do not need
friends.

218 *try*: Test (by making an appeal for help).

219 *seasons him*: Confirms him as, converts him into.

221 *Our wills and fates*: What we want to happen and what
is fated to happen to us.
contrary: In contrary directions.

222 *devices*: Plans for the future.
still: Always.

223 *their ends*: What happens as a result of our *thoughts*.
none of our own: Outside our control.

224 *think*: You may think now.

225 *die thy thoughts*: What you think will come to nothing.

226 *Nor*: Let neither.

227 *Sport*: Recreation.
lock from me: Deprive me of (*Sport and repose*).

229 *An anchor's cheer*: The food of an anchorite (hermit).
The Q2 reading *cheere* is sometimes interpreted as 'chair'.
But both this spelling and the meaning are difficult.
my scope: What I have in prospect.

230 *Each opposite*: Whatever is in opposition.
blanks the face of joy: Changes a happy face to a miserable one.

232 *here and hence*: In the present and in the future (or possibly 'in this world and the next').

240 *protest*: Promise publicly.

242–3 *Have you heard . . . in't*: The King presumably speaks to Polonius, though Hamlet replies to him.

244 *poison in jest*: Poison has not been mentioned so far in the playlet; and Hamlet again anticipates the action by referring to *murder* at 248. Apparently the King begins to reveal his distress or anger *Upon the talk of the poisoning* (298).

245 *offence*: Hamlet's meaning is different from Claudius's at 242: this is only a play; there is no reality in it, so no actual injury is done by this pretence of poisoning.

247 *The Mousetrap*: The new name for the play seems to derive from Hamlet's belief that he could *catch* the King's *conscience* (II.2.603).
   Tropically: Figuratively (like a 'trope', a rhetorical figure). There may be a pun on 'trap'.

248 *image*: Imitation of the reality.

250 *knavish*: Wicked.

251 *free*: Innocent.

252 *galled*: Made sore.
   jade: Ill-conditioned horse (also a contemptuous term for a woman, possibly glancing at the Queen).
   withers: Shoulder-bones (of a horse).
   unwrung: Not chafed.

253 *nephew*: Although the circumstances of the murder in the playlet correspond to the murder of King Hamlet by his brother Claudius, the agent is the murdered man's *nephew*, not his brother. So the playlet could reasonably be interpreted as a threat against Claudius by his nephew Hamlet. Only Claudius knows that it is also an accusation of murder.
   the King: The King in the playlet.

255 *interpret*: Provide dialogue (that is, act as a pander). Hamlet imagines Ophelia and a supposed lover (*love*) as puppets, and himself as presenter speaking the words of their play.

256 *dallying*: Indulging in dalliance (that is love-play).

257 *keen*: Bitter, quick-witted. Hamlet seems to take the
     word as meaning 'eager for sexual intercourse'.

258–9 *It would cost you a groaning to take off mine edge*: You
     would have to pay for it if you were to satisfy my
     sexual appetite, because it would cause you the pangs
     of childbirth.

260 *Still better, and worse*: Your words are getting both
     more witty and more disgraceful.

261 *So you must take your husbands*: 'For better, for worse
     . . .': the marriage service.

     must take: This reading comes from Q1. Both Q2
     and F read *mistake*, from which it is difficult to get any
     satisfactory meaning (unless it is another sneer at his
     mother, who had 'mis-taken' her husbands by going
     from a good to a bad one).

262 *Pox*: A pox on you, may (venereal) disease afflict you.
     The oath is inserted in F.

263 *the croaking raven doth bellow for revenge*: These words
     seem irrelevant to the situation portrayed. They sound
     like a fragment of an 'old play', and something like
     them occurs in the anonymous *True Tragedy of Richard
     III* (printed in 1594). They also seem to be a cue for
     Lucianus, but they do not begin his speech. The word
     bellow applied to the sound of a raven reduces the line
     to burlesque.

264 *apt*: Skilful (perhaps in preparing the poison or in
     pouring it into his victim's ear).

265 *Confederate season*: A helpful opportunity being
     provided which acts as an ally.

     else no creature seeing: No other living creature
     observing me.

266 *rank*: Evil-smelling.

     midnight weeds collected: It was supposed that poisonous
     or magical herbs were especially potent when gathered
     at midnight.

267 *Hecat*: Goddess of the underworld and hence supposed
     to be the ruler of witchcraft (two syllables: 'hekkett').
     ban: Curse.

268 *natural magic*: Inherent magic power.

    dire property: Terribly dangerous power.

270 *estate*: High rank (as king).

275 *false fire*: Blank cartridges.

280–83 *Why, let . . . world away*: This and 290–93 are probably
fragments of an old, lost ballad. Hamlet is contrasting
those who are wounded in some way (*the strucken deer*)
with those who are in a more fortunate position (*The
hart ungallèd*): that is, the King and himself.

280 *the strucken deer*: It was believed that a deer would shed
tears when wounded to death (see *As You Like It*,
II.1.33–40).

282 *watch*: Remain awake (with pain or sorrow).

283 *Thus runs the world away*: It's the way of the world.

284 *this*: Perhaps this refers to Hamlet's skill in play-
revision, or to his managerial ability in selecting a play
and bringing about its intended effect on its audience
(King Claudius). Characteristically Hamlet, while
excitedly triumphing in his theatrical success, has no
thought of any action to deal with the new situation.

    feathers: As worn by actors.

285 *turn Turk*: Make a complete change for the worse (like
a Christian becoming a renegade to the Turks, the great
non-Christian power in the seventeenth century).

285–6 *Provincial roses*: Double rose patterns, made of ribbons,
worn on shoes, and named from Provins, a town in
northern France famous for its roses.

286 *razed*: With 'open work', sometimes showing inside
cloth of another colour.

    fellowship: Partnership (in a company of actors).

    cry: Company. The word is normally used of a pack
of hounds; so Hamlet is thinking of the way they *mouth*
their lines (2).

290 *O Damon dear*: Perhaps Hamlet is thinking of Horatio
and himself as like Damon and Pythias, the legendary
friends.

291–2 *This realm dismantled was | Of Jove himself*:
Presumably he is still thinking of his father (who had
the front of Jove himself, III.4.57), whose kingdom was

usurped by a *peacock* (Claudius) or (as the rhyme suggests) an 'ass'.

291 *dismantled*: Deprived, stripped.

301 *comedy*: The word could be used generally of a play.

302 *perdy*: By God ('*par Dieu*').

309 *retirement*: Withdrawal (from the play to his private apartments).

309–10 *distempered*: Sick (in mind or body).

312 *choler*: Anger (supposed to be caused by bile in the stomach).

314 *signify*: Report.

315 *purgation*: Of the *choler*; one cure was by bleeding.

317 *frame*: Order.

start: Jump away (like a horse that is startled, or not *tame*).

323 *breed*: Sort.

324 *wholesome*: Reasonable.

325 *pardon*: Permission to leave your presence.

328 *What, my lord*: Q2 attributes this to Rosencrantz, but F to Guildenstern (perhaps rightly), waiting until 333 for Rosencrantz to take over the dialogue.

331 *command*: Have for the asking.

332 *to the matter*: Come to the point.

334 *admiration*: Bewilderment.

338–9 *She desires . . . bed*: Rosencrantz and Guildenstern are the messengers of the plot devised by Polonius (III.1.182–6).

339 *closet*: Small private room. It is not a bedroom, though modern directors sometimes turn it into one in order to communicate Hamlet's Oedipal condition.

341 *trade*: Business (an insulting word).

343 *these pickers and stealers*: His hands, or perhaps those of Rosencrantz who is holding them out in protestation. The allusion is to the Catechism in the Prayer Book: 'My duty towards my neighbour is to . . . keep my hands from picking and stealing.' Instead of the usual oath 'by this hand', Hamlet swears one that is not valid, as if the only purpose of hands was theft.

346 *liberty*: Liberation (from your *distemper*). But perhaps

this contains a threat, preparing for the dialogue with the King at III.3.1–26.

deny: Refuse to speak about.

349   *voice*: Vote, support.

351–2   *the proverb*: 'While the grass grows the starving horse dies.'

353–4   *To withdraw with you*: Presumably he takes Guildenstern aside, so that the Player does not hear. Perhaps he gets him at a disadvantage by separating him from Rosencrantz.

354   *recover the wind*: Get to windward (like a huntsman trying to get the quarry to run with the wind, so that the scent of the nets and of the men who have prepared them is not perceived).

355   *toil*: Net.

356–7   *if my duty be too bold, my love is too unmannerly*: This is an evasive response to Hamlet's accusation. It is difficult to work out any exact meaning: perhaps 'if my manner of behaving to you (at 316–26) seemed rather insolent, it was only the strength of my love for you which made me discourteous'. But the antithesis is merely verbal, and it produces Hamlet's tart rejoinder.

365   *ventages*: Finger-holes.

368   *stops*: Hamlet shows how the finger-holes can be covered with his *fingers and thumb*.

374   *sound*: Fathom (with a quibble on 'produce sound from a musical instrument').

375   *top of my compass*: Uppermost range of my notes.

376   *organ*: The recorder.

377   *'Sblood*: By God's blood (on the Cross).

379   *fret*: Punning on the meanings 'a mark on the finger-board of a stringed instrument' and 'irritate'.

383   *yonder cloud*: In an Elizabethan theatre open to the sky, Hamlet's pointing to a cloud would not seem incongruous.

390   *by and by*: At once.

391   *to the top of my bent*: Till I can put up with it no longer (like a bow *bent* to the full).

396   *yawn*: Open wide.

400 *nature*: Natural feelings.

401 *Nero*: The emperor who slew his mother, Agrippina.

404 *be hypocrites*: Deceive her by a show of bitter censure without meaning actually to harm her.

405 *shent*: Shamed.

406 *give them seals*: Confirm my words by actions.

III.3

1 *like him not*: Am nervous about his actions and intentions.

2 *range*: Roam at liberty.

3 *your commission*: The *letters sealed* and the *mandate* (III.4.203–5). It is nowhere made clear that Rosencrantz and Guildenstern are aware of the murderous instructions given in the letters.

dispatch: Quickly prepare (for you to take).

5 *The terms of our estate*: My position as ruler of the state.

7 *brows*: This Q2 reading is difficult. Perhaps the King is thinking of the intensely attentive face, with knitted brows, watching him during the play scene; and so the meaning is something like 'bold opposition'. The compiler of the F text found the word unreasonable, and substituted *Lunacies*; regardless of metre, perhaps an echo of *turbulent and dangerous lunacy* (III.1.4). Emendations proposed include 'blows', 'brains', 'braves', 'brawls', 'frowns' and 'lunes'.

provide: Act with careful foresight.

8–23 *Most holy . . . with a general groan*: This view of kingship, although put into the mouths of the ingratiating Guildenstern and Rosencrantz, was the orthodox Elizabethan one. Its expression here shows the dangerous position into which Hamlet has got himself: his enemies now have political morality on their side and he has offended against it.

8 *religious fear*: Sacred duty.

10 *upon*: That is, at the expense of (like parasites).

11 *single and peculiar life*: Private individual (contrasted with a king).

13 *noyance*: Harm.

14 *That spirit*: The life of a king.

14 *weal*: Welfare.

15 *cess of majesty*: Cessation of royal rule (by the death or deposition of the king). In F the more familiar word *cease* has replaced the unusual *cess*.

16 *Dies not alone*: Is not a single death.
   gulf: Whirlpool.

17–20 *a massy wheel . . . adjoined*: The King is described as resembling the wheel of Fortune.

20 *mortised and adjoined*: Fitted together (like joints of wood).

21 *annexment*: Appendage.
   petty consequence: Unimportant follower.

22 *Attends*: Accompanies.
   boisterous ruin: Tumultuous downfall.

23 *a general groan*: The people share in the misery.

24 *Arm you*: Prepare.

25 *about this fear*: Upon this cause of our fear.

28 *arras*: Again Polonius enjoys spying on Hamlet from a hiding-place.
   convey: Surreptitiously place.

29 *the process*: What happens.
   tax him home: Reproach him unsparingly.

30 *as you said*: In fact the suggestion came from Polonius himself (III.1.185–6).

32 *them*: Mothers.

33 *of vantage*: Perhaps 'in addition', or 'from the vantage-ground of concealment'.

36–72 *O, my offence . . . All may be well*: This is the first time we see the King alone and the only occasion we have a full confession from him (but see III.1.50–54). The conscience-stricken King, unlike Hamlet, knows his theological position exactly, and argues about his situation with clarity of mind. Ironically, only after Hamlet's departure (with the same erroneous belief as ourselves) do we learn that the King has not achieved a state of grace.

37 *the primal eldest curse*: The oldest curse upon mankind.

39 *Though inclination be as sharp as will*: He sincerely desires to pray; he is not merely forcing himself to do so by an act of will.

41 *like a man to double business bound*: He wishes to repent and wishes to persist in his guilty situation.

43 *both neglect*: Fail to deal with either.

44 *thicker*: Deeply covered (made more than double its usual thickness).

45 *Is there not rain enough in the sweet heavens*: 'How fair a thing is mercy in the time of anguish and trouble? It is like a cloud of rain that cometh in the time of drought' (Ecclesiasticus 35:20).

46 *wash it white as snow*: 'Thou shalt wash me, and I shall be whiter than snow' (Psalm 51:7).
   Whereto serves: What is the use of.

47 *confront the visage of offence*: Meet sin face to face.

48 *twofold force*: Double efficacy, in preventing us from sinning and in helping us to win pardon when we have sinned ('lead us not into temptation, but deliver us from evil' (Matthew 6:13)).

49 *forestallèd*: Prevented.

51 *My fault is past*: Once I have appealed to God for mercy, my sin will have been forgiven. (But he knows that appealing to God brings with it certain conditions.)

54 *effects*: Resulting benefits.

55 *mine own ambition*: That is, the fulfilment of my ambition.

56 *retain th'offence*: Continue to enjoy what has been gained by the wicked deed.

57 *corrupted currents*: Corrupt ways of behaviour.

58 *Offence's gilded hand*: The hand of an offender bearing gold as bribes to the judges.
   shove by: Thrust aside.

59–60 *the wicked prize itself | Buys out the law*: What has been gained by wicked actions -- such as power and riches -- is used to obtain exemption from the laws against those very actions.

60 *above*: In heaven.

61 *There . . . There*: In heaven (emphasized).
   shuffling: Trickery.

61–2 *the action lies | In*: Probably 'legal action can be brought

against us according to', as well as 'the wicked deed is
revealed in'.

62 *his*: Its.

62–4 *we ourselves . . . evidence*: In the law courts a man may
not be constrained to give evidence that will incrimi-
nate himself; but before God's seat of judgement it is
different.

62 *compelled*: Are compelled.

63 *to the teeth and forehead*: In the very face.

64 *give in*: Provide.
What rests: What remains for me to do?

65 *can*: Can do.

68 *limèd soul*: The soul is like a bird which has been caught
by the laying of 'lime', a glue-like substance.

69 *engaged*: Entangled.
Make assay: Make a vigorous attempt (probably
addressed to himself rather than to the angels or to his
knees).

70 *strings of steel*: He imagines his heart-strings have hardened to steel as a result of his crime.

73 *pat*: Neatly, opportunely.

74 *'a goes to heaven*: At first Hamlet uses the conventional phrase, meaning 'he dies'. Then he begins
to analyse it literally. He supposes that the King is
in a state of contrition, and so his death at this
moment will, quite literally, enable him to go *to
heaven*.

75 *would be scanned*: Needs to be subjected to scrutiny.

77 *sole son*: Only son (and therefore the only person upon
whom the duty of revenge lies).

79 *hire and salary*: Like a payment for services, instead of
punishment for crimes.

80 *took*: Took at a disadvantage and killed.
grossly, full of bread: In a condition of gross unpre-
paredness, without having had an opportunity of a peni-
tential fast.

81 *crimes*: Sins. See the first note to I.5.12.
broad blown, as flush as May: In full bloom, like the
vigorous vegetation in the month of May. Hamlet is

recalling that the Ghost said he was *Cut off even in the
blossoms of my sin* (I.5.76).

82 *audit*: Account (with God).

83 *our circumstance and course of thought*: The exact
    meaning is difficult to decide, but, roughly inter-
    preted, Hamlet is saying 'so far as we, here on earth,
    can judge' or 'according to our evidence and spec-
    ulation'.

86 *seasoned*: Prepared.

    passage: To the next world.

88 *Up*: That is, come out of your sheath.

    a more horrid hent: A grasp causing more horror (that
    is, when he is about to execute a more terrible deed of
    vengeance upon Claudius).

89 *drunk asleep*: Dead drunk.

91 *game*: Gambling.

91–2 *some act | That has no relish of salvation in't*: This is
    what Hamlet ultimately achieves at V.2.316–21, stab-
    bing the King when he is engaged in acts of murderous
    treachery.

92 *relish*: Savour.

93 *trip him*: Take him by a quick act of treachery (still
    addressing his sword).

    his heels may kick at heaven: Hamlet imagines his enemy
    as receiving a deadly blow and sprawling forwards, so
    that in his death throes his legs bend upwards from his
    knees.

95 *stays*: Awaits me.

96 *This physic but prolongs thy sickly days*: The spiritual
    medicine you (the King) are now taking (by praying
    to God, and in *the purging of his soul*, 85) only gives
    you a respite; you are like a sick man who takes medi-
    cine, but thereby only postpones the inevitable
    approach of death.

97 *My words fly up, my thoughts remain below*: The King
    has been uttering the *words* of prayers, but has not been
    thinking about them. His mind has been busy with
    thoughts of his worldly affairs. So he has not been in
    a state of contrition.

III.4

This scene takes place in Gertrude's *closet* (III.2.339).

1 *lay home*: Talk severely.

2 *broad*: Unrestrained.

4 *heat*: Anger (of the court, and of the King in particular). *silence*: This is the reading of both Q2 and F. Editors often accept the emendation 'sconce' (hide). But *silence* may be right, as a stroke of irony against the *foolish prating knave* who can only be *still* when dead (215–16).

5 *round with*: Plain-spoken to.

7 *Fear me not*: Do not doubt that I will do what you have suggested.

9 *Now, mother . . .* : Q1 makes Hamlet say *but first weele make all safe*. This may be a genuine memory of a piece of stage business by which Hamlet bolts the door.

10 *thy father*: Your stepfather.

12 *idle*: Foolish.

15 *forgot me*: Forgotten that I am your mother. *the Rood*: Christ's Cross.

18 *I'll set those to you that can speak*: Presumably she rises, resentful of Hamlet's insult.

21 *see the inmost part of you*: The Queen interprets this as a threat of personal violence. But Hamlet means merely 'see the bottom of your soul'.

23 *Help, ho*: That Hamlet behaves in a way that genuinely frightens his mother is suggested by the absurd lines which the reporter of Q1 based on his memory of the action: *I first bespake him faire,* | *But then he throwes and tosses me about,* | *As one forgetting that I was his mother* (to the King at IV.1.8).

25 *Dead for a ducat*: I would wager a ducat that I have killed it.

31 *As kill a king*: The Queen's amazement and horror both remind the audience of the terrible nature of the King's crime and confirm our impression of her innocence of any knowledge of it.

34 *busy*: Interfering (like a busybody).

38 *damnèd custom*: Vice that has become habitual. See Hamlet's lines on *that monster custom* (162–71).

brassed: Q2 reads *brasd*, which probably indicates *brassed*, 'hardened like brass'. But F reads *braʒ'd*, which makes it possible that 'brazed' ('made brazen') is correct.

39 *proof*: Impenetrable.

   sense: Feeling.

40 *wag*: Move (not a ludicrous word).

41 *act*: Presumably incest; the accusation of adultery is scarcely evidenced.

43 *Calls virtue hypocrite*: Makes all virtue seem a mere pretence.

43–4 *takes off the rose . . . innocent love*: Presumably he is thinking of his love for Ophelia, and is summarizing his interview with her at III.1.89–150. Cf. Laertes's language at IV.5.120–22: *brands the harlot* | *. . . between the chaste unsmirchèd brows* | *Of my true mother.*

45 *blister*: Mark made by the branding iron. Criminals, including harlots, were branded on the forehead.

47 *contraction*: Witnessed ceremony and contract of marriage.

48–9 *sweet religion makes* | *A rhapsody of words*: Probably referring to the marriage service; but Hamlet's attitude is scarcely justified, for the vows undertaken are to last 'so long as ye both shall live'.

49 *rhapsody*: Medley of items strung together without meaningful order.

   words: Merely, and nothing more.

   glow: Blush.

50 *this solidity and compound mass*: The earth.

   compound: Composed of the various elements.

51 *heated*: F has *tristfull* ('sad'), which many editors adopt.

   as against the Doom: As if the Day of Judgement were at hand.

52 *thought-sick*: Sick with horror.

53 *index*: Table of contents (as in a book – the index was formerly at the beginning, not at the end – and so 'prelude to what you are going to say').

54 *upon this picture, and on this*: It is uncertain whether these are miniatures or large pictures hanging on the

wall. Miniatures have generally been preferred; Hamlet
wears one and his mother another, and he can force
her to gaze upon them as he puts them together.
Moreover, two large pictures would be inconvenient
stage properties, quite apart from the indecorum of the
Queen's having portraits of both her husbands in her
closet. Nevertheless, the pose described at 55–63 would
best suit a full-length portrait; and in the first illustra-
tion of this scene (in Rowe's edition, 1709) wall
portraits (but half-lengths) are shown. Some actors have
preferred to suppose the pictures to be in the mind's
eye only, but *counterfeit presentment* (55) is strongly
against this.

55 *counterfeit presentment*: Presentation by artistic portraiture.

57 *Hyperion*: See the second note to I.2.140.
   front: Forehead.

59 *station*: Stance.
   Mercury: The winged messenger of the gods, and so
   an image of graceful movement and poise.

60 *New lighted*: Newly alighted.

61 *combination*: Of the elements.

62 *every god did seem to set his seal*: This seems to be a
   reminiscence of the classical story of the creation of
   man, in which each of the gods gave something.

63 *assurance*: Confirmation.

65 *ear*: Of wheat.

66 *Blasting*: Blighting.

67–8 *this fair mountain leave to feed, | And batten on this moor*:
   The contrast is difficult to explain. Presumably it is
   suggested by *hill* (60) and *mildewed ear* (65). Neither
   mountains nor moors (uncultivated highlands) are especially attractive for sheep-fattening. We should expect
   the contrast to be between the healthful pasturage on
   the hillsides and the unhealthful pasturage in the rank
   lower ground.

68 *batten*: Fatten (like sheep).

70 *heyday*: Time of wildness in youth.
   blood: Passion, sexual urge.

71 *waits upon*: Obeys.

72 *Sense*: The exact meaning is uncertain; perhaps 'control of the senses', or 'ability to apprehend and distinguish', or 'sexual desire'.

74 *apoplexed*: Paralysed (as by a stroke).

75 *ecstasy*: Madness.
   thralled: Enslaved.

76 *reserved some quantity*: Preserved some small element.

78 *cozened you at hoodman-blind*: Tricked you in playing blind-man's buff (into choosing the very worst).

80 *sans all*: Without using any of the other senses.

82 *so mope*: Behave so aimlessly.

84 *mutine*: Make a mutiny.

85–6 *be as wax | And melt in her own fire*: The image is probably of a stick of sealing-wax, which is ignited and then nearly inverted so that drops of the melting wax fall from it.

87 *charge*: Command (to go forward).

88 *frost*: Of middle age.

89 *reason panders will*: Reason (the powers of judgement appropriate to middle age) acts as a pander to lust.

91 *grainèd*: Deeply ingrained.

92 *will not leave their tinct*: Cannot have the stain washed out of them.

93 *enseamèd*: Greasy.

94 *Stewed*: Soaked. ('Stews' were brothels.)

95 *sty*: Place like a pig-sty.

98 *tithe*: Tenth part.

99 *precedent lord*: Previous husband.
   vice of kings: King who behaves like a buffoon (like the Vice in the morality plays of the sixteenth century).

103 *of shreds and patches*: As if he were wearing the clown's motley.
   Enter the Ghost: Q1 has *Enter the ghost in his night gowne* (i.e. dressing-gown), probably reflecting stage practice. It appears at the climax of Hamlet's tirade, presumably as he is about to tell his mother the circumstances of the murder.

106 *he's mad*: It is clear from this and 125 and 133 that the

Queen cannot see the Ghost.

108 *lapsed in time and passion*: Having allowed time to slip by and his passionate commitment to his task of revenge to cool (also sometimes interpreted as 'deteriorated into mere emotion').

109 *important*: Urgent.

113 *amazement*: Distraction (at Hamlet's behaviour, not at the Ghost).

114 *fighting soul*: Mind in agony.

115 *Conceit*: Imagination.

118 *bend*: Aim.

vacancy: Space, thin air.

119 *incorporal*: Incorporeal.

120 *Forth . . . peep*: That is, you look astonished.

121 *in th'alarm*: When an alarm is sounded.

122 *bedded*: Normally lying flat (like *soldiers* on their beds).

hair: This is sometimes emended to 'hairs', but the plural forms *Start* and *stand* may be influenced by *excrements*.

excrements: Outgrowths (hair grows out of the body, but has no independent *life*).

123 *an*: On.

127 *form and cause*: Physical appearance (which inspires pity) and the reason he has for appealing to us.

conjoined: United.

128 *capable*: Of responding to what he said.

129 *this piteous action*: These gestures (like an actor's) stirring pity.

129–30 *convert | My stern effects*: Transform the results of my stern intentions.

131 *want true colour*: Lack its proper appearance (look pale and bloodless; with a quibble on *colour* meaning 'motive').

tears . . . for blood: Shedding tears instead of blood.

136 *his habit as he lived*: His familiar everyday clothing.

138 *very coinage*: Complete invention.

139 *This bodiless creation*: This kind of hallucination.

139–40 *ecstasy | Is very cunning in*: Madness is very skilful in creating.

141 *temperately keep time*: Beat steadily.

144 *re-word*: Repeat word for word.

145 *gambol*: Capriciously lead me astray.

146 *that flattering unction*: The soothing balm of that flattery.

149 *mining*: Undermining.

151 *what is to come*: Further opportunities of sinful behaviour.

154 *fatness*: Grossness.

   pursy: Short-winded (and so in bad condition morally).

156 *curb*: Bow.

   him: Vice.

161 *Assume*: Acquire.

162 *who all sense doth eat*: Which destroys all sensibility.

163 *Of habits devil*: Being the evil genius of our habits. For
   devil many editors prefer the emendation 'evil'; the
   meaning is then 'custom, which deprives one of all
   feeling for the evil nature of habits'.

   angel yet: Nevertheless our good genius.

164 *use*: Habitual practice.

165 *frock or livery*: (New) dress or uniform.

166 *aptly*: Easily.

169 *stamp of nature*: Inborn characteristics of personality.

170 *And either master the devil*: Q2 omits the verb, doubtless accidentally. (The passage is not in F.) The fourth
   Quarto edition (1611) has *And maister the devil*; and,
   although this Quarto's changes have no known
   authority, the choice of this word to fill the gap could
   be due to stage practice. Other plausible suggestions
   are 'curb', 'lay', 'oust', 'quell', 'shame' or 'tame', or
   to replace *either* by 'exorcize'. Perhaps, however, the
   use of *either . . . or* demands a word contrasting with
   throw . . . out, such as 'aid', 'house' or 'speed'.

172–3 *when you are desirous to be blest,* | *I'll blessing beg of
   you*: That is, I shall not ask for your blessing (as a son
   would normally do on departure) until you are repen-
   tant and seek God's blessing.

174 *heaven hath pleased it so*: Such has been the will of
   heaven. Hamlet seems to transfer the responsibility for
   Polonius's death to Providence.

175 *this*: Polonius's corpse.

176 *scourge and minister*: Both the lash which inflicts punishment and the officer who administers it.

177 *bestow*: Put away somewhere.

  answer: Account for.

179 *only to be kind*: Purely to fulfil my filial love for my father and to effect a reformation of character in you.

180 *This bad begins*: This calamity (the killing of Polonius) is a beginning of trouble.

183 *bloat*: Bloated.

184 *wanton*: Wantonly.

  mouse: A common term of endearment.

185 *reechy*: Dirty (literally, 'smoky').

186 *paddling*: Playing wantonly.

187 *ravel . . . out*: Disentangle, make clear.

188 *essentially*: In my essential nature.

189 *in craft*: By cunning.

  'Twere good: Sarcastic.

191 *paddock*: Toad.

  gib: Tom cat.

192 *Such dear concernings*: Matters that concern him so closely.

193 *sense and secrecy*: Instinct and your impulse towards secrecy.

194–7 *Unpeg the basket . . . down*: This story is not known from any other source. It can be reconstructed as follows: an ape steals a wickerwork cage (*basket*) of birds and carries it to the top of a house. Out of curiosity, or by accident, he releases the pegs of the cage, and the birds fly out. The ape is prompted to imitate them; he creeps into the basket and then leaps out, supposing that he will be able to fly like the birds. But, of course, he falls to the ground and breaks his neck.

  Hamlet's application of the fable is as follows: if you reveal my secrets to the King, you will be like this ape. You will gain nothing by it; and if you imagine you can act with the King as cleverly as I can, independently of me, you will be like the ape trying to fly, and so will come to grief.

196 *try conclusions*: See what will happen.

197 *down*: In the fall.

205 *mandate*: Command.

sweep my way: Prepare the way for me (literally, sweep a path before me).

206 *marshal me to knavery*: Conduct me into some trap. Hamlet guesses that the King is plotting some treachery.

work: Go forward.

207 *enginer*: Maker of military 'engines'.

208 *Hoist*: Hoisted (here, 'blown up').

petar: Bomb.

208–9 *'t shall go hard | But I will delve*: It will be unlucky if I don't succeed in delving.

209–10 *delve one yard . . . moon*: Hamlet imagines that, like the garrison of a besieged town whose walls have been mined, he will dig a counter-mine below the attackers' mine and so blow them up.

211 *in one line two crafts directly meet*: Like mining and counter-mining. Perhaps Hamlet is quibbling on *crafts* meaning 'ships'.

212 *set me packing*: Make me start plotting (with a quibble on the other meaning, 'cause me to be sent away quickly').

217 *draw toward an end with you*: Conclude my conversation with you (who were such a *prating* fellow).

IV.1

As there is clearly no real lapse of time between this and the previous scene, the traditional act division is unreasonable; but it is preserved here for readers' convenience.

1 *matter*: Significance.

heaves: Heavy sighs.

2 *translate*: Explain.

10 *Whips*: He whips.

11 *brainish apprehension*: Headstrong illusion.

12 *heavy*: Grievous.

13 *us . . . we*: The royal plural. Claudius knows that the blow was intended for him.

16 *answered*: Explained.

17 *laid to*: Blamed upon.

providence: Foresight.

18 *short*: Under control.

out of haunt: Away from public places.

22 *divulging*: Becoming known in public.

25 *O'er whom his very madness*: Over which his madness itself.

ore: Vein of gold.

26 *mineral of metals base*: Mine of non-precious metals.

27 *'A weeps*: Probably an invention of Gertrude's to palliate Hamlet's conduct.

29 *The sun . . . touch*: A reminder that it is still the middle of the night.

32 *countenance*: Assume responsibility for.

40 *So haply slander*: There is a gap in the Q2 text here (F omits the whole sentence). Some extra words are needed for both metre and sense. Those printed here, proposed by eighteenth-century editors, seem more satisfactory than other suggestions.

41 *the world's diameter*: The extent of the world from side to side.

42 *level*: Straight.

his blank: Its point of aim (the 'white' in the middle of the target).

44 *woundless*: Invulnerable.

IV.2

Again, no time elapses between this and the previous scene.

1 *Safely stowed*: By hiding the body, Hamlet makes his murder of Polonius seem to be an act of madness.

6 *Compounded it with dust*: Hardly true; Hamlet has only *stowed* it in a cupboard on the stairs: IV.3.35–6.

Compounded: Shakespeare normally accents this word on the first syllable, so Q2's *Compound* may be correct.

11 *I can keep your counsel and not mine own*: Hamlet's riddling speech is as baffling to us as to Rosencrantz. Perhaps *counsel* means 'secret', and Hamlet is referring to his not betraying their confession at II.2.292 that they had been *sent for*. His own *counsel* (or 'secret') is the whereabouts of the body.

12 *to be demanded of*: On being questioned by.

replication: Reply (a legal term).

15 *countenance*: Favour.

16 *his authorities*: The exercise of his powers. Doubtless
Hamlet is speaking scornfully of their position of new
authority over him.

17–18 *like an ape an apple*: F's reading is *like an Ape*; Q2 has
like an apple. Each gives only a very strained meaning.
Q1 transfers this conversation to follow III.2.379 and
reads *hee doth keep you as an Ape doth nuttes,* | *In the
corner of his Iaw, first mouthes you,* | *Then swallowes you.*
It is tempting to adopt the clear reading of Q1 ('as an
ape doth nuts'). But it seems most likely that the Q2 and
F readings are each a confusion of *like an ape an apple*.

18 *first*: At first.
mouthed: Taken into the mouth.

19 *last*: At last.

23–4 *A knavish speech sleeps in a foolish ear*: A sarcastic remark
is wasted upon an unintelligent hearer.

27–8 *The body is . . . body*: Hamlet may mean 'the body is
now in the next world with the King (my father
Hamlet), but King Claudius has not yet been killed'.
Or he may be talking deliberate, sinister nonsense.

28–30 *The King is a thing . . . Of nothing*: Again Hamlet is
using suggestive threatening language, echoing the
passage in the Psalms about the transitoriness of mortal
life: 'Man is like a thing of nought. His time passeth
away like a shadow' (144:4; Prayer Book version).
Claudius is doomed to death.

30–31 *Hide fox, and all after*: These words in F are not in Q2,
and may be an interpolation to introduce a bit of exit
business, such as Hamlet's eluding his captors and
running offstage. This has become common theatrical
practice, but is not justified by Hamlet's entry at IV.3.15.
The words probably refer to some children's game of
hide-and-seek.

IV.3

0 *attendants*: Presumably a group of counsellors or
supporters, perhaps the *wisest friends* of IV.1.38.

4 *of*: By.

4 *distracted*: Unreasonable, unstable.

5 *like not in*: Choose not by.

6 *scourge*: Punishment. Claudius supposes that the people will not allow Hamlet to be punished for murdering Polonius.

7 *bear all smooth and even*: Conduct the affair so as not to give offence or seem high-handed.

9 *Deliberate pause*: The result of deliberately and unhurriedly considering the matter.

9–11 *Diseases desperate grown . . . at all*: A proverbial idiom, which occurs in the form: 'A desperate disease must have a desperate cure.'

10 *appliance*: Remedies.

11 *all the rest*: Probably, in Shakespeare's theatre, any extras who could be spared to stand in as courtiers.

20 *convocation of politic worms*: There is doubtless a punning allusion to the Diet of Worms (a city on the Rhine), opened by the Emperor (see 21) Charles V in 1521, which brought together the dignitaries of the Holy Roman Empire.

  convocation: Parliament.

  politic: Crafty.

  e'en: Even now.

21 *fat*: Fatten.

23 *but variable service*: Just different courses of a meal.

30 *progress*: The usual word for a monarch's official journeys through his kingdom.

35 *nose*: Smell.

39 *thine especial safety*: Claudius is presumably referring to possible retribution upon Hamlet by Polonius's son or friends rather than to Hamlet's judicial prosecution for murder.

40 *tender*: Feel concern for.

  dearly: Keenly.

42 *With fiery quickness*: As quickly as spreading flames.

43 *at help*: Ready to help.

44 *associates*: Companions (Rosencrantz and Guildenstern).

  tend: Await you.

  bent: Prepared (like a drawn bow).

50 *cherub*: A heavenly spirit with exceptional powers of vision: Ezekiel 1:18 and 10:12.

54 *man and wife is one flesh*: Hamlet ironically uses the language of the marriage service.

56 *at foot*: Close behind him.

58 *everything is sealed and done*: Claudius is here referring ostensibly to *the demand of our neglected tribute* (III.1.171) but, in his thoughts, to the letters ordering *The present death of Hamlet* (66–7). There is an emphasis on the secrecy of these instructions. Hamlet has to *unseal | Their grand commission* at V.2.17–18 and seal the new one with his *father's signet* (V.2.49).

59 *leans*: Depends.

60 *England*: (Probably) King of England.

61 *As*: For so.
   thereof may give thee sense: May well give you a just appreciation of the importance of that love.

62 *cicatrice*: Scar.

63 *free awe*: Awe of us which is still felt though without military occupation.

64 *coldly set*: Set a low value upon.

65 *sovereign process*: Royal instructions.
   imports at full: Calls in detail for.

66 *congruing*: Agreeing. Claudius seems to be referring to a second letter with more explicit instructions. Nothing further is made of this. F reads *coniuring* ('earnestly requesting'), which would correspond to *earnest conjuration* (V.2.38).

67 *present*: Immediate.

68 *hectic*: Persistent fever.

70 *Howe'er my haps*: Whatever my fortunes may be.
   were ne'er begun: This is the F reading. Q2 reads *will nere begin*, which is perhaps better grammar, but fails to rhyme.

IV.4

0 *Fortinbras*: We have not heard about old Norway and Fortinbras since II.2.60–80. The vigour of Fortinbras, like that of Laertes, is an adverse reflection upon Hamlet's inactivity, as he himself recognizes (46–53).

3 *the conveyance of*: Escort during.

   promised: Previously agreed (II.2.80–82, where a favourable answer to the Norwegian request is implied).

5–6 *If that his majesty . . . eye*: Fortinbras expresses his respect for the King of Denmark and accepts his authority, in accordance with the vow (shown now to be sincere) he had given to his uncle (II.2.70–71).

5 *would aught*: Wishes to have any communication.

6 *in his eye*: By presenting myself (*us*, the royal plural) personally before him.

8 *Go softly on*: This is probably addressed to his troops, not to the Captain.

   softly: Slowly, leisurely (perhaps; but the word seems to imply the respectful march of the army through the Danish territory).

9 *powers*: Troops.

15 *main*: Central part.

16 *frontier*: Frontier-fortress.

17 *addition*: Fine words to exaggerate the matter.

19 *name*: Reputation for having conquered it.

20 *five ducats, five*: The repeated numeral emphasizes its smallness: it would not be worth paying an annual rent of a mere five ducats (a coin worth about nine shillings) for the lease of the land as a farm.

22 *ranker rate*: Higher rate of interest (on the purchase money).

   in fee: As a freehold property.

25–6 *Two thousand souls . . . straw*: It has been plausibly suggested that these two lines belong to the Captain, who is in a better position to speak of *Two thousand* and *twenty thousand* than is Hamlet. Perhaps the repetition of *straw* at 55 supports this.

25 *Two thousand souls*: His estimate of the size of the armies involved.

   twenty thousand ducats: His estimate of the expenditure on the war.

26 *Will not debate the question*: Are not enough to settle the dispute.

   straw: Trivial matter.

27 *imposthume*: Abscess. The consequences of the luxury of society and its vices accumulate unperceived during peace, like the pus in a swollen abscess.

28 *inward...without*: Internally...externally (of the body).

32–66 *How all occasions . . . worth*: The importance of this soliloquy is that it enables Hamlet to make a strong impression on the audience before his long absence, and gives a reassurance that he is still true to his oath of vengeance. It is the most 'reasonable' of his soliloquies, and is probably intended to reveal his developing maturity.

32 *occasions*: Such dissimilar chance meetings as with the players and with this Norwegian army.

inform against me: Denounce me, provide evidence to my discredit (as in a lawsuit).

34 *market*: Profitable employment.

36 *large discourse*: Wide-ranging faculty of understanding.

37 *Looking before and after*: Able to review the past and to use experience as a guide in facing the future.

38 *capability*: Capacity of mind.

godlike: Because shared with the Creator Himself.

39 *fust*: Go mouldy.

40 *Bestial oblivion*: Animal-like inability to retain past impressions.

craven scruple: Cowardly scrupulousness.

41–3 *thinking . . . coward*: Anxiety about the precise consequences of one's actions is due to cowardice much more than to prudence (a remarkably unillusioned analysis by Hamlet of his own feelings and motives).

41 *event*: Outcome.

44 *to do*: Still to be done.

45 *Sith*: Since.

46 *gross*: Weighty.

47 *mass and charge*: Size and expense.

49 *puffed*: Swollen (not necessarily derogatory).

50 *Makes mouths at*: Scorns.

52 *dare*: Could inflict upon him.

53–6 *Rightly to be . . . stake*: True greatness does not consist in rushing into action on account of any trivial cause;

but when the cause is one involving honour, it is noble
to act, however trivial the subject of dispute may be.

54 *argument*: Cause.

55 *greatly*: Nobly.

58 *Excitements*: Incentives.
   blood: Passions.

60 *twenty thousand men*: Hamlet has confusedly transferred
   the number of ducats at 25 to the men (who were then
   only *Two thousand*).

61 *trick of fame*: Whim of seeking fame. Probably *of fame*
   goes with both *fantasy* and *trick*.

62 *plot*: Of ground.

63 *Whereon the numbers cannot try the cause*: Where there
   is not enough space for the two armies to fight out the
   dispute.

64 *continent*: Receptacle (that is, earth to cover the bodies
   of those who are killed in battle).

66 *thoughts*: He speaks only of *thoughts*, not of deeds.

IV.5

There is clearly a considerable lapse of time between
the previous scene and the opening of this.

1 *I will not speak with her*: The Queen is reluctant to see
  her son's beloved, the daughter of the man he has
  murdered.

2 *distract*: Distracted.

3 *mood will needs be*: Mental condition cannot fail to be.

5 *hems*: She makes a noise like 'hmm', confirming her
  knowledge that *There's tricks i'th'world*.

6 *Spurns*: With her foot.
  enviously: Spitefully.
  straws: Trifles.
  in doubt: Ambiguous.

7 *Her speech is nothing*: She talks nonsense.

8 *unshapèd*: Uncontrolled.

9 *to collection*: To gather something of a meaning.
  aim at it: Make a guess at its meaning. This is the F
  reading (*ayme*). Q2 has *yawne*, which can hardly be
  right, though in an appropriate context 'yawn' can mean
  'let the mouth gape open with surprise'.

10 *botch*: Patch clumsily.

   fit to their own thoughts: To suit their own inferences
   (about her state of mind and the meaning she is trying
   to convey).

11 *Which*: Her words.

   yield them: Deliver (interpret) her words.

13 *nothing*: Not at all.

   much unhappily: Very unskilfully.

15 *Dangerous conjectures*: About the murder of Polonius
   and ill-treatment of herself.

16 *Let her come in*: Q2 attributes these words to Horatio.
   If this were retained, the Queen must give some silent
   assent to Horatio's request.

17 *as sin's true nature is*: That is, as is characteristic of
   someone in a state of sin.

18 *toy*: Trifling event. Apparently she does not yet take
   Ophelia's madness as a serious thing.

   amiss: Misfortune.

19 *artless jealousy*: Uncontrolled suspicion.

20 *spills*: Reveals and destroys.

   Enter Ophelia: Q1 has *Enter Ofelia playing on a Lute,
   and her haire downe singing*. This doubtless is a memory
   of a performance.

21 *Where is the beauteous majesty of Denmark*: This may
   mean merely 'Where is the Queen?', or possibly 'Where
   has your queenly beauty gone?' (addressed to the
   Queen, who, now conscience-ridden, may be looking
   very different from the happy woman of the scenes up
   to III.4).

23–40 *How should I . . . showers*: In these snatches of ballads
   Ophelia seems to be confusing recollections of her lost
   lover with her dead father. They hint that the cause of
   her madness is not only her father's death but her
   estrangement from Hamlet and his banishment.
   Shakespeare does not reveal whether she knows that
   Hamlet killed her father. Her song to the Queen about
   your true-love and *another one* may seem to hint at the
   difference between her first and second husbands. The
   next two stanzas remind the Queen of the death of

King Hamlet as well as of Polonius. For the music of
Ophelia's songs see F. W. Sternfeld's *Music in
Shakespearean Tragedy* (1963).

25 *cockle hat*: A hat with a cockle shell on it signified that
the wearer had made a pilgrimage to the shrine of St
James at Compostela (in north-west Spain), famous
medieval place of pilgrimage.
staff: Pilgrim's walking-staff.

26 *shoon*: Shoes (archaic plural).

28 *Say you*: What do you say?

38 *Larded*: Garnished.

39 *ground*: F and Q1 read *graue* (*grave*), which many
editors prefer.
did not go: It has been suggested that the original song
had 'did go' (which would give an easier rhythm) and
that Ophelia inserts *not* because of her father's not
having received an adequate funeral ceremony (*In
hugger-mugger to inter him*, 85 below).

40 *showers*: Of tears.

42 *God dild*: May God reward ('yield').

42–3 *They say the owl was a baker's daughter*: This may refer
to a folktale in which Christ begged for a loaf of bread
and punished the baker's daughter, who insisted on his
being given only a small one, by transforming her into
an owl. Perhaps Ophelia is trying to say that she knows
she is changed from what she was but is not so badly
done by as that other wicked daughter.

43–4 *we know . . . may be*: Presumably this is a comment on
the transformation of the baker's daughter.

44 *God be at your table*: Perhaps the emphasis is on *your*:
'The benediction before eating may save you from such
a fate as that of the inhospitable baker's daughter.'

45 *Conceit upon her father*: These imaginings of hers about
her father (Claudius is interrupted by Ophelia). Or
perhaps this is an aside, spoken in anxiety about what
Ophelia may reveal. Or it may be addressed to the
Queen, a kind of warning about her son's dangerous
violence.

48–67 *Tomorrow is . . . bed*: The song seems to be prompted

by her imagining herself to have been disobedient to
her father about associating with Hamlet.

48 *Saint Valentine's day*: 14 February, when the birds
choose their mates, according to popular tradition.
There were also folk-customs: the first girl seen by a
man was his 'Valentine'.

49 *betime*: Early.

53 *dupped*: Opened (by lifting *up* the latch).

57 *la*: A very mild substitute for an oath.

57–8 *make an end on't*: Finish the song (in spite of its im-
modesty).

59 *Gis*: Jesus.
Saint Charity: The personification of the virtue.

62 *Cock*: God (probably with a quibble on the popular
name for the penis).

63 *tumbled me*: Took my virginity.

72 *Come, my coach*: Perhaps she imagines herself to be a
stately princess or Hamlet's queen.

73 *ladies . . . Sweet ladies*: The only female present is the
Queen (unless she has attendants).

75 *Follow her . . . you*: There is no indication whom the
King is addressing; but except for Gertrude (and,
possibly, unspecified attendants) Horatio is the only
other character onstage, and editors usually leave the
King and Queen alone for their obviously private
conversation.

76–7 *It springs | All from her father's death*: Claudius does not
consider – or wish Gertrude to consider – that Ophelia's
love for Hamlet has anything to do with her madness.

81 *author*: Originator.

82 *remove*: Removal.
muddied: Turbulent with suspicion (stirred up, as a pool
of water becomes muddy).

83 *Thick and unwholesome*: Like bad blood.
whispers: Malicious gossip.

84 *greenly*: In an inexperienced way.

85 *In hugger-mugger*: With haste and in secrecy. The King
could not allow an inquiry into the circumstances of
Polonius's death, exposing Hamlet's guilt; for he knows

that Hamlet has the secret of the fratricide. To the
Queen he must pretend that his actions are prompted
by a desire to protect Hamlet from the consequences
of his crime.

87 *pictures or mere beasts*: That is, lacking a soul.

88 *as much containing*: Quite as important.

89 *come from France*: This indicates the passage of some
time since the night of Polonius's death and the morning
of Hamlet's departure (IV.4).

90 *Feeds on his wonder*: Nurses his shocked grievance
(perhaps). For *his* Q2 reads *this*, which is even more
difficult; it can hardly refer to Ophelia's distraction
(and in any case it is implied that Laertes does not know
of it until he sees her at 155); and the *hugger-mugger*
funeral of Polonius is grammatically too far away to
be referred to by *this*.

   keeps himself in clouds: Holds himself sullenly aloof.

91 *wants*: Lacks.

   buzzers: Rumourmongers.

93–4 *Wherein necessity . . . arraign*: In this gossip, as the
speakers have nothing definite to go on, they are obliged
to invent things and so do not scruple to spread accu-
sations against me.

95 *In ear and ear*: In many ears one after the other.

96 *murdering-piece*: Mortar or cannon which scattered a
variety of lethal small shot and pieces of metal instead
of a single shot.

99 *Attend*: A call to his guards, imagined as just offstage.

   Switzers: Swiss mercenary soldiers were employed in
many European courts to form a royal bodyguard
(they survive in the Vatican). Their mention here
implies that Claudius is usually well guarded; so
Hamlet's task is not easy.

101 *overpeering of*: Rising above.

   list: Boundary, barrier (perhaps the shore).

102 *Eats not the flats*: Shakespeare is doubtless thinking of
the advancing tide of such places as the Essex coast
and the Thames estuary, where it moves a considerable distance in a short time.

impiteous: Probably this is another form of 'impetuous', influenced by the meaning of the word 'piteous'. But perhaps Shakespeare uses it to mean 'pitiless'.

103 *head*: Onset.

104 *officers*: Household servants and guards.

105 *as the world were now but to begin*: As if civilized life were only now to be created (instead of having been in existence from time immemorial).

107 *The ratifiers and props of every word*: Traditional practices, inherited from earlier times, are the things which give authority and stability to society. This leisurely comment hardly suits the excited tone of the speech. Editors have often emended *word*. It may mean 'pledge, honourable undertakings according to promise', or 'oath of allegiance', or 'title of rank'. But all these interpretations are strained.

108 *Choose we! Laertes shall be king*: Claudius had intimated that Hamlet was the people's favourite (IV.3.4–5). The fickleness of the *multitude* is illustrated by their support for Laertes when the opportunity is offered. The demand *Choose we!* is remarkable. It implies that the election of Claudius was an oligarchic move, not a popular one. But Laertes soon comes to terms with Claudius, and this hint of a democratic revolt is immediately forgotten.

109 *Caps*: Which they wave or throw into the air.

111 *How cheerfully on the false trail they cry*: Gertrude, with unusual bitterness of language, imagines the intruders as a pack of baying hounds pursuing a false scent (*false* because the King is not guilty of Polonius's murder).

112 *counter*: Hunting the trail backwards (like hounds going in the direction contrary to the game). The Danes elected Claudius as their king, and now are going back on their oaths of allegiance.

you false Danish dogs: Presumably Shakespeare took it for granted that the queen-consort of the monarch was a foreigner.

false: Perfidious.

117 *Keep*: Guard.

118 *Give me my father*: Apparently Laertes does not yet know that it was Hamlet who killed Polonius.

121 *the chaste unsmirchèd brows*: See the note to III.4.43–4.

122 *true*: Faithful in marriage.

124 *fear our*: Fear for my royal.

125 *divinity*: Alluding to the doctrine of kings as divine representatives on earth, the Lord's anointed. Claudius's brave assertion of this doctrine in order to intimidate Laertes comes ironically from one who is himself a regicide.
    hedge: Protect as with a rampart.

126 *peep to*: Claudius's language belittles the power of treason by supposing it to peer furtively out of, or over, its hiding place or *hedge*.

127 *Acts little of his will*: (And) performs little of what it intends.

132 *juggled with*: Deceived.

134 *grace*: The grace of God.

135 *To this point I stand*: I have gone so far as this.

136 *both the worlds I give to negligence*: I care nothing of what happens to me in this world or the next.

138 *throughly*: Thoroughly.

139 *My will, not all the world's*: Nothing in the world shall stop me, except my own decision (when my desire for revenge is satisfied).

140–41 *for my means . . . little*: I will employ my resources so economically that I shall be able to make them go a long way.

142–3 *certainty | Of*: Truth about.

143 *writ*: Specified.

144 *swoopstake*: Gambling term used when a winner took the stakes of all his opponents.
    draw: Take from.

148 *life-rendering*: Giving life to its young. The pelican was supposed to feed its young with the blood that flowed from self-inflicted wounds upon its breast. No one, as far as I can discover, has yet suggested that Laertes, with his arms stretched out in the form of a cross and with the blood flowing from his wounded breast, is a

Christ figure. Yet the religious metaphor seems clear: Laertes's image of himself feeding his father's friends with his own blood is offensive bombast, typical of the man.

149 *Repast*: Feed.

152 *most sensibly*: With very intense feeling.

153 *level*: Plain (like a path on the level).

'pear: Appear. Q2 reads *peare*, which some editors have interpreted as 'peer'. F reads *pierce*.

155 *Enter Ophelia*: Presumably Ophelia behaves in such a way as reveals immediately to Laertes that she is mad. It is not clear whether she still carries her lute or whether she now has a bunch of flowers instead. Perhaps it is intended that she has gone to collect the flowers for her father's grave (178–85). Q1 has *Enter Ofelia as before*, but this may refer only to her madness. In her first speech in Q1 she says *I a bin gathering of floures*.

156 *heat, dry up my brains*: Laertes is probably referring to his own fiery anger.

157 *Burn out the sense and virtue*: (Let scalding tears) destroy the sense and power.

158 *paid with weight*: Paid for in full measure.

159 *our scale turn the beam*: His revenge will weigh heavier than Ophelia's madness.

beam: Horizontal bar of a balance.

rose of May: The English wild rose first flowers in May; Ophelia is in her early bloom.

163–5 *Nature is fine . . . loves*: Filial love is, by nature, very sensitive; and such is its sensitivity that it sends some most precious token of itself to the object of its love – in this case, Ophelia's sanity departs with her father Polonius. Laertes's language is typically strained. These three lines are not in Q2.

169 *my dove*: Perhaps Laertes.

171 *move thus*: Persuade me as strongly as your madness does.

172–3 *A-down a-down, and you call him a-down-a*: Perhaps Ophelia is thinking of Polonius as having been called *down* to his grave, and therefore says that this is a

preferable refrain to *Hey non nony* . . . It is possible that
the correct reading is 'You must sing "A-down a-
down", and you call him a-down-a' (if you refer to
Polonius as being dead).

173 *wheel*: Perhaps the spinning-wheel, to which she imagines she is singing the song; or perhaps *wheel* means
'refrain' ('how appropriate is that refrain "A-down a-
down" to my song of woe!'); or perhaps it is a movement in her dance.

173–4 *the false steward, that stole his master's daughter*: This
story (perhaps a ballad) is unknown. It may be that the
three lines sung by Ophelia at 166–8 above are from
the ballad, of which she is here giving the title or
subject.

175 *This nothing's more than matter*: This nonsense has more
significance than any coherent sense could have.

176–85 *There's rosemary . . . violets*: Presumably these flowers
are distributed by Ophelia to be taken to her father's
undecked grave. We can only guess who are the recip-
ients, nor do we know whether the flowers are intended
to be real or fantasies of Ophelia's disordered brain.

176–8 *rosemary . . . for remembrance . . . pansies . . . for thoughts*:
These are probably gifts to a lover. Perhaps she imag-
ines Laertes to be her lover, and gives these flowers to
him.

177–8 *pansies . . . thoughts*: The name comes from French
'pensées'.

179 *document in madness*: Something from which one can
gain instruction in the study of madness.

179–80 *thoughts and remembrance fitted*: By *thoughts* Laertes
probably means 'melancholy thoughts': 'she appropriately brings together melancholy and memories (of
happier things)'.

181 *fennel*: Suggests flattery and *columbines* ingratitude
or marital infidelity. Perhaps these are given to the
King.

182 *rue*: Perhaps she gives this to the Queen, as suggesting
contrition, and then to herself, as suggesting sorrow.

183 *herb of grace o'Sundays*: As 'herb (of) grace' is an ordi-

nary name for *rue*, the idea that such a pious-sounding
name is appropriate for use on Sunday seems to be a
mere fancy.

184 *with a difference*: The heraldic phrase refers to an alteration or addition to a coat of arms to distinguish one
branch of a family from another. But it is only remotely,
if at all, applied here: the rue has a different significance for each of the wearers.

daisy: The flower of dissembling; perhaps given to the
Queen.

185 *violets*: These represent faithfulness in love, and Ophelia
now has none to give. Perhaps in her fantasy she gives
them to Hamlet – all faith in love has disappeared after
the murder of Polonius.

185–6 *They say 'a made a good end*: If she is thinking of
Polonius, the statement is strikingly untrue; he was
killed suddenly, with no opportunity for contrition and
for receiving the sacraments.

187 *For bonny sweet Robin . . . joy*: The words of this song,
probably relating to Robin Hood, are lost; but the tune,
which was exceptionally popular, survives.

188 *Thought*: Gloomy thought.

passion: Suffering.

hell itself: Presumably 'torment of soul'.

189 *favour*: Beauty.

196 *flaxen was his poll*: His head was pale like flax.

198 *cast away moan*: Are wasting our time in grieving.

201 *Do you see this? O God*: Q2 reads *Doe you this ô
God*. F reads *Do you see this, you Gods?* F's *Gods* is
unsuitable in a Christian play, especially immediately after Ophelia's exit line; but its *see* is probably
right. There is no punctuation in Q2 to help us
decide whether Laertes, in an expostulatory tone, is
asking God to observe what is going on here on
earth ('Do you see this, O God?') or whether he is
making two broken-hearted utterances, first a general
appeal and then an anguished interjection. On the
whole the second seems more likely. Perhaps *you*
refers to the King, who responds.

202 *commune with your grief*: Have your grief in common
with you.

commune: Accented on the first syllable.

204 *whom*: Whichever among.

206 *collateral hand*: Indirect agency.

207 *touched*: Infected with guilt (of the murder of Polonius).

209 *in satisfaction*: As recompense.

210 *lend your patience to us*: Be patient for a while at my
request.

213 *His means of death*: The manner of Polonius's death.

obscure: Accented on the first syllable.

214 *trophy, sword . . . hatchment*: Memorial emblems, such
as the knightly sword and the coat of arms, accompanied the coffin in the funeral procession. The *hatchment* (or 'achievement') was an escutcheon blazoning
the arms of the dead person. Many of these old painted
escutcheons still hang in churches in England.

215 *ostentation*: Ceremony.

217 *That*: So that.

call't in question: Demand an explanation of it.

218 *where th'offence is, let the great axe fall*: The Queen can
hardly fail to hear this threat to Hamlet. But Claudius
is doubtless thinking of his secret instructions to the
King of England *not to stay the grinding of the axe* but
Hamlet's *head should be struck off* (V.2.24–5). He comes
to terms with Laertes for his own safety. Not until
IV.7.43 does the news come that Hamlet, contrary to
expectations, is returning to Elsinore; and then Claudius
sees the advantages of allying himself with Laertes
against Hamlet.

IV.6

6 *greeted*: Addressed in a letter.

10 *th'ambassador*: The sailor does not name Hamlet,
presumably as a disguise. He can hardly be unaware
of his identity.

14 *overlooked*: Looked over.

means: Of access.

16 *appointment*: Equipment.

17 *put on a compelled valour*: Decided to assume an appear-

ance of courage, because we had no alternative.

20 *of mercy*: Merciful. There seems to be a slight allusion
to the thieves crucified with Christ, as is supported by
the phraseology of *they knew what they did*.

20–21 *knew what they did*: Were aware that Hamlet was a
prince, who would have influence to get them pardoned
if they treated him well.

22 *repair*: Come.

25 *much too light for the bore of the matter*: Weak in comparison with the importance of the matter, like a small
projectile in a gun with a large *bore*.

26 *will bring thee where I am*: This may suggest that Hamlet
is in hiding, but the idea is not developed.

31 *I will give you way for these your letters*: Cf. IV.7.39–41.

IV.7

This scene continues the talk between the King and
Laertes which was broken off at the end of IV.5. In
the interval, the King has been able to give Laertes an
account (which the audience does not need) of Hamlet's
misdeeds.

1 *my acquittance seal*: Confirm my acquittal (as guiltless
of the misdeeds you had attributed to me).

3 *with a knowing ear*: Laertes is an intelligent listener, says
the ingratiating King.

6 *feats*: Deeds.

7 *capital*: Punishable by death.

8 *your safety*: Your care for your own safety.
greatness: This word is omitted in F, probably in order
to reduce the line to ten syllables.
wisdom: Political prudence.

9 *mainly*: Strongly.
two special reasons: The King omits the really powerful
reason: if he were to take public proceedings against
Hamlet for the murder of Polonius, Hamlet would be
likely to reveal the fratricide. The King is confident in
dealing with Laertes because he expects shortly to
receive from England the news of Hamlet's death.

10 *unsinewed*: Without strength.

13 *My virtue or my plague, be it either which*: Whether it is

a good side of my character or a serious misfortune (that I have these feelings contrary to my self-interest).

14 *conjunctive*: Closely united (also an astronomical term, and so leading to the image in the next line).

15 *the star moves not but in his sphere*: In astronomy, before Copernicus, the earth, at the centre of the universe, was believed to be surrounded by a series of hollow transparent concentric spheres. On the surface of each a planet was fixed. The sphere revolved around the earth and carried the planet with it.

16 *I could not but by her*: (Because she is, as it were, my sphere, and with her motion I move) I could not live without her.

17 *count*: Trial.

18 *general gender*: Common people.

20 *Work*: Act.

the spring that turneth wood to stone: Several of these lime-laden springs, able to 'petrify' (with a limestone deposit) objects placed in them, were known in Shakespeare's time.

21 *Convert his gyves to graces*: Would make the fetters he wore as a prisoner seem to be emblems of his personal honour.

22 *Too slightly timbered for*: Too light in weight to be effective in.

loud: Suggesting popular clamour on Hamlet's behalf.

23 *reverted*: Returned.

26 *desperate terms*: A condition of despair.

27 *if praises may go back again*: If one may praise what has been and is now no more.

28 *Stood challenger . . . of all the age*: Was able to challenge all competitors in the world nowadays.

on mount: Conspicuously, for all to see. An alternative reading is 'challenger-on-mount' ('a challenger mounted and ready in the lists'), but this usage is difficult to parallel.

30 *Break not your sleeps for that*: Laertes need not worry about taking vengeance for his father's murder, for the King has already arranged for Hamlet's death. He is,

up to this point, only concerned with pacifying Laertes,
not with arousing him to revenge.

32 *let our beard be shook with danger*: Allow such insulting
behaviour to come close to me.

33 *You shortly shall hear more*: Claudius has in mind the
news he expects of Hamlet's execution in England. But
soon quite different news arrives.

37 *This to the Queen*: No more is heard of this letter.

40 *Claudio*: An odd name for Shakespeare to use, as the
King's name is Claudius.

41 *you shall hear them*: The King is showing off his confidence in Laertes, and his openness: he will read the
letter without previously examining its contents.

43 *naked*: Without resources, or unarmed, rather than
without clothes.

44 *Tomorrow*: The time-scheme of the play scarcely allows
this. Some interval of time is assumed between the end
of this scene and V.1, allowing for the inquest on
Ophelia. See the headnote to V.1.

46 *more strange*: Than *sudden*.

48 *What should this mean*: The King receives the news
with consternation, as it shows that his English plot has
failed. But Laertes is delighted.
    all the rest: Rosencrantz, Guildenstern and others in the
party for England.

49 *abuse*: Deception.

50 *character*: Handwriting.

51 *alone*: Perhaps Hamlet is avoiding suspicion of having
raised support for himself.

52 *devise me*: Explain it for me. The King is surprised, but
is thinking rapidly, and by 58 has made up his mind
about his next move.

53 *lost in*: Perplexed at.

56 *didest*: Q2 has *didst*, possibly a misreading of 'diest'.
    it: Hamlet's return, rather than Laertes's impulse to
revenge.

57 *how should it be so? How otherwise*: The King is almost
incredulous of Hamlet's return, yet the evidence of the
letter is strong.

58 *Will you be ruled by me*: The King has recovered his equilibrium. Now he must stir Laertes to revenge against Hamlet.

59 *So you will not*: Provided that you do not.

60 *thine own peace*: Peace of mind achieved by taking full vengeance, not the 'reconciliation' rejected by Laertes in the previous line.

61 *As checking at*: Because he has turned aside from (like a hawk swerving aside from its prey and pursuing some inferior object).
   that: If.

63 *ripe in my device*: Matured in my invention.

66 *uncharge the practice*: Be unable to make any accusation as a consequence of our plot (or 'not suspect a plot').

69 *organ*: Agent.

72 *Your sum of parts*: All your talents put together.

75 *siege*: Rank.

76 *A very riband in the cap of youth*: A typical accomplishment of a young man, like a ribbon worn as an ornament in his hat.

77 *needful*: It being a necessary accomplishment for a man to defend himself with his sword.
   no less becomes: Is no less suited by.

78 *livery*: Garments.

79 *his sables and his weeds*: Its (dark) fur-lined garments.

80 *Importing health*: Indicating a care for health (or perhaps *health* means 'prosperity' in general: 'giving an impression of being well-to-do').

81 *Normandy*: As the play is vaguely set in late Anglo-Saxon times, the introduction of a Norman is appropriate enough.

83 *can well*: Are very skilful.

84 *in't*: In his horsemanship.

86 *As had he*: As if he had.

86–7 *incorpsed and demi-natured* | *With the . . . beast*: Grown to have one body with the horse, and so half-man and half-beast. Shakespeare is doubtless thinking of the centaurs.

87 *topped my thought*: Surpassed my estimate.

88–9 *I, in forgery of shapes and tricks,* | *Come short of what he did*: Whatever I am able to describe as figures and tricks (in managing a horse), he exceeded in actual execution.

91 *Lamord*: F reads *Lamound*, which editors often spell as 'Lamond'. If *Lamord* is accurate, it is curiously ominous ('*mort*', 'death'), especially when accompanied by the oath *Upon my life*.

92–3 *brooch . . . gem*: Ornament . . . jewel.

94 *made confession of you*: Felt compelled, although he was a Frenchman, to acknowledge the truth about you.

95 *masterly report*: Report of your masterly skill.

96 *For art and exercise in your defence*: In respect of your knowledge and skilful practice in the use of your sword.

99 *one could match you*: An equal opponent could be found for you.

   scrimers: Fencers (pronounced to rhyme with 'rhymers').

100 *motion*: Attack (as distinct from *guard*, 'parrying').

101–4 *this report . . . with you*: There is no other mention in the play of Hamlet's envy of Laertes. It sounds like a ruse of Hamlet, giving himself an excuse for improving his swordsmanship. Or perhaps the actor can convey that the whole thing is an invention of the King's. Cf. *Since he went into France I have been in continual practice* (V.2.204–5).

104 *sudden*: Immediate.

   play: Fence.

   you: Grammatically we might have expected 'him' (which is, in fact, the F reading).

109–22 *Not that I think . . . hurts by easing*: This discourse of the King on the effects of time upon will-power is an interesting and ironical comment on Hamlet's situation. Hamlet had given his view of the matter at IV.4.32–66, and had acknowledged to the Ghost that he, *lapsed in time and passion, lets go by* | *The important acting of your dread command* (III.4.108–9). Claudius seems, moreover, to be repeating the assertion of the Player-King at III.2.198–225, that *Purpose is but the slave to memory*.

110 *love is begun by time*: Circumstances give rise to love
     (and they change).

111 *in passages of proof*: By definite incidents that prove the
     truth of what I am saying.

112 *qualifies*: Moderates.

114 *snuff*: The image is that of a candle; the *snuff* is the
     charred part of the candle wick, which, if neglected,
     spoils and eventually puts out the flame.

115 *is at a like goodness still*: Remains at the same constant
     level of goodness.

116 *pleurisy*: Excess. The word is spelt *plurisy* in the early texts,
     by association with Latin '*plus*', 'more', and not with Greek
     '*pleura*', 'rib', from which is derived modern 'pleurisy',
     inflammation of the pleura (coverings of the lungs).

117 *his*: Its.

117–18 *That we would do | We should do when we would*: When
     we want to do something, we should do it immediately
     we know we want to do it.

119 *abatements*: Diminutions of energy.

120 *As there are tongues, are hands, are accidents*: As the
     ways in which we are influenced by what people say,
     and by what they help us to do or restrain us from
     doing, and by the mere chances of life.

121–2 *this 'should' is like a spendthrift sigh, | That hurts by
     easing*: A sigh is a relief to our feelings, though it also
     harms us (alluding to the belief that with every sigh a
     drop of blood was lost); likewise, when we say 'I know
     what I ought to do', it may ease the conscience but the
     self-reproach also weakens our will-power. (This is the
     probable explanation of a difficult passage.)

122 *the quick o'th'ulcer*: That is, the main point.

124–5 *in deed ... More than in words*: Contrasting with Hamlet.

125 *cut his throat i'th'church*: Laertes's words contrast
     strongly with Hamlet's unwillingness to kill the King
     while he was at his prayers (III.3.73–96).

126 *No place ... should murder sanctuarize*: For a murderer
     (such as Hamlet) there should be no rights of sanc-
     tuary; so there would be no objection to your killing
     him anywhere, even in church.

127 *Revenge should have no bounds*: This is Hamlet's
    doctrine, expounded by him at III.3.73–96.

128 *keep close within your chamber*: Presumably the King is
    guarding against the possibility that Hamlet might win
    Laertes over to his side.

130 *We'll put on those shall praise*: I will arrange that some
    persons shall praise.

132 *fine*: Conclusion.

133 *remiss*: Careless (as not expecting any treachery).

134 *Most generous, and free from all contriving*: Claudius is
    not speaking the truth, for he knows that Hamlet has
    already engaged in a complicated contrivance, *The
    Mousetrap*.

135 *foils*: Blunt-edged swords with buttons on the point for
    use in fencing.

136 *a little shuffling*: Some little trick of substitution.

137 *unbated*: Without a button on the point.
    in a pass of practice: This probably means 'in making
    a treacherous thrust at him', rather than 'while playing
    a practice-bout' or 'while making a pass in which you
    are well practised'. But perhaps the King is deliber-
    ately ambiguous.

139–47 *I will do't . . . death*: Part of the treacherous plan comes
    from Laertes; in Q1 the proposal to poison the sword
    comes from the King himself. This may represent what
    happened in a performance earlier than the Q2 text,
    the change being intended to indicate the deterioration
    of Laertes under the King's influence. At V.2.307–14
    Laertes does not confess that the envenoming of the
    sword was his own idea.

140 *unction*: Ointment.
    of a mountebank: From a quack doctor (or itinerant
    drug-seller).

142 *cataplasm*: Poultice.

143–4 *Collected . . . Under the moon*: It was believed that herbs
    were especially efficacious when gathered by moon-
    light (see III.2.266). But perhaps *Under the moon* goes
    with *have virtue* and merely means 'anywhere on earth'.

143 *simples*: Medicinal herbs.

146 *gall*: Graze.

148–9 *Weigh what convenience both of time and means | May
     fit us to our shape*: Consider carefully what arrange-
     ments of time and of opportunity may suit us in
     assuming the roles we have decided to act.

149 *shape*: Role.

150 *drift*: Intention, plan.
    look through: Become visible.

151 *assayed*: Attempted.

152 *back*: Support.
    hold: Stand firm.

153 *blast in proof*: Like a gun exploding when it is tested by
    being fired.

154 *cunnings*: Respective skills in fencing.

157 *As*: And therefore.

158 *preferred*: Proffered. This seems to be the meaning of
    Q2's reading, *prefard*. But F reads *prepar'd*, which may
    well be right.

159 *chalice*: A special ceremonial cup.
    nonce: Occasion.

160 *stuck*: Thrust.

161 *may hold there*: Will be achieved by that.

161–2 *But stay, what noise? | How, sweet Queen*: Q2 has only
     the first sentence, F only the second. One or other may
     be an accidental omission. It seems best to include both
     in the text; a director can choose either or both.

165 *O, where*: Presumably these words represent a numbed
    reaction to the deeply felt calamity. Or Laertes may
    speak as if about to run to her.

166 *willow*: The emblem of forsaken love, appropriately.
    askant: Sideways, leaning over. F has *aslant*, a more
    usual word.

167 *shows his hoar leaves in the glassy stream*: The under-
    side of the willow leaf is greyish, and this, not the
    green upper side, would be reflected in the *glassy stream*
    underneath.

168 *Therewith*: Of the willow. F reads *There with*, and alters
    make to *come*.
    fantastic: Extravagant.

169 *crowflowers*: Buttercups.
      long purples: Purple orchises.
170 *liberal*: Free-spoken.
      grosser: More obscene.
171 *cold maids*: Distinguished from *liberal shepherds*; the
      maidens are chaste and therefore ignore obscene names
      for flowers.
      dead-men's-fingers: So named from the pale tuber-like
      roots of some kinds of orchids.
172–3 *There . . . | Clambering to hang*: As one forsaken in
      love, Ophelia tries to hang her garland on a willow
      tree. Or perhaps she imagines herself to be decorating
      her father's monument.
172 *crownet weeds*: Garlands made of weeds.
173 *an envious sliver broke*: There is no word here of Ophelia's
      death's being suicide, though the strong suspicion of this
      is voiced in the next scene (V.1.1–25 and 223–34).
      envious: Malicious.
      sliver: Branch.
175 *clothes*: Ophelia is imagined as wearing the elaborate
      farthingale of an Elizabethan court lady.
177 *tunes*: Q2 has *laudes*, a strange word in this context,
      but just possible, referring to parts of the Psalms sung
      at the service of Lauds. The F reading *tunes* is supported
      by Q1, *Chaunting olde sundry tunes*.
178 *incapable of*: Unable to comprehend.
179–80 *indued | Unto that element*: Having the qualities appro-
      priate for living in the water.
182 *lay*: Song.
187 *our trick*: The way of us men.
187–8 *Nature her custom holds, | Let shame say what it will*:
      Nature follows her usual course, even though our shame
      (at being unmanly) rebukes us.
188–9 *When these are gone, | The woman will be out*: After my
      tears are over, the woman-like side of my human nature
      will cease to appear.
191 *this folly*: These foolish tears.
      drowns: So Q2; F reads *doubts*, which could be inter-
      preted as 'douts' (puts out).

192 *calm his rage*: Not a true statement of what has happened.

V.1

It seems that this remarkable scene was an after-thought. V.2 would follow naturally upon IV.7, where we are told (44) that Hamlet will arrive at the court *Tomorrow*. V.2 opens with Hamlet's narration to Horatio of what had happened to bring him back to Elsinore.

0 *Enter two Clowns*: This is the direction in Q2 and F. But Q1 has *enter Clowne and an other*. This probably indicates the principal comic actor and his 'feed', who appear as rustics ('clowns'). The First Clown plays the part of a gravedigger: he is addressed as *Goodman Delver* (14) and called a *sexton* (88 and 160) and *grave-maker* (140). It would be wrong to regard the Second Clown as another; for two men cannot easily dig the same grave.

1 *in Christian burial*: With the authorized funeral services of the Church and in consecrated ground (as was not permitted to suicides).

2 *salvation*: He presumably should say 'damnation', but he has muddled notions of her presumptuousness in dying and going to heaven before her due time.

4 *straight*: Straightaway.

4–22 *The crowner ... law*: The Clowns give a burlesque of the arguments in the coroner's court over Ophelia's death.

4 *crowner*: Coroner. This colloquial form occurs in common Elizabethan usage, and not only in unedu-cated speech.

sat on her: Conducted an inquest into the cause of her death.

4–5 *finds it*: Has given his verdict that the cause of her death does not prohibit.

8 *'tis found so*: This verdict has been given by the coroner.

9 *se offendendo*: He means '*se defendendo*' ('in self-defence'), the phrase used in a plea of justifiable homi-cide. But it is, of course, comically misapplied in a case of suicide. Q2's reading, *so offended*, may be a further

comic corruption of the phrase, rather than a misprint.

11 *branches*: Divisions of an argument. Shakespeare is doubtless making fun of the over-systematic distinctions and quibbles of lawyers.

12 *Argal*: The Clown is attempting the Latin '*ergo*', 'therefore'.

14 *Goodman*: A polite form of address to a working-man. *Delver*: Gravedigger.

17 *will he nill he*: Willy-nilly.

22 *crowner's quest law*: That is, according to the formalities governing a coroner's inquest (*quest*).

26 *there thou sayst*: What you say is true.

27–9 *great folk . . . even-Christian*: This looks forward to the Priest's remarks at 223–34, including the revealing information that *great command o'ersways the order*.

27 *countenance*: Social and legal privilege.

28–9 *even-Christian*: Ordinary fellow Christians (who are all equal, whatever their social rank, in the sight of God).

31 *hold up*: Continue.

33 *arms*: Both 'a coat of arms' and 'arms to hold a spade with'.

34 *none*: No coat of arms.

36 *the Scripture*: Genesis 2:15 and 3:19.

37 *Could he dig without arms*: This mocks the absurd claims of writers on heraldry about the antiquity of their branch of knowledge.

39 *confess thyself*: To be a fool. Or perhaps this is the first half of the proverb 'Confess yourself and be hanged', which may prompt the Second Clown to guess *gallows-maker* (43) as the answer to the riddle.

40 *Go to*: An interjection of impatience: 'Come on!'

43 *frame*: The 'framework' of the gallows.

52 *unyoke*: After this great effort, you can have your yoke taken off, like a beast of burden whose day's task is done, and can give your brain a rest.

55 *Mass*: By the mass.

60 *stoup*: Pronounced like 'stoop'; a flagon containing two quarts.

61–119 *In youth . . . meet*: The Clown sings three garbled

stanzas of a well-known poem attributed to Thomas
Lord Vaux (1510–56), first printed in the book of *Songs
and Sonnets* (by the Earl of Surrey and others) published
by Tottel in 1557, with the title 'The Aged Lover
Renounceth Love', and printed separately as a ballad
in 1563.

63 *O . . . a*: Presumably grunts made by the digger at his
   labours rather than interpolated vowels in the song.
   behove: (That is, 'behoof') benefit, advantage.

65 *feeling of his business*: Response to the sombre nature
   of his job.

67–8 *in him a property of easiness*: Natural for him to carry
   out his distressing task without any painful sensations.

70 *hath the daintier sense*: Is more fastidious (than the hard
   hand of a working man).

74 *such*: As I was in my youth.

76 *jowls*: Thrusts or knocks forcibly (presumably with a
   play upon *jawbone*).

77 *Cain's jawbone, that did*: The jawbone used by Cain.
   According to legend, he used an ass's jawbone to
   murder his brother Abel. Hamlet's mind reverts to fratricide, as does the King's (III.3.37–8).

78 *politician*: This word generally had a derogatory
   meaning: 'schemer'.
   this ass: The gravedigger.
   o'erreaches: Gets the better of (perhaps with a pun on
   the sense 'reach over').

79 *circumvent*: Outwit.

83–4 *praised my Lord Such-a-one's horse when 'a meant to beg
   it*: Shakespeare gives an instance of this kind of devi-
   ousness in *Timon of Athens*, I.2.210–16.

87 *my Lady Worm's*: It belongs to my Lady Worm.

87–8 *chopless*: Without the lower jaw.

88 *mazzard*: Skull (the upper part).

89 *revolution*: Reversal of fortune brought about by time.

89–90 *trick to see*: Knack of seeing.

90 *cost no more the breeding but*: Cost so little to raise that
   men are willing.

91 *loggats*: A game played by throwing pear-shaped pieces

of wood – *loggats* – at wooden pins stuck in the ground.
Mine: My own *bones*.

93 *For and*: (An emphatic form) and.

97 *quiddities*: Subtleties.
quillets: Small distinctions.

98 *tenures*: Modes of holding property from a superior
owner, or periods of time during which it may be so held.

100 *sconce*: Head.

101 *action of battery*: Suing for physical violence upon himself.

102 *statutes*: Legal documents acknowledging debts, by
which creditors acquired rights over the debtors' lands
and goods.

102–3 *recognizances*: Certain kinds of statutes.

103 *fines*: Legal documents by which entailed property was
changed into freehold possession.
double vouchers: Persons (generally two) who played
their part in the legal devices of *recoveries*.
recoveries: The process including *fines*.

104 *fine of his fines*: End of his *fines* (103). In this sentence
Hamlet achieves four puns on the word *fine*.
recovery: Successful attainment.

106 *vouch him . . . of*: Guarantee his legal title to.

107–8 *the length and breadth of a pair of indentures*: Two of
his legal documents would together be of the same size
as his grave.

108 *indentures*: Joint agreements. The document was cut or
torn into two parts so that the exact fitting together of
the irregularly indented edges was a proof of genuine-
ness. Perhaps Hamlet is punning, referring to the two
teeth-bearing jaws.

108–10 *The very conveyances . . . more*: The documents themselves, symbols of ownership, are too bulky to go into
this grave (or coffin), and must the owner of all these
lands occupy no more space.

108 *conveyances*: Documents legalizing the transfer of
ownership of property.

109 *box*: Grave, or coffin, compared to the box in which a
lawyer keeps his documents.
inheritor: Owner.

114 *sheep and calves*: Foolish fellows.

114–15 *assurance*: Security (with a pun on the legal sense, 'documentary conveyance of property').

115 *in that*: By trusting to legal documents, which are only made of parchment.

115–16 *Whose grave's this*: Horatio, as well as Hamlet, is ignorant of Ophelia's death, having left the court at the end of IV.6.

120 *thou liest*: Hamlet jestingly uses the formula of insult among gentlemen.

126 *a quick lie*: A lie that will return from me to you quickly.

126–7 *'Twill away again from me to you*: The Clown 'gives him the lie' back again.

135 *absolute*: Positively precise (in language).

135–6 *by the card*: Precisely, as if according to the directions given on a seaman's chart or on his compass (divided into thirty-two points).

136 *equivocation*: Deliberate use of ambiguity in words. It was notorious in Shakespeare's time as a device, attributed to the Roman Catholics, for taking oaths with mental reservations and double meanings.

137 *the age*: Our contemporaries of all classes (both *peasant* and *courtier*).

138 *picked*: Over-refined.

138–9 *the toe of the peasant comes so near the heel of the courtier*: A curious echo of the Queen's image at IV.7.163: *One woe doth tread upon another's heel.*

139 *kibe*: Chilblain.

145 *that very day that young Hamlet was born*: There seems to be a curious symbolism in the gravedigger's having entered upon his occupation at the same time as Hamlet entered into being, as if preparation for death began from the day of birth.

158 *Upon what ground*: From what cause? (But the Clown chooses to take *ground* literally.)

160 *thirty years*: This seems conclusive that at this point Shakespeare intended Hamlet to be aged thirty. See the notes to I.1.171 and 170–71 below.

163 *pocky corses nowadays*: The ravages of the 'great pox'

(venereal diseases) were serious in Elizabethan
England.

164 *hold*: Last out.

169 *sore*: An intensifying epithet: 'terrible'.

170 *lien*: (An old form) lain.

170–71 *three-and-twenty years*: Q1 has a passage which combines
139–46 and 170–71 and gives about twelve years since
Yorick's death, so that in Q1 Hamlet could be in his
late teens.

177 *Rhenish*: See the note to I.4.10.

178 *Yorick*: This (like *Osrick* in V.2) is a Scandinavian-
sounding name, suggesting Jörg (George) and Eric.

182 *fancy*: Imagination.

183–9 *He hath . . . grinning*: This passage is a wonderful
glimpse of the privileged position of the jester in a
great Elizabethan household.

189 *grinning*: As a skull appears to be.

chop-fallen: With the lower jaw hanging down (as if
miserable).

189–90 *get you to my lady's table*: There were engravings of
Death (represented by a skeleton) coming into a young
lady's bedchamber while she sits at her dressing-table.
For *table* F reads *Chamber*, which may be right; *table*
could be due to a repetition from 188.

190–91 *paint an inch thick*: The frequent hostility to face-
painting; cf. III.1.51 and 143–5.

191 *favour*: Facial appearance.

194 *Alexander*: The Great.

202 *too curiously*: With unreasonably minute attention.

203 *follow him*: In imagination.

204 *with modesty*: Moderately and reasonably (that is, not
too curiously, which would make the idea improbable).

207 *loam*: Mortar or plaster made of clay and straw.

209–12 *Imperious Caesar . . . winter's flaw*: Perhaps this
impromptu verse-epigram (a characteristic specimen
of its kind) serves, like the love poem to Ophelia
(II.2.115–18), to identify Hamlet as a 'university wit'.

209 *Imperious*: Imperial.

211 *earth*: Piece of earth, that is, Caesar's remains.

212 *expel the winter's flaw*: Keep out a sudden gust of winter wind.

215 *maimèd*: Incomplete.

217 *Fordo*: Undo, destroy.

   it: Its.

   some estate: Rather high social station.

218 *Couch we*: Let us lie down and so be concealed.

219 *What ceremony else*: Laertes irritably repeats his question, following an embarrassed or indignant silence by the Priest.

222 PRIEST: For his two speeches Q2 has the heading *Doct*. This presumably means 'Doctor of Divinity' and would point to a Protestant rather than a Catholic cleric. But Laertes calls him a *priest* at 236.

   enlarged: Extended.

223 *warranty*: Authorization.

   doubtful: Owing to the suspicion of suicide. There was nothing, however, in the Queen's description of Ophelia's death (IV.7.166–83) to suggest that it was suicide; and we are told at V.1.4–5 that the coroner gave his judgement that it was to be *Christian burial*.

224 *great*: That is, of the King.

   order: Regulations prescribed by the ecclesiastical authorities.

226 *For*: Instead of.

227 *Shards*: Broken pieces of pots.

228 *crants*: Garlands (an unusual and foreign word, apparently Germanic, whose use may be a bit of local colour).

229 *strewments*: Flowers strewn on the grave or coffin.

   bringing home: Ophelia's funeral has followed the usual custom of being made to resemble a wedding festival. Instead of being taken to her husband's house, she is brought to her 'last home'.

230 *Of*: With.

   burial: Burial service.

234 *peace-parted souls*: Those who die piously in peace ('Lord, now lettest thou thy servant depart in peace' (Luke 2:29)).

238 *howling*: As a damned soul in hell.

244 *Whose wicked deed*: The killing of Polonius, to which
   alone Laertes seems to attribute Ophelia's loss of
   reason.

   ingenious sense: Naturally quick (or perhaps 'noble')
   powers of mind.

246 *caught her . . . in mine arms*: This implies an open coffin.

249 *Pelion*: A mountain in Thessaly; presumably it is *old*
   because of its reputation in ancient literature.

250 *blue*: Presumably like a distant mountain.

252 *Conjures*: Puts a magic spell upon.

   wandering stars: Planets (contrasted with the 'fixed
   stars').

   stand: Stand still.

253 *wonder-wounded*: Awe-struck.

   This is I: Presumably he throws off his cloak or *sea-
   gown* (V.2.13).

254 *Hamlet the Dane*: A defiant way of describing himself,
   asserting his princely rank or his claim to the throne.

   The devil take thy soul: Perhaps with this Laertes leaps
   out of the grave and flies at Hamlet. Before it, Q1 has
   the direction *Hamlet leapes in after Leartes*, but this turns
   Hamlet into the physical aggressor, though the text
   (256 and 259) indicates otherwise.

257 *splenitive*: Of an angry temperament. In sixteenth-
   century physiology the spleen was regarded as one of
   the seats of emotion, particularly of choler.

259 *Which let thy wisdom fear*: Which your good sense
   should cause you to fear.

263 *wag*: Move (not a ludicrous word). The movement of
   the eyelids is among the last visible ones to cease in a
   human being.

265 *I loved Ophelia*: Hamlet is shown briefly as having lost
   most of his self-consciousness and as being moved
   by serious feelings. Or perhaps it is another self-
   dramatization?

   Forty: Its use as an indefinitely large number seems to
   derive from its frequent biblical use.

266 *quantity*: Comparatively small quantity.

269 *forbear him*: Refrain from conflicting with him (Hamlet).

271 *Woo't*: Wouldst thou.

272 *eisel*: Vinegar. This is the common emendation of the
word *Esill* in Q2 and *Esile* (italicized, as if the printer
thought it might be a proper name or a foreign word)
in F. The difficulty is that something more violently
absurd may be expected than the notion of eagerly
drinking vinegar. This has prompted such conjectures
as 'Nilus' (the river Nile – which might have suggested
Eat a crocodile), 'Yssel' in Flanders, 'Weissel' (Vistula),
which flows into the Baltic, and others.

   crocodile: Regarded as a venomous beast; perhaps
alluding also to its hypocritical trick of counterfeiting
tears.

275 *quick*: Alive.

278 *burning ʒone*: Part of the sky representing the path of
the sun between the tropics of Cancer and Capricorn.

279 *Make Ossa like a wart*: Hamlet derides Laertes's mention
of *Pelion* (249) by naming the other mountain of
Thessaly, always associated with Pelion: when the
giants made war upon the gods of Olympus they tried
to scale heaven by piling Pelion upon Ossa.

280 *mere*: Pure.

282 *Anon*: Soon afterwards.

   dove: Symbol of peace and quiet.

283 *golden couplets*: The newly hatched two chicks of a
dove are covered with a yellow down.

   disclosed: Hatched.

285 *use*: Treat.

288 *cat . . . dog*: Presumably Hamlet is comparing Laertes
to a cat for his whining lamentation and to a dog for
his snarling. But perhaps *dog will have his day* refers to
Hamlet: 'My turn will come soon.'

290 *Strengthen your patience in our last night's speech*: Let
thoughts of our conversation last night enable you to
preserve your patience (under such provocation by
Hamlet).

291 *the present push*: An immediate test.

293–5 *This grave shall . . . be*: The King speaks these lines
publicly, but they have an additional meaning for

Laertes, as continuing 290–91: Hamlet will soon be in his
grave, too, and then we can rest safe; but meanwhile,
looking forward to the duel, we can remain patient.

293 *living monument*: Enduring memorial (but the King
knows that Laertes will take his remark ironically).

294 *An hour of quiet shortly shall we see*: The King expects
that Hamlet's death, which he has plotted, will solve
his anxieties. But he himself will soon find *quiet* in death.

V.2

1 *this*: Possibly the letter to England given to Hamlet, *the
other* being the *commission* given to Rosencrantz and
Guildenstern (26); the contrast shows the King's
treachery.

4 *fighting*: Agitation.

5–6 *Methought I lay | Worse than the mutines in the bilboes*:
It seemed to me that I felt more uncomfortable in my
bed than do mutineers in their iron fetters.

6 *Rashly* . . .: After five lines of interpolation, the sentence
is resumed, not quite logically, at 12: *Up from my cabin*.

7 *praised be rashness*: The praise of impetuous conduct
and the confidence in divine providence are ill
connected logically. Hamlet speaks eloquently, but
without philosophical competence, of the old dilemma
of human action and reliance on the will of God. At
V.1.257 he boasted *I am not splenitive and rash*.

8 *indiscretion*: Lack of judgement.

9 *pall*: Fail.
learn: Teach.

10–11 *There's a divinity . . . will*: This is the first evidence of
Hamlet's new piety or Christian patience, preparing us
for 213–18. Perhaps Shakespeare is interesting the audience by showing, after the excited reasoning of
IV.4.32–66, the meditative force of V.1.65–212, and the
anxieties of V.1.250–88, a new kind of irresponsibility
in Hamlet.

11 *Rough-hew*: Like a piece of timber.

13 *sea-gown*: Described in the 1611 dictionary of Cotgrave
as 'a coarse, high-collared, and short-sleeved gown,
reaching down to the mid-leg'.

13 *scarfed about me*: Wrapped around me like a sash. He had not dressed properly, but merely put his gown around him without using the sleeves.

14 *them*: Rosencrantz and Guildenstern.

15 *Fingered*: Stole.
   in fine: Finally.

18 *grand*: Sarcastic.
   commission: The *commission* of III.3.3 and the *letters sealed* of III.4.203. See the note to IV.3.58.

20 *Larded*: Garnished.
   many several: A variety of different.

21 *Importing*: Deeply concerned with.

22 *bugs and goblins*: Terrors and dangers (spoken contemptuously, for Hamlet believes them to be imaginary).
   bugs: (Literally) bogies, bugbears.
   in my life: If I am allowed to live (or perhaps 'in my daily behaviour').

23 *supervise*: Viewing.
   no leisure bated: Without any delay being permitted.

24 *stay*: Wait for.

26 *Here's the commission*: Presumably he hands it to Horatio.

29 *be-netted*: Ensnared.

30 *Or*: Before.
   make a prologue to my brains: Go through the initial steps of submitting the problem to my intelligence (as often with Hamlet, a theatrical metaphor).

31 *They*: His *brains*, without his conscious will.

32 *fair*: In a clear hand, like a professional scrivener.

33 *statists*: Men involved in business of state.

34 *A baseness to write fair*: Evidence of ungentlemanly birth to have a clear handwriting, like a professional.

36 *yeoman's service*: The kind of admirably loyal and reliable military service which an English yeoman rendered to his feudal lord.

37 *effect*: Import.

38 *conjuration*: Appeal or injunction (as from a person able to rely upon some special authority).

40 *As*: So that (whereas the *As* at 39 means 'because').

like the palm might flourish: Hamlet is mocking the high-flown style of diplomatic correspondence, which borrowed biblical phrases: 'The righteous shall flourish like the palm tree' (Psalm 92:12).

41 *wheaten garland*: Emblematic of *peace*.

42 *comma*: This, the reading of both Q2 and F, is difficult. Perhaps it is used in the sense 'a short part of a sentence'. But the word may be wrong. The suggested emendations ('commere', 'cement', 'column', 'concord', 'calm', 'compact', etc.) are unsatisfactory.

    amities: Perhaps Hamlet is ironical; for England's *cicatrice looks raw and red | After the Danish sword*: (IV.3.62–3), and Shakespeare could hardly have been ignorant of the terrible conflicts between the Anglo-Saxons and the Danes.

43 *as's of great charge*: Hamlet characteristically puns on 'asses bearing heavy burdens'.

44 *That*: Follows *conjuration* (38).

46 *those bearers*: Rosencrantz and Guildenstern.

47 *shriving time*: A period of time for confession and absolution before execution.

48 *ordinant*: In control (cf. 10–11).

49 *signet*: Seal.

50 *model*: Replica.

    that Danish seal: Probably pointing to the seal on the commission now in Horatio's hand. Hamlet seems to be saying that, by good luck, he had his father's seal, and, equally luckily, the Danish seal of state of the new monarch was not (as one would expect) different from that of his predecessor.

52 *Subscribed it*: By forging King Claudius's signature.

    impression: Of the seal.

53 *changeling*: Like a human child taken by the fairies and replaced by one of their own.

53–4 *the next day | Was our sea-fight*: Shakespeare makes it clear that Hamlet's substitution of the *commission* to be carried to England had nothing to do with his accidental return to Denmark.

54 *our sea-fight*: This is described at IV.6.15 as *Ere we were*

two days old at sea. So the substitution of the commission took place during the first night aboard ship.

56 *to't*: To their death.

57 *did make love to this employment*: Were willing and active
collaborators in Claudius's schemes against me.

58 *defeat*: Destruction.

59 *insinuation*: Intrusive intervention.

61 *pass*: Thrust (of the rapier).
fell incensèd points: Fiercely angered sword-points.

62 *mighty opposites*: Hamlet and Claudius.

63 *Does it not . . . stand me now upon*: Is it not now my
duty.

66 *angle*: Fishing-hook.
my proper life: My very life.

67 *cozenage*: Cheating by inspiring confidence in one's
victim.
is't not perfect conscience: May I not with a clear
conscience.

68 *quit*: Pay back.
be damned: Act sinfully.

69 *canker*: Cancer, ulcer.
nature: Human nature.

69–70 *come | In*: Grow into.

74 *a man's life's no more than to say 'one'*: The probable
meaning is that the *short* time will be enough: he needs
only a single successful thrust of his rapier into Claudius
to end his life (*one* is the swordsman's claim to have hit
his opponent's body). But perhaps it is another of
Hamlet's newly acquired fatalistic generalizations, like
There's a divinity . . . (10) and *The readiness is all . . .*
(216), and so refers to his own life, not the King's.

78 *favours*: Friendship.

79 *bravery*: Bravado.

80 *Osrick*: The first form of the name in Q2 is *Ostricke*,
and this is used for his speech headings in the duel
scene. In view of the many references to birds in this
episode, it is tempting to suppose that 'Ostrick' was
Shakespeare's original intention. But at 343–4 Q2 has
Osrick, and F has *Osricke* (*Osr.*) throughout. Q1 has

Enter a Bragart Gentleman, which indicates how he appeared on the stage. Hamlet's easy wit in ragging poor Osrick, showing a mind free from vacillation and anxiety, confirms the change of mood revealed in the earlier part of the scene.

83   *waterfly*: Vain and meddlesome creature.

85   *state*: Of soul.

    more gracious: Happier (as being in a state of grace).

87   *Let a beast be lord of beasts, and*: If a man, however contemptible he may be, owns large flocks and herds and is therefore rich (he will be received at the royal court). Wealth brings its position at court, regardless of merit.

    crib: Manger.

88   *mess*: A division of the company at a banquet.

    chough: Jackdaw (which is able to make a chatter resembling human speech).

89   *spacious in the possession of dirt*: The owner of many acres of land.

92   *diligence of spirit*: Attention. Hamlet begins to mock Osrick's style of speech.

93   *Put your bonnet to his right use*: It was customary to wear hats indoors. Probably Osrick's excessive cap-doffing was an affectation of respect. But he politely pretends he has taken his hat off for his comfort in the hot weather.

    bonnet: Any kind of headwear.

    his: Its.

97   *indifferent*: Fairly.

98–9 *for my complexion*: This is F's reading. Q2 has *or* instead of *for*; this could be right if one puts a dash after *complexion* and supposes that Hamlet is interrupted by Osrick before he can finish his sentence with 'judges it wrongly' (or something of the sort).

99   *complexion*: Bodily state.

105 *Nay . . .*: Osrick apparently wins, and does not put on his hat until he departs at 179.

107–11 *an absolute gentleman . . . see*: Osrick's panegyric has been arranged by the King (IV.7.130).

107 *absolute*: Perfect.

    differences: Distinguishing qualities.

108 *soft society*: Sociable disposition.

    great showing: Impressive appearance.

109 *card*: Accurate guide, to be used as a seaman uses his chart or compass (see V.1.135–6 and note).

    calendar: Directory which one may consult for information.

    gentry: Gentlemanliness.

110 *continent*: Embodiment.

110–11 *what part a gentleman would see*: Every quality a gentleman would like to see.

112 *his definement suffers no perdition in you*: He loses nothing by being described by you.

113 *divide him inventorially*: List his qualities one by one.

113–14 *dizzy th'arithmetic of memory*: The number of his qualities would be so large that one's memory would become confused in trying to remember them.

114 *yaw*: Move unsteadily (of a boat).

    neither: For all that.

115 *the verity of extolment*: Praising him truly.

116 *article*: Importance.

    infusion: Mixture of good qualities.

117 *dearth and rareness*: 'Dearness' (preciousness) and rarity.

    make true diction of: Speak truthfully about.

118 *his semblable is his mirror*: The only thing that resembles him is his own image in a mirror.

    who: Whoever.

119 *trace*: Follow in his footsteps (that is, imitate).

    his umbrage: (Is) a shadow of him.

120 *infallibly*: Accurately.

121 *concernancy*: Purpose of all this (apparently a word invented for the occasion).

122 *more rawer breath*: Too little refined way of speech.

125 *You will to't*: You can succeed, if you try.

126 *imports the nomination of*: Is your purpose in naming.

134 *approve me*: Demonstrate the truth about me (or perhaps 'be to my credit').

137 *compare*: Vie.

138–9 *to know a man well were to know himself*: This exercise
in logical nonsense seems to be based on an extension
of 'Judge not, that you be not judged' (Matthew 7:1).
It would be wrong for Hamlet to judge Laertes's excellence, unless he were to consider himself worthy to be
judged to be of equal excellence, and that would be a
presumptuous self-opinion, for he cannot really *know
himself*; therefore he cannot really know (or estimate)
Laertes's excellence.

139 *himself*: Oneself.

140 *for*: With.

140–41 *imputation*: Reputation.

141 *by them*: By people in general. Some editors, following
Q2's punctuation, read 'by them in his meed' ('by those
who are in his pay, his retainers'), but this seems to
indicate an irony that is beyond Osrick.

141 *meed*: Merit (probably, but the word is difficult).
unfellowed: Without a rival.

145–6 *Barbary horses*: North African horses were much
esteemed.

146 *he has impawned*: Laertes has wagered.

147 *poniards*: Daggers.
assigns: Appurtenances.
as: Such as.

148 *hangers*: Straps by which the sword (or its scabbard)
was attached to the man's belt (*girdle*).
carriages: An affected word for *hangers*.

149 *very dear to fancy*: Probably 'delightful to think about'.
responsive to: Perhaps 'matching' or 'in keeping with';
the two items 'go well together'.

150 *delicate*: Finely wrought.
of very liberal conceit: (Perhaps) tasteful in design and
decoration.

152–3 *I knew you must be edified by the margent*: I expected
that you would fail to understand something he said
and have some word or phrase explained. (Explanations
of difficult words or phrases were usually printed in
the *margent* (margin) rather than at the foot of the
page.)

152   *edified*: Enlightened.

155–6 *germane to the matter*: Appropriate to the thing itself
      (*the matter* contrasts with *The phrase*).

156–7 *I would it might be 'hangers' till then*: I had rather we
      kept the word 'hangers' until that time comes (when
      we can carry cannons at our sides and not merely
      rapiers).

162   *laid*: Wagered.

162–4 *in a doȝen passes . . . he shall not exceed you three hits.
      He hath laid on twelve for nine*: These odds are difficult
      to interpret, but must have been immediately intelli-
      gible to Shakespeare's audience, familiar with the art
      of fencing and with the conventions of fencing matches.
      It seems that the King wagers that, in twelve bouts or
      rounds, Laertes's score will not exceed Hamlet's by
      three. That means that if the score were Laertes 8 and
      Hamlet 4, Laertes would win; and that if the score were
      Laertes 7 and Hamlet 5, Hamlet would win. This expla-
      nation seems to be supported by Q1, where the reporter
      is doubtless remembering what he saw on the stage.
      Hamlet asks *And howe's the wager?* and receives the reply
      *Mary sir, that yong Leartes in twelue venies | At Rapier
      and Dagger do not get three oddes of you.* In the event
      Hamlet wins the first two bouts (275 and 280 below).
      The score of two-nil against him is serious for Laertes,
      for it means he must win at least eight of the remaining
      ten bouts in order to win the match. The King there-
      upon says *Our son shall win* (281). But what is the
      meaning of *He hath laid on twelve for nine*? By the
      natural run of the sentences *He* would be the King.
      The actor might convey that *He* was Laertes. It would
      be natural to take *twelve for nine* as being related to
      Hamlet's 'advantage' of *three hits*. Perhaps *for nine*
      means 'instead of nine': Laertes wants a larger number
      of bouts than usual, in order to achieve a lead of at
      least four hits over Hamlet. Unfortunately there is no
      evidence that nine was the usual number of bouts.
      Perhaps the wager is that Laertes will not achieve twelve
      hits before Hamlet has achieved nine. If so, they might

have to fight as many as twenty bouts; for the score,
after the nineteenth, could be 11 to 8.

163   *passes*: Probably means 'bouts' or 'rounds', which ended
when one of the contestants scored a hit.

165–6   *vouchsafe the answer*: Accept the challenge. But Hamlet
deliberately misunderstands the words as merely 'give
a reply'.

167   *How if I answer no*: A moment of suspense, when
Hamlet comes near to spoiling the treacherous plot.

168–9   *I mean . . . in trial*: Osrick assumes that it is unthink-
able that a gentleman should refuse to respond to a
challenge of this kind, and so he pretends that Hamlet
may have misunderstood him.

171   *breathing time*: Time for taking exercise.

174   *the odd hits*: My small score of successful hits.

175   *re-deliver you*: Report what you have said.

176   *flourish*: Verbal decoration.

178   *I commend my duty*: This is a merely complimentary
phrase, and Hamlet's immediate response is conventional too. But after Osrick has left he plays with the
words, taking them separately and literally as 'I praise
my performance of duty'.

182–3   *This lapwing runs away with the shell on his head*:
Presumably Osrick puts his hat on at his departure.
The image is of a precocious young bird which, just
hatched, starts running away with a piece of its shell
still clinging to its head.

184   *comply . . . with his dug*: Behave with ingratiating good
manners towards his nurse's breast ('he was born a
courtier').

185   *bevy*: Covey of birds. Q2 has *breede*, which is accept-
able; but the appropriateness of F's *Beauy* ('bevy') is
strongly in its favour.

186   *drossy age*: Present times, which are worthless.
dotes on: Makes a cult of.

186–7   *got the tune of the time*: Acquired the fashionable
mannerisms of speech.

187   *out of an habit of encounter*: By practice in having
constant conversational contact with other gallants. F

reads *outward habite of encounter* ('exterior manner of address'), which is parallel to *the tune of the time*.

187–8 *yeasty collection*: Frothy accumulation (of modes of expression).

188 *carries*: Sustains.

through and through: Right through.

189 *fanned and winnowed*: Carefully considered. Q2 reads *prophane and trennowed*, which does not make sense. F reads *fond and winnowed*; but *fond* is difficult, for the meaning the context requires is the opposite of 'foolish'. The emendation to 'fand', that is, *fanned* ('sifted'), is commonly accepted, though it is rather close to *winnowed* in meaning. An equally probable emendation is 'profound'.

190 *are out*: Soon burst.

192 *attend*: Await.

194 *that*: If.

196 *his fitness speaks*: His (the King's) readiness is declared.

199 *In happy time*: It is an opportune moment (a polite phrase).

200–201 *gentle entertainment*: Friendliness of attitude.

204–5 *Since he went . . . continual practice*: This is more or less consistent with the King's words at IV.7.101–4; nevertheless at II.2.296–7 Hamlet told Rosencrantz and Guildenstern that he had *forgone all custom of exercises*.

205 *at the odds*: With the advantage given me (at 162–4).

209–10 *gaingiving*: Misgiving.

212 *repair*: Coming.

213 *We defy augury*: I shall disdain forebodings. For a moment Hamlet becomes almost like his admired Horatio (III.2.75–81 – though Horatio's stoicism has no religious foundation). But it is perhaps felt to be a moment of carelessness, rather than heroism, before the catastrophe of the duel.

213–14 *There is special providence in the fall of a sparrow*: 'And fear ye not them which kill the body, but are not able to kill the soul; but rather fear him which is able to destroy both body and soul in hell. Are not two little sparrows sold for a farthing? And one of them shall

not light on the ground without your father. Yea, even
all the hairs of your head are numbered. Fear ye not,
therefore; ye are of more value than many sparrows'
(Matthew 10:28–31). The phrase is also influenced by
augury, which originally meant the foretelling of the
future by observing the behaviour of birds.

214 *it*: My death.

216–17 *The readiness is all: Since no man knows of aught he
leaves, what is't to leave betimes*: Q2 places *knows* after
leaves. F reads: *the readinesse is all, since no man ha's
ought of what he leaues. What is't to leaue betimes?* Many
amendments have been suggested. On the whole, the
simplest is to suppose that *knows* in Q2 has got out of
place. The meaning is then: 'To be ready (for death)
is all that matters. As no one has knowledge of what
happens after his death, what does an early death
matter?'

218 *Let be*: Do not try to postpone the fencing match.
Alternatively *Let be* may be part of the previous
sentence, giving the meaning 'since a man cannot find
out from anything on earth (*of aught he leaves*) what
is the appropriate moment for his dying, don't bother
about it'. The words are in Q2, not in F.

Enter the King and Queen . . . all the state: Q2 and F
differ slightly; see the fourth list of collations, An
Account of the Text.

state: That is, courtly attendants.

220–38 *Give me your pardon . . . hurt my brother*:Hamlet is
loyally carrying out his mother's request (200–201) and
adopts her explanation of his behaviour (V.1.280–84).

222 *presence*: Royal assembly (or perhaps only the King and
Queen).

223 *punished*: Afflicted.

a sore distraction: The excuse of madness must be
regarded as disingenuous. In the episode of the killing
of Polonius, Hamlet is conspicuously sane in his
discourse and expressly denies to his mother that he is
really mad (III.4.140–45).

225 *exception*: Right to take exception.

232 *faction*: Contending party.

237 *That I have*: As if I had.

238 *my brother*: As Ophelia's brother, Laertes might have
   been Hamlet's brother-in-law. But the allusion would
   be awkward, and perhaps, rather, the echoes of the
   fratricide are heard even here.

   in nature: So far as my personal feelings are concerned
   (but not as regards my position in society).

239 *Whose motive*: The impulse from which.

240 *terms of honour*: Condition as a man of honour.

241 *will*: Desire.

243 *voice*: Opinion.

   precedent of peace: Knowledge of a precedent for my
   making peace with you.

245 *receive*: Accept.

246 *will not wrong it*: Laertes's plain speaking is the extreme
   of treachery.

   embrace: Welcome.

247 *frankly*: Without ill-feeling.

249 *foil*: A characteristic pun: 'the gold-leaf used to set off
   the brightness of a gem' and 'a blunted sword'.

251 *Stick fiery off*: Shine out brightly in contrast.

257 *But since he is bettered, we have therefore odds*: Perhaps
   since means 'since then', giving the meaning: 'Since I
   saw you both fence, Laertes has improved himself.
   Therefore we are giving three points to Hamlet.'
   Another suggestion is that the King's stake is so much
   more valuable than Laertes's that he has asked for
   favourable odds. But it is difficult to see how this could
   be communicated to an audience.

   bettered: More skilful than you (or perhaps 'improved
   by his training' in France). Q2 has *better* for F's *better'd*.

258 *Let me see another*: This begins the process (also covered
   by the King's elaborate speech at 261–72) through which
   Laertes secures the *Unbated and envenomed* rapier.

259 *likes*: Pleases.

   a length: One and the same length. From surviving
   rapiers it seems that the length of the blades varied
   considerably. Hamlet's question increases the suspense

by suggesting that he may, contrary to the King's expectation (IV.7.135), inspect the weapons and so discover the plot.

263 *quit in answer of the third exchange*: (Probably) win the third bout, which will pay Laertes back for his having won the first and second. The King is thinking of the need to bring into effect his *back or second* (IV.7.152) and to get Hamlet to drink from the poisoned cup as soon as possible.

266 *cup*: The *chalice* of IV.7.159.
union: Large pearl.

268 *Denmark's crown*: Presumably that which he is now wearing.

269 *kettle*: Kettledrum.

273 *judges*: Of whom Osrick is the only active one.

274 *Judgement*: Appealing to the *judges* for a decision.

275 *Drum, trumpets, and shot*: Presumably the King or an official gives the order.
piece: Piece of ordnance, cannon.

276 *this pearl is thine*: Presumably this is the moment when the King throws the poison into the cup, as Hamlet later believes (320). We would assume that the King has drunk from the cup first, but the placing of *Here's to thy health* suggests that he throws in the poison and takes a sip before it has time to dissolve; the cup will have been shaken and enough time will have elapsed before it reaches Hamlet.

278 *I'll play this bout first*: Presumably a grave discourtesy, a refusal of the King's amity.

281 *He's fat and scant of breath*: The word *fat* (in both Q2 and F) is incongruous. There is slight evidence that it could mean 'sweaty', but the usual meaning was the same as today. Possibly the Queen's tone is bantering, giving expression to her motherly happiness at her now well-behaved son. But the word may be wrong. What the sense needs is something like 'he sweats and scants his breath'. None of the emendations suggested so far (e.g. 'faint', 'hot') is satisfactory.

282 *take my napkin*: This move of the Queen can appear

significant: she openly goes over to Hamlet's 'side', leaving the throne and the King. It may be a relic of the old motivation which appears in Q1: having secretly allied herself with Hamlet against the King, she suspects some treachery and is warning her son.

napkin: Handkerchief.

283 *The Queen*: As well as the King.

284, 286 *do not drink . . . It is the poisoned cup. It is too late*: At this sudden turn of events the King, for all his usual skill and promptitude, cannot summon the energy to face the peril of abandoning the plot by saving his Queen.

289 *I do not think't*: Perhaps this is almost a moment of despair in the King, though he retains his self-control as he waits for the Queen to show the effects of the poison.

292 *pass*: Make your thrusts.

293 *make a wanton of me*: Are playing with me as if I were a child (unworthy of your serious swordsmanship). Perhaps the implication is that Laertes's bad *conscience* is affecting his skill.

296 *Have at you now*: This is usually interpreted as indicating that Laertes suddenly thrusts at Hamlet, without warning, and wounds him, thus apprising him of the treachery.

In scuffling . . . poisoned weapon: Q2 has no stage direction for the exchange of rapiers. F has *In scuffling they change Rapiers*. The compiler of Q1 remembered the situation as *They catch one anothers Rapiers, and both are wounded, Leartes falles downe, the Queene falles downe and dies*. Probably Burbage displayed a virtuoso piece of swordsmanship as Hamlet. When in a tight corner a swordsman would throw down his own weapon and seize the blade of his opponent's, securing enough leverage to wrench it away. The opponent then had no alternative but to pick up the other weapon, by which time his opponent would have recovered himself.

Part them: The King wishes to save Laertes.

297 *Ho*: Perhaps this is Osrick's cry to stop the duel in

accordance with the King's instructions. Q2 reads *howe* here and *how* at 305; this was a common spelling of 'ho', though 'how' could be an exclamatory interrogative.

300 *as a woodcock to mine own springe*: A curious echo of Polonius's *springes to catch woodcocks*, I.3.115.

302 *She swounds to see them bleed*: He tries to keep up appearances and to cover the cause of the Queen's collapse. Knowing that the Queen, Hamlet and Laertes will soon be dead, he can still hope to escape exposure.

swounds: Swoons.

304 *poisoned*: The terrible word arouses Hamlet's fury.

She dies: There is no indication in Q2 or F; perhaps the Queen, speechless, hears and sees some of the later words and actions before dying. Hamlet's *Follow my mother* (321) implies that he knows she is dying, if not dead; his *Wretched Queen, adieu!* (327) may be an immediate response, accompanied by some gesture, to her death.

311 *Unbated . . . practice*: An echo of the King's words at IV.7.137.

practice: Plot.

314 *can no more*: Can say no more. But in fact Laertes is able to give the first public evidence of the King's guilt.

316 *Then, venom, to thy work*: Hamlet never really becomes a contriving revenger. He kills the King, as he had killed Polonius, on the spur of the moment.

318 *but hurt*: Only wounded. Perhaps he is intended to suppose that the poison on the sword-point has been used up on Hamlet and Laertes.

320 *Is thy union here*: Hamlet is probably still making a pun, referring to his uncle's *union* in marriage with his mother.

321 *The King dies*: Claudius dies without contrition or forgiveness, unlike Laertes.

322 *tempered*: Compounded.

326 *make thee free*: Acquit you of the guilt.

328 *You that look pale . . .*: The courtiers and attendants.

329 *mutes*: Actors with wordless parts in a play.

330   *as*: Which I have not, because.
      sergeant: An officer of the sheriff, responsible for arrests.

331   *arrest*: Doubtless a final pun: Death stops him from
      proceeding with his story.

334   *the unsatisfied*: Those who are in doubt about my
      conduct.

335   *more an antique Roman than a Dane*: The common
      notion that, among the Romans, suicide was an accept-
      able way of escaping from an intolerable situation
      derived from the many stories in which stoical Roman
      nobles foiled the dishonour they suffered from wicked
      emperors. A Christian *Dane* would know that *the
      Everlasting had . . . fixed | His canon 'gainst self-slaughter*
      (I.2.131–2). But Horatio's Roman allusion is congruous
      with the classical education he showed at I.1.113–25.
      Here he temporarily loses the imperturbability of one
      who *Fortune's buffets and rewards* has *ta'en with equal
      thanks* (III.2.77–8).

338   *wounded name*: Damaged reputation.

339   *shall I leave behind me*: This is the Q2 reading. F has
      shall liue behind me, and Q1 *wouldst thou leaue behinde*.
      The excellent suggestion has been made that the Q2
      reading is a mistake for an original 'shall't leave behind
      me', which improves the scansion and the meaning.

341   *felicity*: Hamlet refers to the happiness of release from
      life's miseries (cf. III.1.63–4) rather than to the joys of
      heaven.

343   *and shout within*: This is only in F. Many editors have
      emended *shout* to *shot* or *shoot*, to connect with the
      warlike volley at 346.
          Both Q2 and F have an entry for Osrick at the end
      of the line, though there has been no reasonable point
      of exit for him. Probably no more is implied than that
      he comes forward to give his explanation of the *warlike
      noise*.

344   *with conquest come from Poland*: This is the first news
      of the outcome of Fortinbras's expedition (II.2.72–80,
      IV.4).

345   *the ambassadors of England*: The Englishmen coming

as ambassadors to the King of Denmark (see 71–2). The dramatic time has been drastically shortened.

347   *o'er-crows*: Triumphs over (like the victor in cock-fighting).

349–50   *But I do prophesy . . . Fortinbras*: This does not mean that there is any connection between *the news from England* and *the election* (to the Danish throne). Rather, Hamlet turns aside from the triviality of the fate of Rosencrantz and Guildenstern to his serious concern for the future of the Danish crown. Perhaps some stage business is required: he is handed the crown of Denmark (taken from the dead Claudius), and his dying thoughts, self-forgetful and calm, are upon its inheritance by a worthy successor.

    Shakespeare does not intend us to regard Fortinbras as a tyrant, or his assumption of power as arbitrary. The praise bestowed on him by Hamlet (*a delicate and tender prince*, IV.4.48) is important, confirming the good impression of Fortinbras given throughout the play (II.2.68–80 and IV.4.1–8). In many respects Fortinbras seems to embody Hamlet's ideal of kingship.

  lights | On: Alights upon.

350   *voice*: Vote.

351   *occurrents, more and less*: Incidents, great and small.

352   *solicited–*: Incited me to –. Probably Hamlet breaks off in mid-sentence, intending to continue with something like 'my various actions over the last few months'.

  silence: F somewhat incongruously adds *O, o, o, o* (presumably indicating the actor's dying groans).

354   *flights of angels sing*: May companies of angels sing.

355   *his train*: As there are now four dead bodies on the stage, requiring at least eight men for their simultaneous removal, Shakespeare has good reason to bring on a stage-army. It provides a splendid military finale.

  drum: Drummer.

  colours: Military ensigns.

358   *quarry cries on havoc*: Heap of dead proclaims that the hunters have carried out their slaughter (rather than '. . . cries out for revenge').

359 *toward*: In preparation.
       thine eternal cell: The grave.

361 *dismal*: Calamitous (a strong word).

363 *The ears*: Claudius's.

366 *Where should we have our thanks*: The Ambassador seems to be politely inquiring about the succession to the throne of Denmark.
       his: Claudius's.

367 *Had it th'ability of life*: Even if it could utter words.

369 *jump*: Exactly.
       question: Conflict.

371 *give order*: Presumably addressed to Fortinbras, who has his military power with him.

372 *stage*: Platform.

373 *let me speak*: Horatio is proposing to speak to the people, rather like Mark Antony in *Julius Caesar*, III.2.

375 *carnal, bloody, and unnatural acts*: The murder of King Hamlet by his brother Claudius and the Queen's re-marriage; the plot against Prince Hamlet which was to lead to his execution in England.

376 *accidental judgements, casual slaughters*: The unpremed-itated killing of Polonius behind the arras; Ophelia's drowning; the Queen's unintended death by poison; the killing of Laertes by his own *Unbated and envenomed* sword.

377 *deaths put on by cunning and forced cause*: The intended death of Hamlet by execution in England; the conse-quent deaths of Rosencrantz and Guildenstern.

377 *put on*: Instigated.
       forced: Not genuine.

378 *in this upshot*: As a final result of this.

378–9 *purposes mistook | Fallen on th'inventors' heads*: The death of Laertes by the unbated sword intended for use on Hamlet; the Queen's death by the poison intended for Hamlet; the King's death by the poisoned sword and drink.

383 *I have some rights of memory*: Fortinbras's claims to the Danish throne have not hitherto been mentioned, nor are we told what they are. But we remember that old

Fortinbras forfeited his personal lands to old Hamlet (I.1.80–104 and I.2.17–25) and so his son might regard himself as the residual heir to the throne after the expiring of the Hamlet lineage. It is notable that Fortinbras speaks only of *rights of memory* in Denmark. He is not like Malcolm in *Macbeth* or Richmond in *Richard III*, the rightful heir to the throne who ousts a regicide and usurper and so can cleanse the kingdom of corruption. A peaceful transfer of the throne to a strong, worthy and rightful claimant, and so an avoidance of political disorder, is what the ending of this tragedy requires (and perhaps supplies).

of memory: 'Not forgotten' (by you) or 'ancient' (claims). Perhaps both meanings are implied.

384 *Which*: This kingdom.

my vantage: Good fortune.

386 *from his mouth*: See 350–51.

whose voice will draw on more: Denmark being an elective monarchy, Fortinbras's claims will be dependent upon his winning support. The approval of him by the popular Prince Hamlet as he died will win him many votes in the election.

387 *this same*: Horatio's proposal that he give *to the yet unknowing world* a full account, which will include Hamlet's recommendation of Fortinbras.

presently: Immediately.

389 *On plots and errors*: On top of the plots and misjudgements. Horatio fears disorder as a result of the disasters to the ruling house.

391–2 *he was likely, had he been put on,* | *To have proved most royal*: The tribute over the dead body of the tragic hero is conventional. It does not necessarily cast a light over the whole of the preceding play. A similar problem faces us in *Julius Caesar*, where Mark Antony praises Brutus as 'the noblest Roman of them all' (V.5.68–75), and in *Coriolanus*, where Aufidius praises Coriolanus: 'he shall have a noble memory' (V.6.155). But Fortinbras's strong words are consistent with Ophelia's *Th'expectancy and rose of the fair state* (III.1.153).

391 *put on*: Put to the test (by his accession to the throne, rather than by following a career as a soldier).

392 *passage*: From this life to the other world.

393 *The soldiers' music and the rites of war*: A military funeral is described by Aufidius at the end of *Coriolanus*, V.6.149–52:

> Take him up.
> Help three o'th'chiefest soldiers; I'll be one.
> Beat thou the drum, that it speak mournfully.
> Trail your steel pikes.

394 *Speak*: Let them speak.

396 *field*: Battlefield.

397 *shoot . . . a peal of ordnance is shot off*: This again reminds us, unhappily or ironically, of Claudius's partiality for gunshot (I.2.124–8, I.4.8–12 and V.2.269–72).